Giorgio Piola

Formula1
technical analysis
2006-07

THE 2006 SEASON

Renault R26

1°

The 2006 season was one of the hardest fought of recent years and focused on the battle between Renault, which started out as the favourite, and Ferrari, the protagonist of a pursuit that culminated in the summer with a hand to hand battle with its French rival. A confrontation that turned into numerous controversies of a technical and sporting nature, as happened for example at Monza, with serious accusations being made against the Prancing Horse by Fernando Alonso and Flavio Briatore. The Grand Prix of Italy will also be remembered for the official announcement of Michael Schumacher's retirement, made by the driver during the post race press conference.

As well as for Fernando Alonso's and Renault's second world titles, the 2006 season will be remembered in a technical sense for the prickly matter of the mass damper, which rumbled on throughout the summer. The mass damper, which was frequently fitted to the Renault and then copied by other teams, was revealed to the general public during the Grand Prix of Monaco weekend, but the real controversy blew up five races later in Germany. Introduced the previous season by Renault and approved by the scrutineers at all the races at the beginning of the year, the mass damper was then outlawed on the eve of Hockenheim and was definitively banned by the appeals tribunal of the Federation. A solution which, unlike those who subsequently followed the example of the French team, had rather negative consequences on the yield of the Renault R26, the development project of which – especially as far as its suspension was concerned – was strictly linked to the use of that particular component at both the front and rear ends. This mobile ballast, the application of which should have been prohibited from the moment it first appeared, optimised the suspension yield as well as the exploitation of the tyres and aerodynamics of the various cars.

SEASON OF SUSPICIONS
The season was peppered with suspicion and disputes, which started at the first race in Bahrain with Ferrari's use of small carbon fairing in the external area of the rims of the rear wheels, considered by the rival teams to be mobile aerodynamic devices and, therefore, irregular. On that subject, it should be said that the new definition of brake air intakes, which were in introduced in mid-2005, permitted the integration of these aerodynamic devices as a part of these cooling devices. It was no coincidence that the 2005 Technical Analysis included a number of extreme cases (page 49) of the shape of such intakes and the aerodynamic appendages fitted to them, which had given way to the restrictions brought in on the subject by the Federation before the Grand Prix of Canada. They, however, became more permissive after a subsequent meeting of the Working Technical Group (WTG). From here the perfect conformity of the rings applied to the rear rims, which were immediately imitated by Toyota and Toro Rosso. Ferrari then introduced an even more extreme version at the Grand Prix of Turkey, with fairing extended so that it covered almost the entire rim. The second raised flap also created discontent: it appeared on the Ferrari's nose and was discovered while watching television pictures of the Grand Prix of Malaysia, which clearly showed transverse movement in the central anchorage point. Suspicions that were immediately allayed by a more precise fitting of the flap from the following race.

In the traditional description of the various aspects of the cars there is no New Developments chapter for the simple two-fold reason that, either such developments were the subjects of protest (see the mass damper and the faired rims) or they were focused on aerodynamics, and, as such, are included in the Controversies or Aerodynamics chapters.

ENGINES FROM 3000 CC TO 2400 CC
Fortunately, disputes were not the only feature of the 2006 season but they were extremely animated from the technical point of view, starting with the replacement of the 10-cylinder, 3000 cc engine with the smaller 2400 cc V8, an attempt to limit costs and power output. This was a decision that did not go down well with many engineers, but in the end it did enliven the technical panorama, with Cosworth in the early races and Mercedes-Benz in considerable difficulty, compared to their rivals Renault and Ferrari. The only cars that kept their 10-cylinder 3000 cc units were Toro Rossos, which competed with the previous year's Red Bull engines: the 10-cylinder Ford was also the only unit that did not have variable trumpets, which enabled it to suffer less in terms of power generation than its rivals, due to this limitation.

GREAT AERODYNAMIC REFINEMENT
There was a certain stability of regulations in the aerodynamics field during the 2006 season, which saw the almost total disappearance of the single keel feature for front suspension anchorage, a feature that was only used by Ferrari and Toro Rosso, the latter, as mentioned, on the 2005 Red Bull cars. It was only Red Bull that used the open V keel brought in by Renault in 2005. All the other teams adopted a 'no keel' layout, the greater number of them using the solution introduced by McLaren the previous season. There was also a notable refinement of aerodynamics in 2006, with micro-developments in search of maximum efficiency. Instead of looking for the highest degree of downforce, the designers attempted to optimise the cars aerodynamics by reducing advancement resistance as much as possible, also in an effort to counter the loss of maximum power due to the reduction of the engines' cubic capacity. So a great deal of development work was carried out,

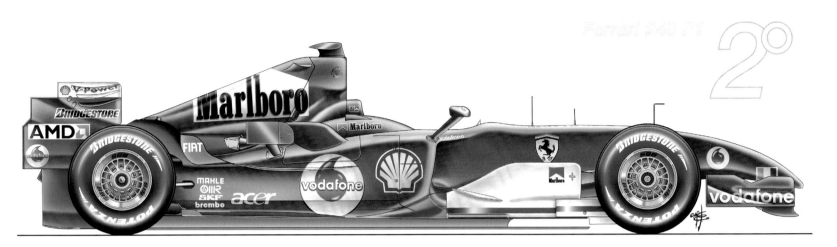

Ferrari 248 F1   2°

resulting in the introduction of new aerodynamic packages, often made up of many small, almost imperceptible modifications in all areas of the car. Contrary to that which had happened in the past, new features were also seen on the top cars, sometimes copied from second level teams. That was the case with the curious fins on the upper part of the sidepods first used the previous year by BAR Honda and then by almost all teams during 2006.

THE DISAPPOINTMENT OF THE SEASON

The biggest disappointment of 2006 was the McLaren MP4-21, which, amazingly, was not among the main contenders and did not even win a Grand Prix, a situation that certainly facilitated Kimi Raikkonen's decision to move to Ferrari for 2007. The results achieved by the Anglo-German team were decidedly inferior, not so much for the places lost in favour of Ferrari in the constructors' championship as for the 72 points fewer than those scored by the team in 2005, a factor that, compared to the previous season, meant McLaren lost

more world title points than any other team. The car inherited from Adrian Newey, who moved to Red Bull, was often stopped by its eight-cylinder Mercedes-Benz engine, which was less powerful than those of the competition, and still afflicted by too many reliability problems, despite a project packed with interesting ideas, like the horizontal front brake calipers. That was a feature copied from Honda, which took on a third brake caliper supplier called Akebono of Japan in addition to Brembo and A+P. Toyota and Williams also slid down the championship table, the two having fallen from 4th to 6th and from 5th to 8th respectively in the classification, but, in particular, with 53 and 55 fewer points. This was caused by two cars that were hardly competitive – especially in the case of Toyota – and a not very reliable as far as Williams was concerned.

THE DEBUT OF BMW, HONDA AND SUPER AGURI

Two major car manufacturers joined Formula One in 2006: BMW acquired Sauber after a surprising divorce from Williams, and Honda

absorbed its engine customer, BAR. Both teams had decidedly better seasons compared to the previous year. Honda went from 7th to 4th and BMW from 8th to 5th in the championship table. Unfortunately, the 2006 season saw the loss of Jordan and Minardi, which had already been announced in 2005: they were replaced by Midland and Toro Rosso respectively. While, in practice, the former acquired the technical material of the old team, the heads of the latter dispensed with engineer Gabriele Tredozzi's ambitious new Minardi car, which had made its debut at the Grand Prix of San Marino. The new owners preferred to enter the antiquated and not very competitive 2005 Red Bull, a car that soon showed its limits.

The number of teams competing for the championship went up by one with the arrival of Super Aguri, a team that perplexed many people because of its decision to revert to an old Arrows chassis that dated back as far as 2002. But the newcomer improved in technical and team terms during the second part of the season with the considerable support of Honda.

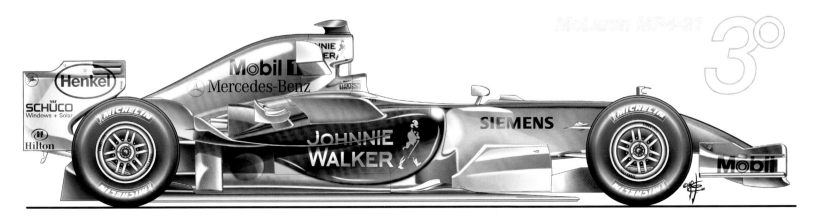

McLaren MP4-21   3°

THE RETURN OF THE TYRE CHANGE

The abolition of the races' single set of tyres rule, which became necessary after the clamorous happenings at Indianapolis in 2005, countered the handicap derived from the less powerful 2400 cc engine, guaranteeing better performance in lap and race terms compared to the previous season. The tyre change also re-launched Bridgestone from the Grand Prix of the United States onwards, as the company overtook its rival Michelin, making the battle between Ferrari and Renault even more uncertain and strictly connected to the performance of their tyres on the various circuits. Grand Prix victory was often influenced by the abilities of the two tyre makers, with the exception of unforeseen mechanical problems. A battle we shall no longer see from

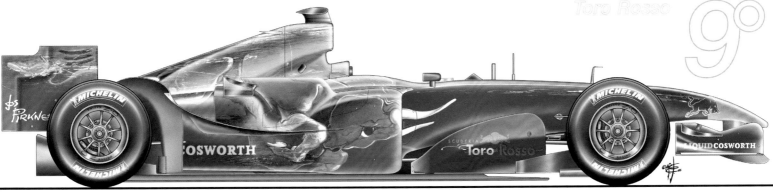

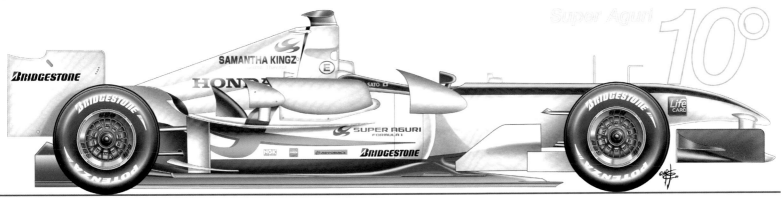

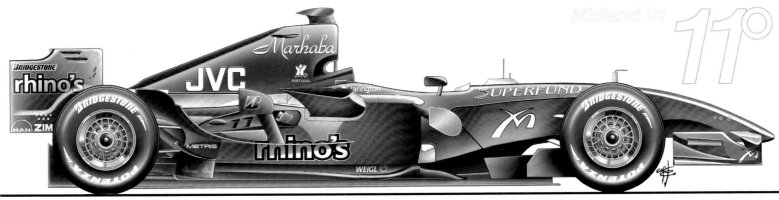

2007 with the imposition of the mono-tyre situation as required by the Federation. That meant the inevitable retirement of the French manufacturer, which was seriously affected by the tragic death of its president Edouard Michelin in a boating accident.

To help recount the 2006 season, we have taken advantage of invaluable contributions from engineers Mauro Forghieri and Mauro Coppini for the engines chapter, which also includes a new table by Michele Merlino on one of the most salient aspects of the season – the use of engines that were obliged to run for two races. This contribution will enable readers to evaluate all the defections that took place during the 18 races that made up the championship. Kazuiko Kasai, Mark Hughes also contributed chapters on tyres.

In the third season with the parc fermé regime in force between qualifying and the race, there was a further reduction in the use of the T-car and spare chassis during the season. The teams only used their spare cars when absolutely necessary and after being authorised by the scrutineers. The number of chassis built also fell drastically – in 2004 Toyota built a record 11 units. In 2006 the teams building the most chassis were Ferrari, McLaren and Toyota with 7 apiece. Fortunately there were no serious accidents, which helped reduce the number of damaged chassis to a minimum. The graphs relating to the use of chassis during the season have been notably simplified and reduced by an analysis of the two leading players. In this case too it is evident that there was less interest in using different chassis, as in the case of Renault and Alonso with the Spaniard remaining faithful to chassis No. 3 throughout the season. Only two teams created "B" versions: Toyota, which introduced the definitive TF106 at Monaco equipped with a redesigned chassis, and Super Aguri, which also introduced a new chassis at the German Grand Prix, one no longer derived from that of the 2002 Arrows.

Chassis 248 F	250	251	252	253	254	255	256
First run	16-01-2006	06-02-2006	23-02-2006	03-03-2006	04-04-2006	06-07-2006	14-09-2006
Km completed GP	3.615	315	4.805	1.696	5.395	2.686	1.934
Km completed Test	13.978	5.995	3.722	1.5994	3.959	446	3.072

CURIOSITIES

CHASSIS BUILT
The tally of chassis built in 2006 saw Ferrari, McLaren and Toyota out in front with 7. They were followed by Renault, BMW and Williams with 6. Next up with 5 were Honda, Red Bull and Super Aguri (of which only 2 not derived from the Arrows A23 tubs). Spyker built fewest with just 3 examples.

VICTORIOUS CHASSIS
In 2006 GP wins were shared between three teams, Renault, Ferrari and Honda; the season's most successful chassis was Renault 03 used by Alonso to take 7 wins, followed by Ferrari 254 with 5 wins for Schumacher and 252 with a further 2 wins for the German; that chassis was also driven to victory by Massa who also won with chassis No. 256.

WHEELBASES
The car with the longest wheelbase was the BMW (3215 mm), followed by the second version of the Honda (3190 mm, 50 mm longer than the original that raced through to the Turkish GP); then came the Renault (3165 mm) and Toro Rosso (3145 mm). According to measurements taken from photographic sources, the Ferrari had a wheelbase of 3105 mm.

	laps completed (%)	finishes	technical failures	accidents	test km	days
Ferrari	2160 (94,9 %)	31	1 engine	4	43282	80
Renault	2157 (94,8 %)	32	3* hydraulics (1) - engine (1)	1	47825	59
BMW	1985 (87,3 %)	27	4 engine (3) - brakes (1)	4**	40896	57
Honda	1943 (85,4 %)	28	7 engine	1	54816	63
Toro Rosso	1900 (83,5 %)	27	3 eng. (1) - clut. (1) - p. steer. (1)	6	15150	33
Toyota	1833 (80,6 %)	22	12 engine (4) - r. susp. (2)	2	42709	60
Red Bull	1764 (77,6 %)	23	9 gearbox (5) - hydraulics (3)	4	23526	51
Spyker	1715 (75,4 %)	21	5 hydraulics (1) - susp. (1)	2**	13698	36
McLaren	1680 73,9 %)	23	6 gearbox (1) - engine (2)	7	46893	67
Super Aguri	1455 (64,0 %)	17	12 hydraulics (5) - engine (2)	1**	2996	14
Williams	1331 (58,5 %)	16	10 hydraulics (2) - engine (1)	10	35903	65

* Wheel nut
** Disqualified

The most reliable team was Ferrari, which completed 94.9% of the total Championship laps, followed by the championship winning team Renault with 94.8%. The least reliable team was instead Williams, which completed just 58.8% of the total. The second least reliable team was Red Bull with 77.6% (5 gearbox failures and 3 hydraulic problems). The least reliable engine was the Honda 8-cylinder unit with no less than 7 failures on the official works cars and 2 on the Super Aguri, followed by the Toyota with 4, the BMW with 3 and the Mercedes-Benz with 2. The team completing the most private testing days was Ferrari with 80, followed by McLaren with 67, Honda with 63 and Toyota with 60. Renault instead completed 59 days. The team that completed least testing days was Super Aguri with just 14 during the course of the season.

RENAULT • *R26* • N° 1-2

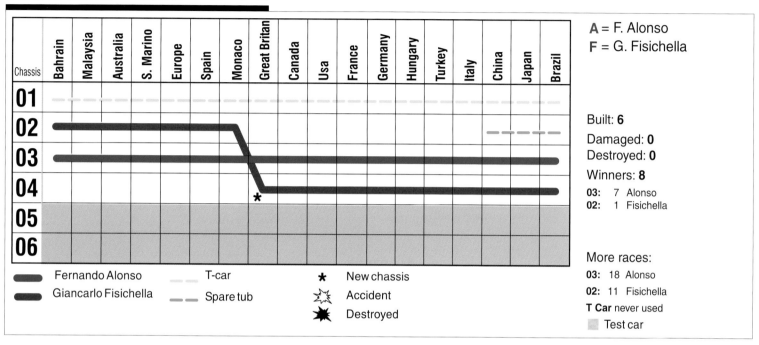

Chassis	Bahrain	Malaysia	Australia	S. Marino	Europe	Spain	Monaco	Great Britain	Canada	Usa	France	Germany	Hungary	Turkey	Italy	China	Japan	Brazil
01																		
02																		
03																		
04								*										
05																		
06																		

Legend:
- ▬▬ Fernando Alonso
- ▬▬ Giancarlo Fisichella
- – – T-car
- – – Spare tub
- * New chassis
- ✸ Accident
- ✸ Destroyed

A = F. Alonso
F = G. Fisichella

Built: **6**
Damaged: **0**
Destroyed: **0**
Winners: **8**
03: 7 Alonso
02: 1 Fisichella

More races:
03: 18 Alonso
02: 11 Fisichella
T Car never used
▨ Test car

FERRARI • *248 F1* • N° 5-6

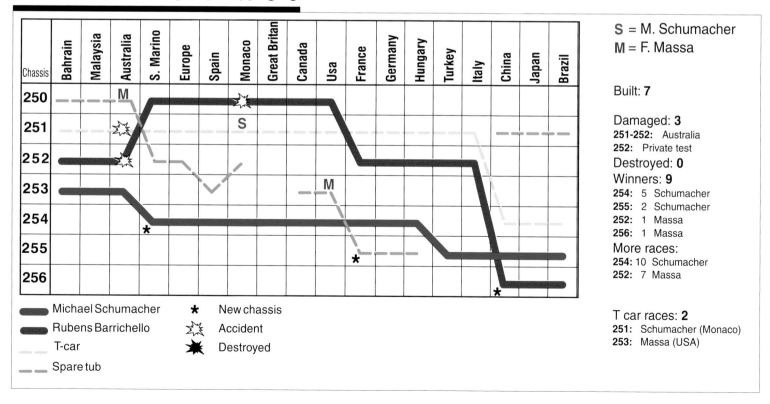

Chassis	Bahrain	Malaysia	Australia	S. Marino	Europe	Spain	Monaco	Great Britain	Canada	Usa	France	Germany	Hungary	Turkey	Italy	China	Japan	Brazil
250			M				✸											
251			✸				S											
252			✸															
253											M							
254			*															
255											*							
256															*			

Legend:
- ▬▬ Michael Schumacher
- ▬▬ Rubens Barrichello
- – – T-car
- – – Spare tub
- * New chassis
- ✸ Accident
- ✸ Destroyed

S = M. Schumacher
M = F. Massa

Built: **7**

Damaged: **3**
251-252: Australia
252: Private test
Destroyed: **0**
Winners: **9**
254: 5 Schumacher
255: 2 Schumacher
252: 1 Massa
256: 1 Massa
More races:
254: 10 Schumacher
252: 7 Massa

T car races: **2**
251: Schumacher (Monaco)
253: Massa (USA)

		1 - 2 RENAULT	5 - 6 FERRARI	3 - 4 McLAREN	11 - 12 HONDA	16 - 17 BMW
CAR		**R26**	**248 F1**	**MP4/21**	**RA 106**	**F106**
	Designers	Bob Bell - Rob White Pat Symonds - Dino Toso	Ross Brawn - Rory Byrne Aldo Costa - Paolo Martinelli	Mike Coughlan - Neil Oatley Paddy Lowe	Geoffrey Willis• Shuhei Nakamoto	Willy Rampf Jorg Zander
	Race engineers	R. Nelson - S. Rennie - R. Taffin (1) A. Permane - D. Greenwood - F. Lom (2)	Chris Dyer (5) Rob Smedley (6)	Steve Hallam M.Slade (3) - P. Prew (4)	Jock Clear (11) Andrew Shovlin (12)	G. Dallara (16) A. Borne (17)
	Chief mechanic	Gavin Hudson	Nigel Stepney	Stephen Giles	Alistair Gibson	Urs Kuratle
CHASSIS	Wheelbase	3165 mm*	3105 mm*	3087 mm*	3140 mm / 3190 mm•	3215 mm*
	Front track	1450 mm	1470 mm	1470 mm*	1460 mm	1460 mm
	Rear track	1420 mm	1405 mm	1405 mm*	1420 mm	1400 mm
	Front suspension	2+1 dampers and torsion bars	2+1 dampers and torsion bars	2+1 dampers and torsion bars	2+1 dampers and torsion bars	2+1 dampers and torsion bars
	Rear suspension	2+1 dampers and torsion bars	2+1 dampers and torsion bars	2+1 dampers and torsion bars	2+1 dampers and torsion bars	2+1 dampers and torsion bars
	Dampers	Penske	Sachs (rotary rear dampers)	McLaren	Koni	Sachs
	Brakes calipers	A+P	Brembo	A+P	Alcon - Akebono	Brembo
	Brakes discs	Hitco	Brembo CCR Carbon Industrie	Carbon Industrie	Alcon	Brembo
	Wheels	O.Z.	BBS	Enkey	BBS	O.Z.
	Radiators	Marston	Secan	Calsonic - IMI	IMI Marston - Showa	Calsonic
	Oil tank	middle position inside fuel tank	middle position inside fuel tank	middle position inside fuel tank	middle position inside fuel tank	middle position inside fuel tank
GEARBOX		Longitudinal Titanium	Longitudinal Carbon con	Longitudinal Carbon	Longitudinal Carbon	Longitudinal Titanium
	Gear selection	Semiautomatic 6 gears	Semiautomatic 7 gears	Semiautomatic 7 gears	Semiautomatic 7 gears	Semiautomatic 7 gears
	Clutch	A+P	A+P	A+P	Sachs	A+P
	Pedals	2	2	2	2	2
ENGINE		Renault RS26	Ferrari 056	Mercedes F01085	Honda RA806E	BMW P86
	Total capacity	2400 cmc	2400 cmc	2400 cmc	2400 cmc*	2398 cmc
	N° cylinders and V	8 - V 90°	8 - V 90°	8 - V 90°	8 - V 90°	8 - V 90°
	Electronics	Magneti Marelli	Magneti Marelli	McLaren el. sys.	Honda Athena 206	Magneti Marelli
	Fuel	Elf	Shell	Mobil	Elf	Petronas
	Oil	Elf	Shell	Mobil	Eneos	Petronas
	Fuel tank capacity	98 kg*	90 kg*	98 kg*	100 kg	98 kg
	Dashboard	Magneti Marelli	Magneti Marelli	McLaren	BAR HONDA	BMW Sauber

7 - 8 TOYOTA	14 - 15 RED BULL	9 - 10 WILLIAMS	20 - 21 TORO ROSSO	18 - 19 SPYKER	22 - 23 SUPER AGURI
TF 106	R. B. 2	FW 28	STR 01	M16	SA 06
Pascal Vasselon Luigi Marmorini	Adrian Newey Mark Smith	Patrick Head - Sam Michael Loic Bigois	Gabriele Tredozzi Alex Hitzinger	James Key - Mike Gascoyne[4]	MarK Preston
Francesco Nenci (7) Ossi Oikarinen (8)	Mark Hutcheson (14) Ciaron Pilbeam (15)	X. Pujolar - J. Boughton (9) T. Ross - M. White (10)	R. Adami (20) S. Sordo (21)	Brand . Joyce (18) Jody Eggington (19)	Gerry Huges (22) Antonio Cuquerella (23)
Gerard LeCoq	Kenny Handkammer	Carl Gaden	Bruno Fagnocchi	Andy Deeming	Phill Spencer
3090 mm	3145 mm	3100 mm	3145 mm	3097 mm*	3090 mm
1425 mm	1440 mm*	1480 mm	1440 mm*	1480 mm	1445 mm
1411 mm	1410 mm*	1420 mm	1410 mm*	1410 mm	1405 mm
2+1 dampers and torsion bars	2+1 dampers and torsion bars	2+1 dampers and torsion bars	2+1 dampers and torsion bars	2+1 dampers and torsion bars	2+1 dampers and torsion bars
2+1 dampers and torsion bars	2+1 dampers and springs	2+1 dampers and torsion bars	2+1 dampers and springs	2+1 dampers and springs	2+1 dampers and springs
Sachs - Toyota	Koni	Williams	Koni	Sachs (rotary rear dampers)	OHLINS
Brembo	A+P	A+P	A+P	A+P	A+P
Hitco	Brembo - Hitco	Carbon Industrie	Hitco	Hitco - Brembo	Hitco
BBS	O.Z.	O.Z.	AVUS Racing	BBS	BBS
Nippon - Denso	Marston	IMI Marston	Marston	Secan	Secan - Marston
middle position inside fuel tank	middle position inside fuel tank	middle position inside fuel tank	middle position inside fuel tank	middle position inside fuel tank	middle position inside fuel tank
Longitudinal Titanium	Longitudinal Alluminium	Longitudinal Alluminium	Longitudinal Alluminium	Longitudinal Magnesium	Longitudinal carbon/aluminium[5]
Semiautomatic 7 gears	Semiautomatic 7 gears	Semiautomatic 7 gears	Semiautomatic 7 gears	Semiautomatic 7 gears	Semiautomatic 7 gears
A+P	A+P	A+P	A+P	A+P	SACHS
2	2/3	2	2	2	2
RVX 06	Ferrari 056	Cosworth CA 2006	Ford Cosworth TJ 2005	Toyota RVX06	HONDA RA 806 E
2398 cmc	2398 cmc	2398 cmc	2998 cmc	2398 cmc	2398 cmc
8 - V 90°	8 - V 90°	8 - V 90°	10 - V 90°•	8 - V 90°	8 - V 90°
Magneti Marellli	Magneti Marelli	Williams F1	P.I.	Magneti Marelli	Honda Eneos
Esso	BP	Petrobras	BP	Esso	
Esso	Castrol	Castrol	Castrol	Esso	
98 kg	95 kg	90 kg	95 kg	95 kg	95 kg*
Toyota	P.I.	Williams	P.I.	P.I.	SA F1

1) G. Willis left the team in summer
2) From Turkish Grand Prix
3) Old V10 2005
4) From summer
5) From German Grand Prix

* extimated value

ENGINES
2006

Almost 40 years on from the Ford Cosworth DFV engine's first Grand Prix victory, Formula 1 returned to the 90° V8 configuration characterising the engine that had propelled Grand Prix cars into the modern era. In 1967, this decision might have been questioned. More extreme configurations would, in fact, have allowed greater power outputs to be achieved and this was the path

chosen by Cosworth's rivals. BRM had abandoned its ineffective H-16 unit, but only in favour of a V12. Eagle, Honda, Matra and, of course, Ferrari were all on the same wavelength. This was despite the continued success enjoyed by the Repco V8 used by Jack Brabham and Dennis Hulme that had raised doubts as to the validity of more exotic configurations. Keith Duckworth and Mike Costin

were instead willing to take a broad-based look at the requirements associated with the general principles of racing car construction and to recognize the importance of parameters such as weight and dimensions that had previously been considered to be marginal, at least with respects to the primary objective of producing as much power as possible. In 2006, the adoption of 90° V8 engines was not

New 2400 cc displacement and mandatory 8-cylinder configuration. These were the principal innovations in the regulations introduced for the 2006 season. The new engines were around 10 cm shorter, as highlighted in yellow in the comparison between the Renault V8 and V10 units.

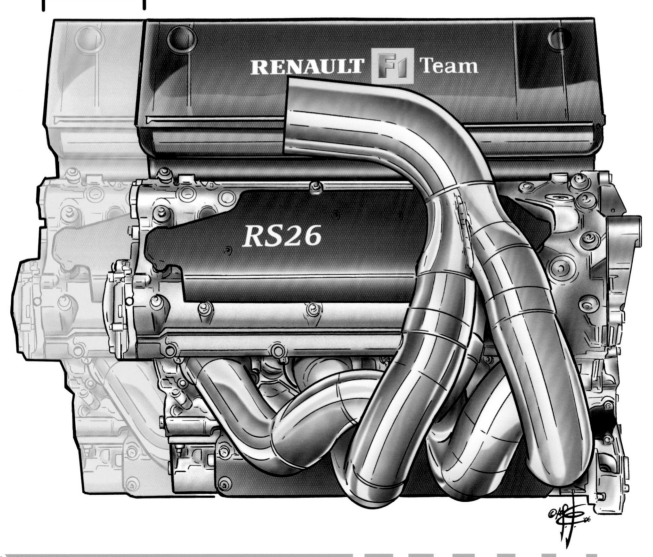

≃ - 10 cm

RENAULT F1 Team

RS26

Driver	Engines
T. Sato	13
F. Massa	12
J. Trulli	12
J. Villeneuve/R. Kubica	12
R. Schumacher	12
C. Albers	11
C. Klien/R. Doornbos	11
D. Coulthard	11
J. Button	11
M. Schumacher	11
M. Webber	11
N. Rosberg	11
V .Liuzzi	11
Y. Ide/F .Montagny/S.Yamamoto	11
F. Alonso	10
G. Fisichella	10
J. P. Montoya/P. De la Rosa	10
K. Raikkonen	10
R .Barrichello	10
S. Speed	10
T. Monteiro	10
N. Heidfeld	9

Engines used during the season

Driver n°		Unit	covered Km	Used in
8	J. Trulli	Toyota RVX-06 (11)	1264	Europe-Spain
21	S. Speed	Cosworth TJ2005-2 (18)	1220	Italy-China
22	T. Sato	Honda RA806E (3)	1216	Bahrain-Malaysia
20	V. Liuzzi	Cosworth TJ2005-2 (1)	1209	Bahrain-Malaysia
11	R. Barrichello	Honda RA806E (9)	1196	San Marino-Europe
2	G. Fisichella	Renault RS26 (15)	1188	Turkey-Italy
20	V. Liuzzi	Cosworth TJ2005-2 (19)	1179	Japan-Brasil
12	J. Button	Honda RA806E (2)	1177	Bahrain-Malaysia
11	R. Barrichello	Honda RA806E (42)	1175	Japan-Brasil
20	V. Liuzzi	Cosworth TJ2005-2 (17)	1168	Italy-China

Engines that covered the most kilometres

23	S. Yamamoto	Honda RA806E (31)	22	Germany
8	J. Trulli	Toyota RVX-06 (29)	86	Germany
23	F. Montagny	Honda RA806E (25)	138	U.S.A.
10	N. Rosberg	Cosworth CA2006 (4)	174	Australia
9	M. Webber	Cosworth CA2006 (22)	185	Brasil
17	J. Villeneuve	BMW P86 (8)	185	Spain
8	J. Trulli	Toyota RVX-06 (19)	200	Great Britain
9	M. Webber	Cosworth CA2006 (16)	214	Hungary
18	T. Monteiro	Toyota RVX-06 (3)	221	Bahrain
15	C. Klien	Ferrari 056 (9)	243	Australia

Engines that covered the least kilometres

With one Grand Prix less than in 2005 – 18 races instead of 19 – engine statistics only changed slightly in 2006, without being subjected to a significant shale-up. In that sense, it is emblematic that the record for the distance covered by a single engine during the year is the same as that of kilometres in 2005: the Toyota RVX-06 number 11, which Trulli used in Europe and Spain, ran for 1,264 km, precisely the same distance as Monteiro's RVX-05 number three in Australia and Malaysia in 2005. Scott Speed came second with about 40 kilometres less than Trulli; he drove 1,220 km with Cosworth TJ2005-2 number 18.

And it is the Cosworth 3000 cc V10, together with the Honda RA806E, that was exploited more than any other during the season: both are present with four engines, a record in the top 10 coverage classification.

On the other hand, the negative record belongs to Sakon Yamamoto, who made his debut in Germany when Super Aguri fielded the SA06 for the first time, and only covered 22 km (five laps of the track) before it broke down. A troubled weekend, seeing that Yamamoto used three different engines and retired during the race with a broken drive shaft after just one lap.

Paradoxically, that breakdown enabled Yamamoto to establish a seasonal record: he used one new engine for a single lap of the track. Super Aguri took the same engine to Hungary, where it only did 254 km before Yamamoto spun. He spun again in Turkey to make his engine the only one that competed during three weekends of 2006 and covered just 675 kilometres.

Only Nick Heidfeld had a perfect season, using nine engines for the 18 races. A man who was rather hard on his power units was Takuma Sato who, as in 2005, was the driver who used most engines – a total of 13. After the Japanese come four drivers: Massa, Villeneuve-Kubica (they drove the same car) and the Toyota duo Trulli and Ralf Schumacher. Praise goes to Renault, who not only managed to use just 10 engines per driver, but they were also top in terms of average distance, with Alonso taking the lead with 975.9 km per engine ad Fisichella fourth with 943.9 km. That yield, or should we say approach, was diametrically opposed to Williams, which established a record for the minimum average covered: only 613 km for Webber and 622 for Heidfeld with their respective Cosworth CA2006 units.

Engine use was a subject of discussion during the Grand Prix of Japan, where Michael Schumacher's breakdown on the 37th lap put an end to his race and championship ambitions. The Ferrari 056 unit number 38 gave up after 1,007 km, a value above average by the German in 2006 and equal to 871 kms. The unit arrived at Suzuka having run for 566 km during Schumacher's victorious weekend at the Grand Prix of China. But these are not values that much exceed the standards adopted by Ferrari in 2006, seeing that on two occasions the seven times world champion covered over 1,100 km with a single engine when he won the Grands Prix of Europe and the United States.

Driver	Engine	km	Average km/engine
F. Alonso	10	9759	975,9
N. Heidfeld	9	8602	955,8
R. Barrichello	10	9537	953,7
G. Fisichella	10	9439	943,9
S. Speed	10	9233	923,3
M. Schumacher	11	9585	871,4
T. Monteiro	10	8479	847,9
J. Button	11	9257	841,5
V. Liuzzi	11	9252	841,1
J. P. Montoya/P. De la Rosa	10	7985	798,5
R. Schumacher	12	9544	795,3
F. Massa	12	9507	792,3
K. Raikkonen	10	7853	785,3
J. Trulli	12	9397	783,1
D. Coulthard	11	8225	747,7
C. Albers	11	8168	742,5
J. Villeneuve/R. Kubica	12	8788	732,3
T. Sato	13	9266	712,8
C. Klien/R. Doornbos	11	7694	699,5
Y. I. de/F.Montagny/S. Yamamoto	11	7607	691,5
N. Rosberg	11	6849	622,6
M. Webber	11	6750	613,6

Average covered in kilometres

so much a valid technical decision but rather the fruit of a regulatory imposition the level of interference of which was unprecedented in the history of motorsport. While the need to limit the costs and performance of the 3-litre V10 engines that in 11 years of development had reached power outputs of between 930 and 960 hp is comprehensible, the path followed by the FIA with the compilation of a veritable design manual is less convincing and would appear to leave little scope for the designer's intuition. This is the inevitable result of a document to which a significant contribution was actually made by the Cosworth engineers, truly skilled in regulating the nerve centres through which the indispensable projects in the search for performance

are bound to move. It was not so much the 20% reduction in cylinder capacity from 3.0 to 2.4 litres, obtained by subtracting two cylinders from the V10 units, and which at least in the initial development phase led to a similar reduction in the maximum power output to values in the order of 730-760 hp, but rather the legislator's interference in defining the principal design parameters that conditioned the engineers. This was, however, an inevitable decision if the total redesign of the engines and the consequent effects on costs was to be avoided. Had no restrictions been put in place, the passage from the V10 to V8 configuration would certainly not have been limited to the elimination of the two "superfluous" cylinders. The contemporary variation in the total displacement and the number of cylinder would inevitably have pushed the designer in the direction of research into new bore/stroke ratios and consequently the birth of a completely new engine. While the Cosworth engineers did not directly impose a

bore/stroke ratio, something that would have been unbecoming to Formula 1, a category that sees itself at the cutting edge of engine design research, that was actually the indirect effect of their prescriptions. By setting the minimum distance between the cylinders at 106.5 mm they effectively restricted the maximum bore to the 98 mm that characterised the previous 10-cylinder power units. In the same way, the imposition of a 90° angle between the banks of cylinder that, with the temporary exception of Renault which had explored alternative paths in order to lower the centre of gravity (111°) and to improve the smoothness of the cycle (72°), effectively froze a format already adopted with the previous V10s.

Then again, a 90° angle represents the optimum configuration from the point of view of smoothness for an 8-cylinder engine while it is decidedly "unnatural" for a 10-cylinder unit in which the angle was defined in relation to a more favourable ratio between the height of the centre of gravity and the transverse dimensions. Further impediments derived from the imposition of a centre of gravity no lower than 165 mm, measured from the base of the sump and from a distance between the crankshaft and the reference plane of no less than 58 mm.

In this way a brake was applied to the race to lower the centre of gravity that would have led to the reduction of the block to a minimum, with negative effects on the durability of the engines. However, the regulations also outlawed interesting solutions such as those conceived by Cosworth for its own V10 with the adoption of a beam-type cylinder head capable of saving considerable weight in the upper part of the engine assembly. To all this has to be added a 95 kg weight limit that was extremely conservative when you consider that the three-litre BMW V10 weighed less than 90 kg and that in the absence of limits Toyota had planned on keeping the weight of its V8 under 88 kg. The prohibition of magnesium and metal matrix composites that had hitherto been widely used for the conrod-piston assembly was designed as an obstacle on the only path available to designers for the recovery of power output: that of increasing engine speeds. This was a well-designed "trap" as the combined effect deriving from the restriction of the bore and the impossibility of reducing the weight of the reciprocating masses represents a significant hurdle. Especially when to all this is added the ban on the use of variable geometry intake manifolds. ¬This was indispensable so as not to narrow the usable bands as specific power outputs increased. Benefits from the new regulations were enjoyed by the chassis and aerodynamic rather than the engine designers. The reduction in the length of the new engines in the order of 80-100 mm and an exhaust pipe configuration that favoured a forward devel-

Another significant restriction concerned the architecture of the engines with the imposition of a 90° V, as had become customary with the 10-cylinder units used through to 2005.

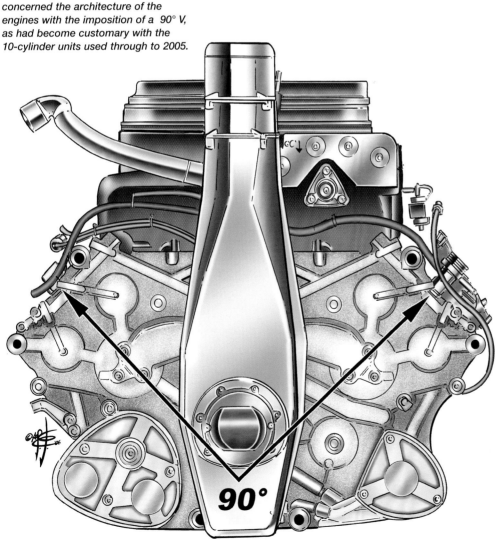

90°

opment effectively translated into a more advanced location thanks to which it was possible to lengthen the wheelbase without significantly altering the centre of gravity. For the same reason the rear bodywork could be more sharply tapered so as to achieve a greater acceleration of the flow of air over the wing surfaces. There were also benefits for the configuration of the sidepods, with smaller air intakes for the cooling of the radiators thanks to the reduced demands of the new engines. It was surprising that the Cosworth engineers limited to four litres or just over the quantity of liquid permitted in the cooling system, a restriction compensated by the more efficient thermal gradient deriving from a pressurised circuit capable of maintaining a running temperature of around 125° C and the exceptional capacity of a water pump with a throughput of 270 l/1'. It should however be pointed out that in this field the decisions made by the designers proved to be cautiously conservative, restricting themselves to a reduction of the cooling surface of around 10% against the 20% that calculations suggest could have been achieved. And yet, despite the raft of limitations the passage from 10 to 8 cylinders did not result in reductions of the specific power output that, in contrast, actually rose further during the course of the season. The new architecture in fact resolved, at least in part, those problems associated with vibration, especially that generated by the timing gear that had tormented the engineers. Mention has already been made of Renault's attempts to resolve the problem by choosing V angles capable of guaranteeing the greatest cyclical smoothness (72°) but the remedy proved to be worse that the disease and the 90° imposed itself as the best possible solution for containing the torsional vibrations of the crankshaft. It was more difficult to guarantee optimum timing gear operation. The proof lies in the fact that Ferrari had to design and build at least ten different versions before finding an answer to the problem, thanks to the adoption of large diameter gears capable of containing the speed of rotation. With the shift to the 8-cylinder engines, accumulated experience proved to be invaluable. In this case, the 90° angle managed to combine a smooth cycle with containment of the vibrations deriving from the adoption of the flat-plane crankshaft. This was an obligatory choice because by dividing the running of the 8 cylinders into two separate four-cylinder units it allowed the exhausts of the two banks to be treated separately while also obtaining greater structural rigidity. It is also surprising that the two most characteristic features of the Cosworth DFV from 1967, the flat-plane crankshaft and the reduced angle between the valves (32°), even at the cost of sacrificing the maximum surface values, still today constitute the basis for the design of a Formula 1 engine. And it was

THE DEVELOPMENT OF SHELL FUEL OILS FOR FERRARI

	fuel	engine oil	gearbox oil
Bahrain	ULG 59L/9	Helix SL-0932*	Spirax L6285
Malaysia	ULG 59L/9	Helix SL-0932	Spirax L6285
Australia	ULG 59L/9	Helix SL-0932	Spirax L6285
San Marino	ULG 62L/3**	Helix SL-0932	Spirax L6285
Europe	ULG 62L/3	Helix SL-0932	Spirax L6285
Spain	ULG 62L/3	Helix SL-0932	Spirax L6285
Monaco	ULG 62L/3	Helix SL-0932	Spirax L6285
Britain	ULG 62L/3	Helix SL-0932	Spirax L6285
Canada	ULG 62L/3	Helix SL-0932	Spirax L-10193
U.S.A.	ULG 62L/3	Helix SL-0932	Spirax L-10193
France	ULG 62L/4	Helix SL-0932	Spirax L-10193
Germany	ULG 62L/4	Helix SL-0932	Spirax L-10193
Hungary	ULG 62L/4	Helix SL-0932	Spirax L-10193
Turkey	ULG 62L/4	Helix SL-0932	Spirax L-10193
Italy	ULG 62/5	Helix SL-0932	Spirax L-10193
China	ULG 62/5	Helix SL-0932	Spirax L-10193
Japan	ULG 62/5	Helix SL-0932	Spirax L-10193
Brazil	ULG 62/5	Helix SL-0932	Spirax L-10193

Shell Helix Racing SL- 0932 was developed as an aggressive oil, used in the final days of the V10 engine, giving a significant power increase over the previous race oil. It was used as the standard lubricant throughout the development of the V8, and further to successful feedback, continued into normal race use during its first season.
**Shell V-Power ULG 62L/3 was produced after an extensive series of tests between Shell and Ferrari. The fuel was designed to have improved power and better gravimetric fuel economy than previous fuels, as a result of changes to the vehicle fuel system.*

actually Cosworth's engineers who, perhaps finding themselves at their ease in a thoroughly explored "environment", achieved the most noteworthy results, at least at the level of pure engine design. They were the first to pass the 20,000 rpm threshold, representing a power output of 755 hp, thanks in part to notable increases in the operating pressures of the injection system, well over 95 bar, and then approached the incredible target of 21,000 rpm, corresponding to an average piston speed of around 27 m/1", piston acceleration of over 10,000 g and inertial forces of over 2.5 tons. While this record did not translate into opportunities for victory it was destined to remain unapproachable for many years, and not only due to regulatory restrictions. The very efficiency of the new engines killed off the nascent polemic caused by the perceived threat from the FIA's decision to admit in a transitory phase the previous season's 3-litre engines, albeit in a penalised form strangled by a 77 mm intake diameter and the limitation of the engine speed to 16,700 rpm. This threat soon proved to be wholly inoffensive given that it was at best a stop-gap measure, necessary to complete the grid and allow Toro Rosso, the only team to have taken up the option of retaining the Cosworth V10, to start the championship. There is nonetheless an interesting comparison to be

made between the characteristics of the two engines that suggests that the lack of competitiveness was, at least in part, caused by the chassis and driver failings rather than true engine deficiencies. The V10's 25 hp drop in power was in fact amply compensated by a weight saving of around 4 kg: just 93 kg against the 97 of the V8 and a decidedly "fuller" power band. Lastly, we should be grateful to a legislator that in bringing the V8 back into Formula 1 fashion allows us to make a direct evaluation of the progress made in forty years of continuous development from the Cosworth DFV of 1967 to the 2006 unit. The specific power output and peak engine speed were more than doubled while the weight was almost halved. The rapidity of this development seemingly ignores the obstacles constituted by the laws of physics and instead resembles the result of a Moore's Law applied to mechanical engineering.

Mauro Forghieri
Mauro Coppini

THE NEW
REGULATIONS

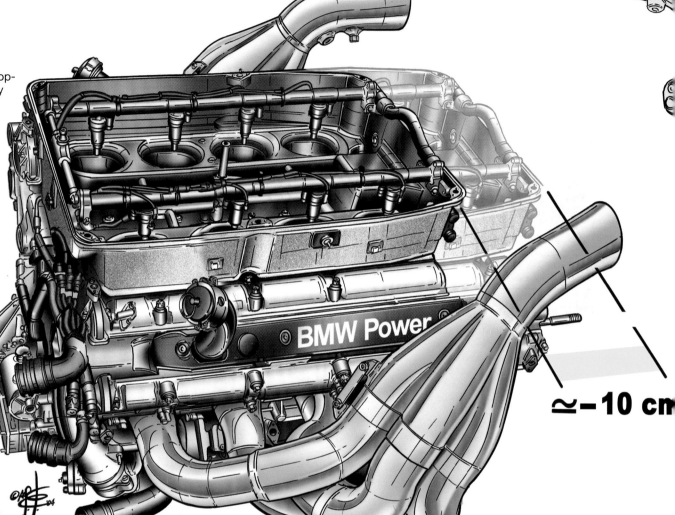

BMW Power

≃ -10 cm

An important development in the history of modern Formula One took place in 2006: the end of the three-litre engine, which was introduced in 1995, and its replacement by the new 2400 cc unit with identical architecture for everyone: and there was also a return to tyre changes during the race. The first revolution by the Federation was dictated by the necessity to reduce costs and performance. But the tyre change decision was a complete U-turn in relation to FIA's position of just a year earlier: a brusque change of direction, brought about first and foremost for safety purposes. This decision was influenced by the serious problems that arose at the 2005 Grand Prix of the United States on the Indianapolis oval. They culminated in the exclusion from the race of all the teams using Michelin tyres, which manifested serious problems during practice. Another rules revolution that also had severe repercussions at a technical level was the new qualifying system, which had the hoped for effect of providing greater spectacle in determining the order of the starting grid. These modifications will be analysed later, starting with the most significant rule limiting the engine's cubic capacity to 2400 cc with a maximum permitted division of eight cylinders and we shall then consider the other regulation limitations sector by sector.

ENGINES (ART. 5.6)
The new cubic capacity of 2400 cc instead of the traditional three-litres came into effect together with the obligation to reduce the cylinder division from the previous 10 to 8. The cylinder bank angle was also frozen at 90° for everyone, as were the bore at 98 mm and the interaction between the cylinders to 106.5 mm. Variable height air trumpets were also prohibited (Art. 5.6) as was the variable geometry of the exhaust manifolds. There was also the new minimum weight regulation, fixed at 95 kg with precise specifications concerning the mechanical components, which contributed to determining that weight. There

were no calculations to define the weight of the car, such as the clutch, electronic management system, oil reservoir, alternator, various liquids, exhaust pipes, the fixings between the chassis and the monocoque, water tank, heat exchangers, hydraulic system that operates the valves and all the components not considered integral parts of the engine. Ballast in excess of 2 kg was removed before weighing the car and determining its centre of gravity. Banning sophisticated materials of which the engines were to be built was strictly linked to the minimum weight of the car, with the parallel objective of reducing costs.

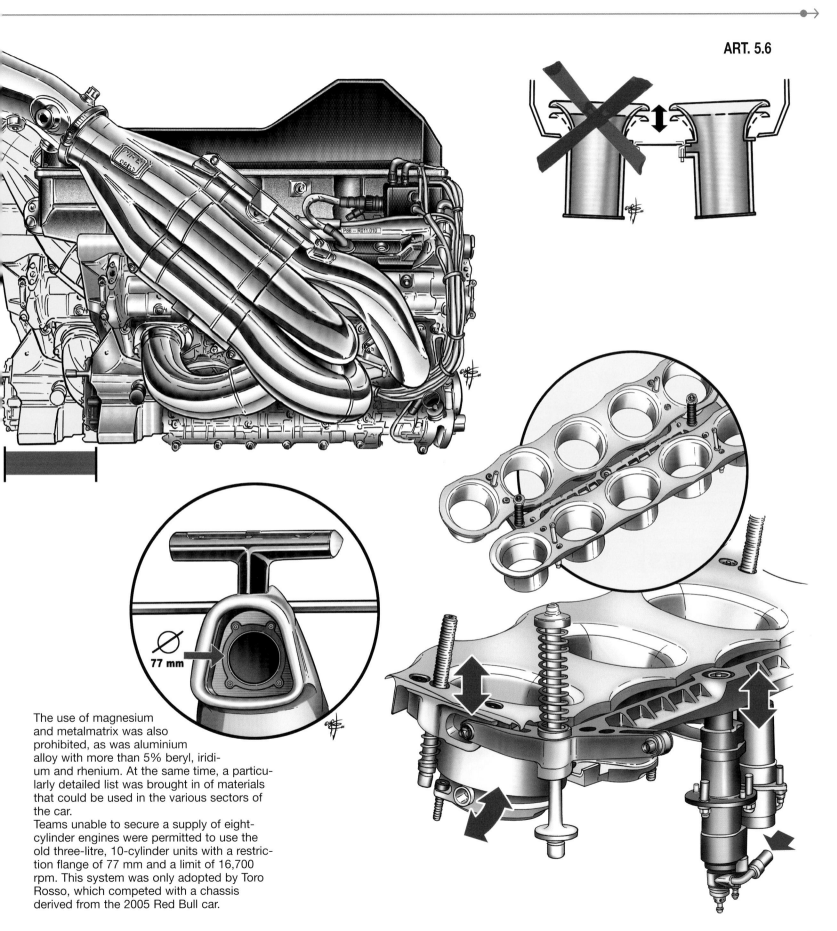

The use of magnesium and metalmatrix was also prohibited, as was aluminium alloy with more than 5% beryl, iridium and rhenium. At the same time, a particularly detailed list was brought in of materials that could be used in the various sectors of the car.

Teams unable to secure a supply of eight-cylinder engines were permitted to use the old three-litre, 10-cylinder units with a restriction flange of 77 mm and a limit of 16,700 rpm. This system was only adopted by Toro Rosso, which competed with a chassis derived from the 2005 Red Bull car.

∅ 77 mm

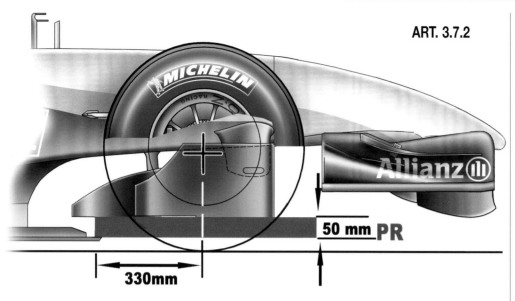

ART. 3.7.2

330mm

50 mm PR

AERODYNAMICS (ART. 3.7.2)

A further limitation to the aerodynamic appendages at the front of the car came in for the 2006 season. This was to limit the ground effect of the various guide vanes on the cars starting with 330 mm on the front axle onwards and was fixed at a height of +40 mm from the reference plane, while previously in the central zone of 50 cm it could drop as far as the plane itself. This limitation turned out to be extremely useful in the reduction of damage to the aerodynamic devices when a car went off the track.

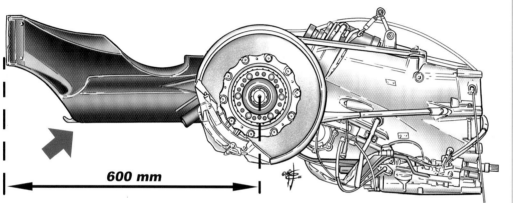

600 mm

CRASH TEST (ART. 16.4)

The Federation continued its campaign to improve safety. The rear crash test was made even more severe for 2006, with an increase in the speed of impact that went from 12 to 15 m/s. To ensure the best absorption, the bulk of the deformable structure behind the gearbox was increased: it was pushed up to 600 mm behind the rear axle – an increase of 100 mm – to guarantee the necessary absorption of a collision, the compression of which had to be contained up to the height of the rear axle. The illustration shows the gearbox of the BMW-Sauber and the massive bulk of the new deformable structure, which was 10 cm longer.

ART. 16.4

(v =12 m/s)   v = 15m/s

R A
A P

780 kg

600mm
(500mm)

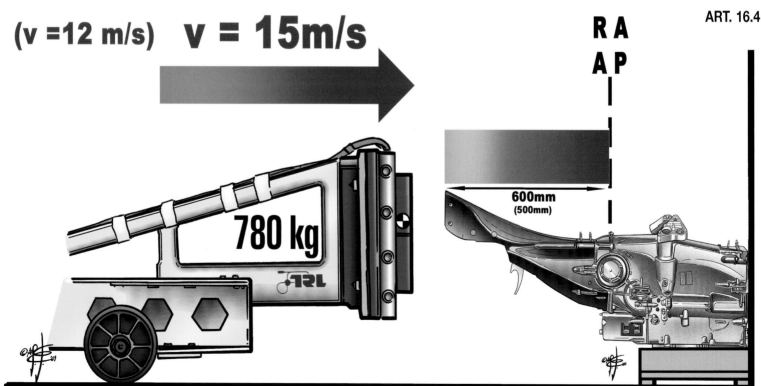

TALKING ABOUT
AERODYNAMICS

There were two principal themes in the aerodynamics sector in 2006: one was the abolition of the twin and single keels – with the exception of Ferrari – for maximum exploitation of the air flow under the front wing, further raised by the 2005 regulations. The other was the search for maximum efficiency at a loss of pure download in an attempt to ensure the car has the most constant possible aerodynamic set-up to exploit to the maximum the extreme development in the tyre sector and so reduce the penalty of the lower power of the new eight cylinder engine. Some developments that could have been worthy of deeper analysis in this chapter ended up in the Controversies section, because they were the subject of protests at the time they appeared; we refer in particular to Ferrari's faired wheels and the "towers" applied to the upper part of the BMW-Sauber chassis. The zero keel technique adopted by most teams found an exception in Renault, followed by Red Bull, preferred to keep the new development of the 2005 season, the V-keel with a highly permeable structure that embodied the structural advantages of the mono-keel without severe aerodynamic restrictions. However not a party to the "conservative" – at least in this sector – Ferrari who, despite a mono-keel, made life difficult for its rival Renault. There were many new aerodynamic developments, especially in the refinement of some features that established trends, like the large fins in the upper area of the sidepods, introduced in 2005 by BAR and copied by many teams, including the great rivals Ferrari and Renault.

_2001_

_2005_

"ZERO KEEL"

BMW-Sauber is the best example with which to show the move to the new zero-keel development, because this team used both solutions in the last two seasons: as far back as 2001 they introduced the twin keel and split front suspension wishbones; then they moved on to the single keel and in 2006 followed McLaren in anchoring the wishbones to the low area of the chassis. Among other things, the raising of the latter, even if not ideal in terms of suspension geometry, worked better for the front wing with the analogous raising imposed by the 2005 regulations.

MONO-KEEL

Ferrari was the only team to retain the central bulb for the monolithic lower wishbone mount. The inferior area of the chassis was further raised and made concave to the point that two protuberances jutted out to fit the pedals. The mandatory lateral safety protection elements required by the regulations are indicated by the second arrow.

FERRARI: FRONT WING

The front wing caused controversy, but it also taught a few lessons, with its raised flap running the entire width. It was copied by many teams, among them Maranello's great rival Renault, from the Grand Prix of Germany. Note the gentle link between the various sections of the main plane, which avoided problems that were discovered with the wing of the F2005, with its heavily stepped central section.

McLAREN

McLaren came up with an interesting new development at the Grand Prix of Monaco. It was a different anchorage point between the central pillar and the planes, something that generally took place with the main plane. In this specific case, the connection was placed midway between the main plane and the flap. It should be mentioned that McLaren further accentuated the narrowing in width of the planes to favour the alignment of the end plates with the tyres, even when steering.

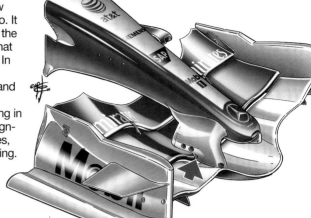

FERRARI DIFFUSER

The award for the most sophisticated rear end certainly goes to Ferrari, especially for the separation of the lower plane (1) of the wing, divided into two sections fixed directly to the high sides (2) of the diffuser. A technique that provided notable aerodynamic advantages, reducing the blocking effect and the loss of efficiency in this area. Note how the considerable height of the central channel permits the extraction of hot air from under the car, even exploiting three channels. Also note the slightly curved shape of the pads (3) in the lower part of the central channel to avoid brusque pitch sensitivity in the case of its eventual approach to the ground. As with last year's car, the drive shafts and the toe-in link were faired with an ample plane (4) in carbon fibre.

RENAULT

A clear derivation of the R25, the rear aerodynamics of the Renault maintained the accentuated fairing of the wing plane of the toe-in link, which acts as an air extractor for the lateral channels. The little flap and the substantial fairing in the drive shaft mount area were almost unchanged, their dimensions limited by the regulations. The new flap mount, introduced two years ago, was further accentuated on the R26.

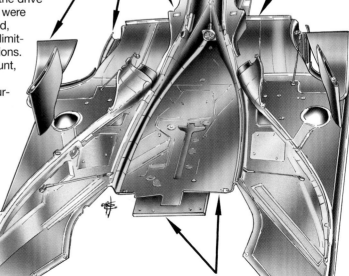

HONDA: LOWER BODY

Honda used a shorter lower body that excluded the initial part of the sidepods (1), as Renault had done. Note how the vertical fins (2) in front of the rear wheels can remain fixed to the underbody when being dismantled. The zone inside the rear wheels is notably curled (3) upwards. There are two mini-channels (4) at the sides of the central channel similar to those that had been used by Ferrari since the 2005 season. The lateral channels also had small Gurney flaps (5).

NEW TRENDS

BAR Honda taught some lessons with the 2005 introduction of fins in the initial upper area of the sidepods (see circle) and they became much bigger and integrated with the shape of the 'pods themselves on the 2006 car. This technique made many converts, but the more interesting thing was that Renault and Ferrari also took up these solutions. The former did so from the Grand Prix of Canada and the latter in China, in the closing stages of the world championship.

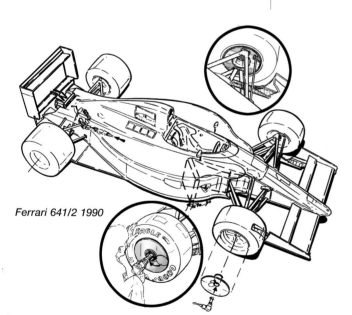

Ferrari 641/2 1990

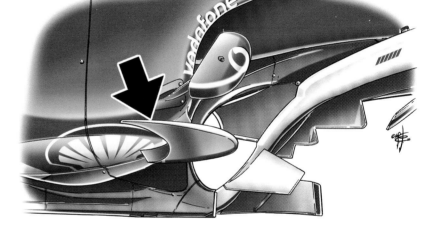

FAIRED WHEELS

One of the unique new developments of the season was the fairing applied to the outside of the Ferrari's rims of its rear wheels, which were then copied by Toyota (see illustration). This feature has, however, a precedent linked to Ferrari dating back to the 1990 season and the 641/2 – the successor to John Barnard's 640 – designed that season by Steve Nichols, when front wheel covers were tested. A step that only brought the Ferrari improvement in penetration at top speed in qualifying: if they had been used in the race, the braking system would have gone up in smoke. They were dropped and taken up again later for the internal part of the rim, along the lines that Barnard did a year earlier but only for the rear wheels at the Grand Prix of Mexico. Ferrari competed with the internal fairing when qualifying for the Grand Prix of Japan. The illustration shows both the intakes with the external disc, which even had a sort of stopper in the central area to create a perfect seal of the whole zone, plus the internal ones. Look closely and you will notice that the internal fairing is not so dissimilar to that now used by all the current cars.

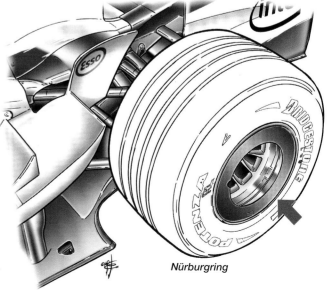

Nürburgring

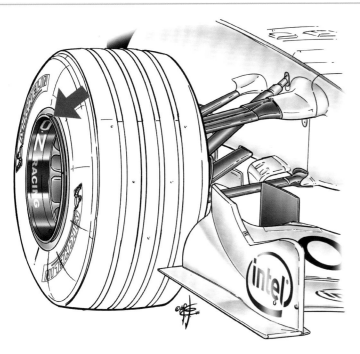

BMW-SAUBER: MONZA

Surprisingly, BMW-Sauber faired their front rims at Monza with a much different solution from that of Ferrari. It was simply a very thin ring that corrected the internal shape of the wheel and had a small protruding Gurney flap in relation to the rim itself. The vortices created by this protrusion interacted with those created by the wheel in movement and improved both the efficiency of the cooling air intake and penetration.

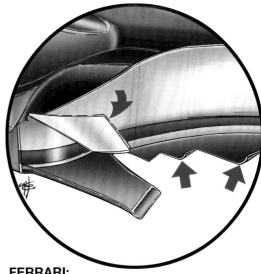

FERRARI: BARGE BOARDS BEHIND THE WHEELS

Ferrari came up with a new feature: these small "curls" applied first at Imola to a single tooth in the lower part of the turning vane behind the wheels and then at the Nürburgring on a second tooth (see illustration). Their purpose was to better manage the vortices that interact in that area to improve the extraction of air from the front wing and clean the flow towards the rear of the car. They worked in correlation with a new, greater incidence of the fin positioned up high, with the shadow plate down low, modified and given a generous lateral Gurney flap.

The evolution of this sector was constant at almost every race. These vortex generators appeared in Germany, shaped like small teeth and applied in the knife edge zone in the lower part of the tapered sidepods. Their task was to speed up the air flow towards the rear of the car ".

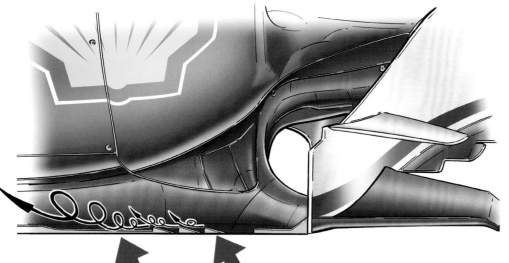

LOUVERS

Another new feature introduced by Ferrari concerned the louvers located near the end plates of the wing in the area close to the rear wheels, the purpose of which was to reduce turbulence. This technique was copied and used by Renault from the Grand Prix of Great Britain.

TOWERS

These vertical turning vanes only lasted for one test session on the Friday at the Grand Prix of France. They were introduced by BMW-Sauber, after which they were, quite rightly, banned by the Federation. They considerably improved the quality of air flow that hit the car, especially when in other cars' slipstreams.

"FOX EARS"

Such is the nickname given by the BAR-Honda technicians to this new aerodynamic feature that first appeared at Imola. Its purpose was to reduce the turbulence in the area at the front of the sidepods and the cockpit.

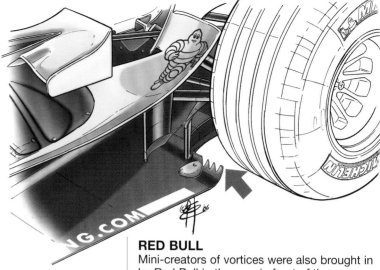

RED BULL

Mini-creators of vortices were also brought in by Red Bull in the area in front of the rear wheels, after which an isolated example remained for the entire season.

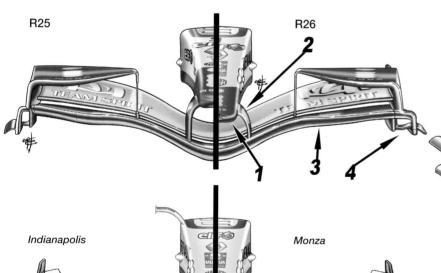

R25   R26

Indianapolis   Monza

Magny Cours   Hockenheim

FRONT WINGS

A comparison between two different front wings: the new one introduced in Canada (see illustration) and the old detached one below. It can be seen how the new solution has passages which are less brusque, to the advantage of the reduction of the lateral flow effect. The old technique guaranteed more load, but it was more sensitive to height variation.

RENAULT FRONT WINGS

Comparison between the various front wings used by Renault. Above, between those of the presentation of the R25, with the central part narrower and higher., (1) and the one used at the start of the season. The two support pillars (2) were more arched and shorter. The progression of the principal plane (3) was more blended, while the external portion (4) of the end plates was slightly bigger. The second comparison is between the wing that was raced until the Grand Prix of Germany and the new one with the full width flap of the Ferrari school, combined with a new main plane that was less V-shaped in the central area. The last comparison is between the two low load wings, which in turn were derived from the one used at Monza in 2005. In Canada and the United States there were small horns in the upper part of the chassis like those of Monza. Note the absence of the raised flap and the reduced chord of the traditional flaps.

TALKING ABOUT
SUSPENSIONS

There were no great innovations in the field of suspension if not the creation of front and rear configurations based on the integration of the mass damper exhaustively described in the 2005 season's Technical Analysis and in the chapters "Disputes" and "Renault". The French team had been thrown into disarray when the device was banned and it had had to modify its suspension configuration ahead of Hungarian Grand Prix. Naturally, all the teams worked hard to optimize the greater potential offered by the tyres in a situation of open competition, a factor that countered the reduction in performance deriving from the reduced power output of the new 8-cylinder engines. Even though there were no new layouts or particular innovations, all the leading teams continually tweaked their suspension geometries, Ferrari for example introducing modifications at the Nürburgring, Imola and Silverstone. The front strut mount on the upright introduced by BAR in 2001 and then reprised by Ferrari was eventually adopted by the rest of the field; however, it should be remembered that the feature had been introduced at the rear by John Barnard with the 412 T way back in 1994. Aerodynamics naturally had a great effect on suspension configurations, especially at the front where the almost total abolition of the dual or single keel revolutionised layouts. Most teams decided to follow the trail blazed by McLaren with the anchoring of the two lower wishbones directly to the lower part of the chassis. The notable exception was Ferrari, which retained a single keel design while Red Bull went with the Renault V-shaped keel configuration. In an interesting variation Midland-Spyker

effectively modified its 2005 chassis with the addition of two lateral mini-keels, nonetheless obtaining a notably clean underbody. The season's other curiosity was the retrograde step taken by Super Aguri in Germany with the introduction of the B version of the car derived from the old Arrows from 2002. The original car was fitted underslung rear brake calipers (reducing the centre of gravity of the unsprung weights), a feature introduced by Minardi in 1998 and then adopted across the board, while the new version represents the only example of a caliper mounted above and to the front of the upright. With the arrival of Mike Gascoyne, Toyota adopted a rear suspension configuration very similar to that of the French car.

RED BULL: V-SHAPED KEEL
Red Bull was the only team to follow Renault's lead with the V-shaped carbon structure for mounting the lower wishbone. This feature allowed the moving parts of the 2005 suspension to be retained together with good stiffness values.

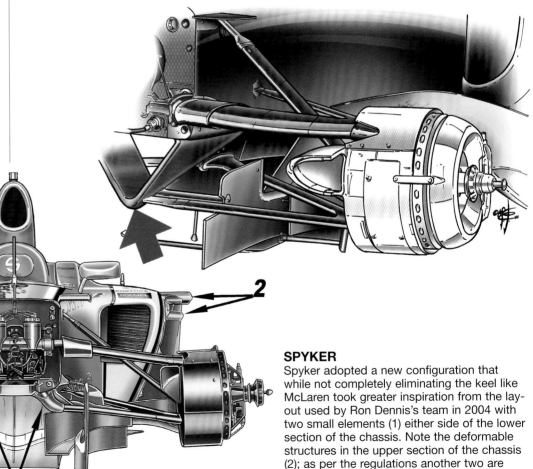

2

1

SPYKER
Spyker adopted a new configuration that while not completely eliminating the keel like McLaren took greater inspiration from the layout used by Ron Dennis's team in 2004 with two small elements (1) either side of the lower section of the chassis. Note the deformable structures in the upper section of the chassis (2); as per the regulations another two are located in the lower section.

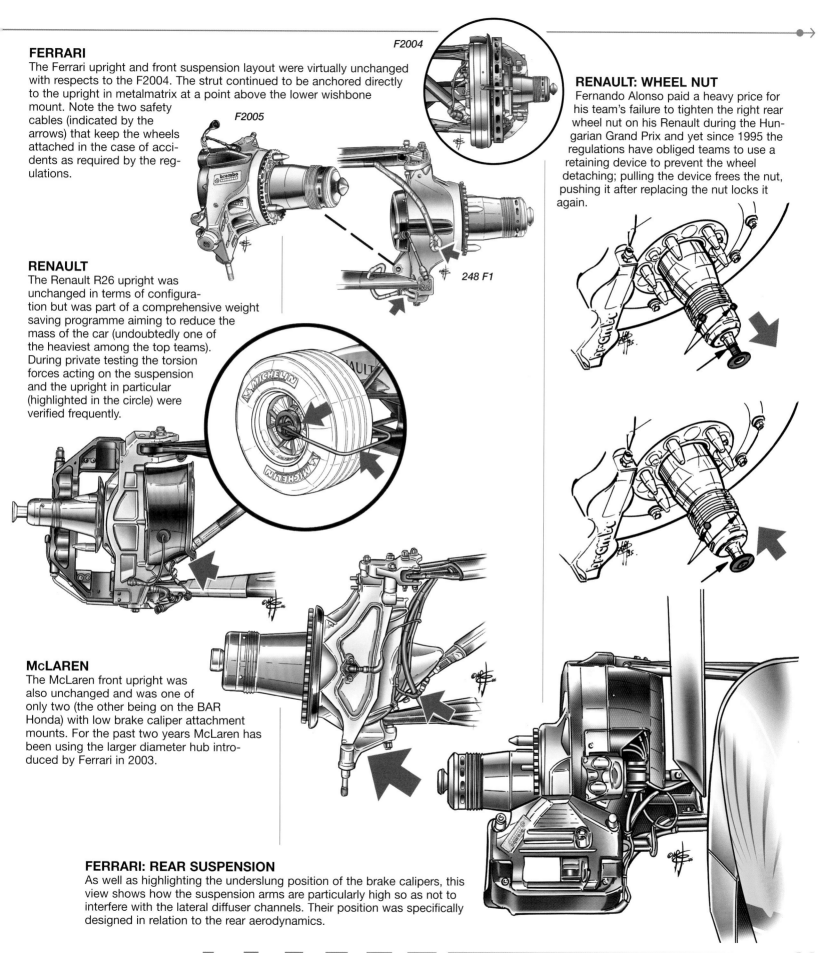

FERRARI

The Ferrari upright and front suspension layout were virtually unchanged with respects to the F2004. The strut continued to be anchored directly to the upright in metalmatrix at a point above the lower wishbone mount. Note the two safety cables (indicated by the arrows) that keep the wheels attached in the case of accidents as required by the regulations.

F2004

F2005

248 F1

RENAULT

The Renault R26 upright was unchanged in terms of configuration but was part of a comprehensive weight saving programme aiming to reduce the mass of the car (undoubtedly one of the heaviest among the top teams). During private testing the torsion forces acting on the suspension and the upright in particular (highlighted in the circle) were verified frequently.

RENAULT: WHEEL NUT

Fernando Alonso paid a heavy price for his team's failure to tighten the right rear wheel nut on his Renault during the Hungarian Grand Prix and yet since 1995 the regulations have obliged teams to use a retaining device to prevent the wheel detaching; pulling the device frees the nut, pushing it after replacing the nut locks it again.

McLAREN

The McLaren front upright was also unchanged and was one of only two (the other being on the BAR Honda) with low brake caliper attachment mounts. For the past two years McLaren has been using the larger diameter hub introduced by Ferrari in 2003.

FERRARI: REAR SUSPENSION

As well as highlighting the underslung position of the brake calipers, this view shows how the suspension arms are particularly high so as not to interfere with the lateral diffuser channels. Their position was specifically designed in relation to the rear aerodynamics.

SUPER AGURI

The unusual brake caliper position (1) introduced by Super Aguri at the German Grand Prix together with the whole new rear end. The gearbox is no longer the Arrows carbonfibre unit but rather a titanium casting. The torsion bars (2) pivoted internally, while the third transverse damper (3) was located above the casting. The dampers and the anti-roll bar were internal (4) with separate fuel tanks (5).

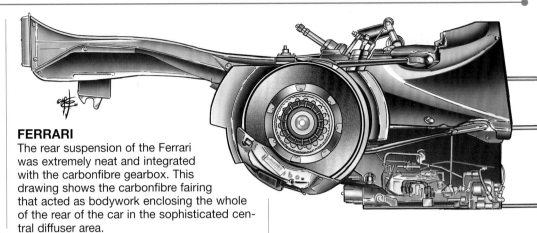

FERRARI

The rear suspension of the Ferrari was extremely neat and integrated with the carbonfibre gearbox. This drawing shows the carbonfibre fairing that acted as bodywork enclosing the whole of the rear of the car in the sophisticated central diffuser area.

FERRARI

The general layout of the Ferrari's rear suspension was unchanged, with modifications to the geometry being made during the season: the difference seen from the outside was the more frequent use of long torsion bars. The third transverse damper was equipped with a separate gas cylinder. Note the carbonfibre fairing acting as a second skin over the whole of the rear area expelling the hot air in the central section of the diffuser.

TOYOTA AND RENAULT

Toyota adopted a rear suspension layout that was very similar to that of the Renault, abandoning the rotating Sachs dampers. The (traditional) dampers (1) were mounted horizontally above the gearbox casting with a third central element (2). The torsion bars were external (3), clearly similar to the Renault layout: the dampers are indicated in (1), the central element in (2); in (3) and (4) you can see the anti-roll bar and the torsion bars respectively. This carbonfibre bulkhead (5) concealed the mass damper.

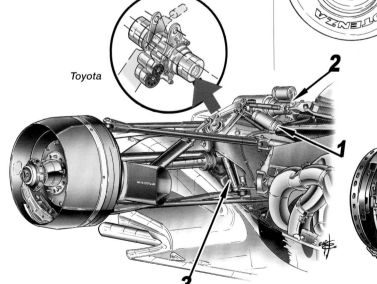

Toyota

Renault

TALKING ABOUT
TYRES AND BRAKES

TYRES

There were two regulation changes for 2006 that had profound effects on the way the final season of the tyre war between Michelin and Bridgestone played out. For one, the new generation of 2.4-litre V8 cars placed a very different set of demands upon the tyres than the previous 3-litre V10s. For another, the regulation that had banned tyre changes during the races in 2005 was repealed, allowing the tyres to be changed at pit stops once more. This removed what had been a key Bridgestone limitation to performance.

Statistically Michelin departed victorious as the tyre supplier to the world title-winning Renault team. But Bridgestone more often appeared to have a performance advantage, particularly in the season's latter half, this helping the Ferrari team launch a very strong comeback.

Although the banning of pit stops appeared to hurt Bridgestone very badly in 2005, there is every reason to believe that with their 2006 range, Bridgestone would have been competitive regardless of the prevailing rules. They followed a radically different construction philosophy to that used in previous years, one that allowed them to take advantage of more exotic compounds.

In previous years Bridgestone tended to have to run harder, less grippy compounds than Michelin because of how their more rigid sidewall construction imposed greater wear rates by forcing the tread to run hotter for a given compound softness. For '06 Bridgestone adopted a more Michelin-like construction with more flexible sidewalls, a direction they had been tentatively going in since the end of 2004. The result was a very evenly matched tyre war over the season.

The new engine regulations made for cars with around 750bhp, as much as 200bhp down on what the best of the V10 engines had given. But in many cases the loss of engine performance was compensated for by greater aerodynamic performance. The new, shorter engines freed up a lot of space at the rear of the cars that was used to increase their downforce, particularly from the underbody. The implication of all this on the tyres was very significant. One the one hand, it meant they had to deal with less longitudinal load (lower accelerative forces because of less engine torque, lower braking force because of the combination of slower straightline and faster corner entry). On the other hand, they had to deal with higher lateral loads from the increased cornering potential of the cars.

In concert with efforts by both Michelin and Bridgestone to have greater peak performance, even at the expense of narrower operating windows, this turned out to be a very tricky combination. It made for tyres that were extremely sensitive to track temperature. Getting the tyres to warm up quickly enough for first lap performance was often very difficult if the track was even slightly cooler than when the tyre selections were made.

Some time in advance of each race teams were given a selection of tyre specifications from which to choose. From this choice they would select two specifications to take to the event, each of which would be tried in Friday practice. The rules stipulated that from Saturday onwards only one tyre specification could be used. So Friday would typically be spent trying to get the necessary durability from the tyre that was faster over one lap. The combination of having to make the tyre selection in advance with the very narrow track temperature window of these tyres meant that both companies tended to formulate tyres for specific track temperature ranges. So whereas in previous years the teams usually had the choice of harder or softer compounds, now it was more a choice of a higher or a lower temperature tyre – and which was chosen depended heavily upon how the weather turned out.

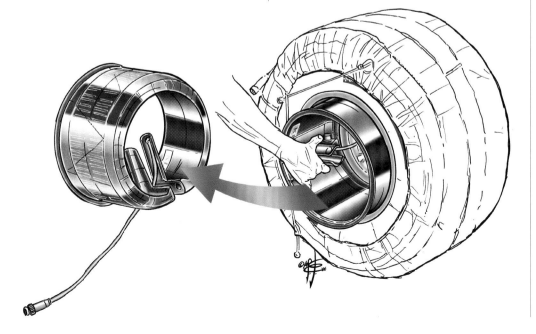

INTERNAL TYRE WARMERS
A new techno-fad swept through Fomula 1 in the 2006 season after being introduced by Toyota at the 2005 Canadian GP: heat blankets applied to the carbonfibre discs that are coupled inside the wheels. In reality the idea had occurred to Gary Anderson in 1991 with elements then supplied by Sparco and now manufactured by KLS. The aim is that of generating different warming temperatures between the tread (with the classic tyre blankets) and the shoulders of the tyres, with a certain influence also being exerted on the tyre pressures so as to bring them close to full operating level for the flying quaification lap. These devices were adopted by Toyota, McLaren, Ferrari, BMW and, in the second part of the season, Williams.

The mechanism determining a tyre's actual compound softness when it's in action is complex and is only partly to do with the base softness resulting from its ingredients. The other two main determinants are the tyre's temperature and the contact frequency (ie, the rubber's frequency of contact with the track). These work in opposing directions.

As temperature rises the compound becomes softer (more rubberised). As contact frequency rises the compound becomes harder (more vitreous). Getting to the point at which the tyre achieves its ideal state (its vitreous transition) is therefore a delicate balancing act. So simple concepts of a harder or softer compound were not as relevant in 2006. These referred just to the base compounds and were no longer adequate.

The higher the contact frequency, the more temperature you need to compensate in order to keep the tyre at its intended compound softness. So how are each of these variables controlled?

Contact frequency is about how the loads react upon the rubber. Because rubber is a visco-elastic material, the way it reacts to loads is not consistent. Up to a point the rubber will accept incoming energy and react against it, trying to spring back in the opposite direction to the load and thereby creating grip. Beyond that point the rubber cannot regain shape quickly enough to absorb the next input of load. This has the effect of stiffening and hardening the compound, breaking the process down and causing the tyre to slide. When the compound is overwhelmed in this way it is often better to go to a harder base compound that will better stand up to the energy being fed into it. So what is ostensibly a harder compound can in effect be a softer one, depending upon the contact frequency.

Tyre temperature is largely to do with the amount of energy the tyre is absorbing – though track temperature plays a significant part. As the tyre accepts the loads, so the energy is absorbed and this creates heat. The temperature at which an F1 tyre typically achieves its vitreous transition and thereby achieves its ideal, intended compound softness is 95-100-deg C. If the base compound is a little too hard, the temperature may fall

short of that ideal. But, as explained in the previous paragraph, sometimes it may be necessary to go to a harder base compound to deal with the effects of the contact frequency. Such is the delicate balancing act to be played.

The 2006 generation of cars, with their high lateral loads but relatively low longitudinal loads, made this balancing act yet more precarious. Contact frequency under lateral load increased (making the compound harder), but under longitudinal load decreased (making it softer). The higher lateral loads will have been making the compound hotter (therefore softer), the lower longitudinal loads will have been making it cooler (therefore harder). These cars placed more variation of demand upon the tyres and the ideal window where contact frequency was in harmony with temperature was thus narrowed even further than before.

When the track temperature proved significantly above or below what was forecast when tyre selections were made, there could be major issues with first lap performance (hurting qualifying and out laps) as the tyres didn't come up to temperature quickly enough because of the opposing mechanisms determining that temperature. Graining, where a layer of the tread tears but remains on the tread surface for several laps before shearing off, also became more of a problem as tyres became too brittle through lack of temperature or too much contact frequency.

On the other hand, heat degradation – where the tyre becomes too hot, the compound therefore too soft to accept the contact frequencies acting upon it – became far less of a problem than in the V10 era. The Montreal circuit used to induce heat degradation in a major way but as Bridgestone's Hisao Suganuma explains, that's no longer the case: "It's incredible. This used to be a very difficult circuit for heat degradation. Controlling that really limited how soft you could go on compounds. But now, we don't even think about heat degradation here; it's just not an issue. So we can go as soft as possible on compounds. The limitation here now is graining – of the rears in particular. Because the cars are turning into the hairpin quite suddenly, it creates graining of the rears." An unintended side effect of that phenomenon was that the tracks tended to rubber-in more this year, grip building up quickly between Friday and Sunday and thereby making tyre choice even more difficult.

What also surprised both tyre and car engineers was that the lower engine power and return of pit stops didn't automatically mean that the base compounds became softer. At tracks where front tyre performance was the limiting factor, it was quite often necessary to

use a harder compound than in '05 such was the increase in cornering performance of the cars. Only at tracks where rear tyre performance is the limitation – traction-type tracks such as Monaco, Hockenheim and Montreal – were softer compounds than before generally used.

With the return of pit stops and typical stint durations of around 20 laps, wear ceased to be the factor it was in 2005. This on its own would probably have allowed Bridgestone to be more competitive than in '05 even had they stayed with the same philosophy of construction. But with more flexible Michelin-like sidewalls absorbing some of the energy that would otherwise be fed into the tread, the '06 generation of Bridgestone had a lower wear rate anyway. In fact, Bridgestone found that their new construction would have been fully capable of doing a full distance in the extreme heat of Bahrain and Malaysia even though they were no longer required to. This was ironic given that the year before, when the regulations insisted they had to do the entire race, they had been incapable of lasting at these two venues.

With much less to distinguish between the technical format of the two makes of tyre than in previous years, which of them came out on top in any given weekend seemed to be more driven by the qualities of the cars using them. There were some weekends where one or the other manufacturer seemed to have an advantage, but this seemed more to do with changes in track temperature taking one type of tyre out of its operating band, but not the other. This was demonstrated quite clearly at Barcelona where on Saturday Bridgestone/Ferrari had a clear advantage over Michelin/Renault, but higher temperatures on Sunday swung the pattern decisively in the opposite direction. At Monaco the pattern worked the other way around – with Bridgestone enjoying an advantage on race day after giving best to Michelin in qualifying. As a generality the Michelins seemed slightly less prone to graining but seemed to have a slightly narrower track temperature band. When track temperature became higher than forecast, it was usually Bridgestone that emerged as quicker.

When this happened however, it frequently became a more marginal tyre too. Its pace advantage over the Michelin may have increased, but the performance became very tricky to access if excessive blistering was to be avoided. At Magny Cours Ferrari opted for a softer tyre than Bridgestone advised. It was very quick, but very delicate, particularly in the early stages with a heavy fuel load. Team play was used to allow Michael Schumacher to drive relatively slowly in the early laps to protect the tyres, with team-mate Felipe

Massa riding shotgun, preventing Michael from attack by Fernando Alonso's Michelin-shod Renault. Mark Webber's Williams showed just how delicate this Bridgestone was when his Williams blew a rear tyre because of internal blistering.

This delicate balance was also evident at Hockenheim, as Suganuma explains: "The main improvement in our '06 performance came from our new construction family. But as the season went on we got more out of the tyre. The difference was in how it was used. Initially we struggled to get the most out of it consistently. But our understanding – and that of our teams – allowed us to understand better just how soft a compound this construction and this type of car allowed us, of how much more the track rubbered in this year and how big the difference in behaviour of the tyre was from Friday to Sunday. Magny Cours and Hockenheim were a big lesson to us in this respect."

This mid-season surge from Bridgestone stung Michelin into further compound developments. Up until this point, constructions had been the main area of development for the French company. Giving some indication of the pace of construction development, they began the year with the same F15/R18 combination they'd ended '05 with but by the time of Brazil they were up to F25 and R31 – representing 10 evolutions of front construction and 13 of rears. This figure is, however, flattered by the fact that each of the six Michelin teams required slightly different qualities of the construction, according to their weight distribution, aero performance and driver style. But the pace of development was also driven by just how differently the V8 generation of cars used their tyres.

"We quickly found that the cars were no longer cornering in three distinct phases of entry, mid-corner and exit," says Michelin's Nick Shorrock. "Instead they were going round in a constant shallow rear end slide. This made for very different rigidity requirements. Getting the casing less rigid to allow the tyre to slide more means you need more rigidity within the rubber itself. So the trade off between casing and rubber stiffness became very different with this generation of cars – and different between cars too."

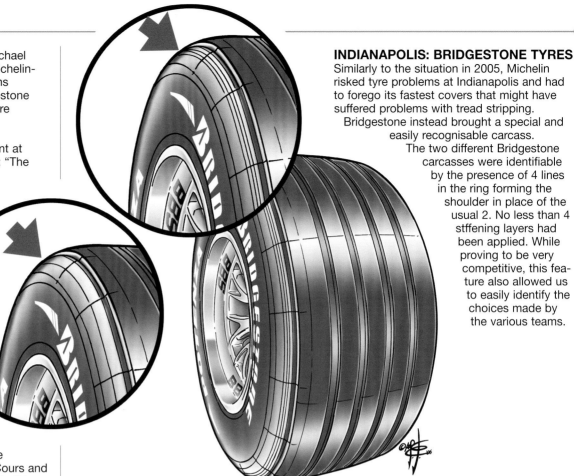

●→

INDIANAPOLIS: BRIDGESTONE TYRES

Similarly to the situation in 2005, Michelin risked tyre problems at Indianapolis and had to forego its fastest covers that might have suffered problems with tread stripping. Bridgestone instead brought a special and easily recognisable carcass.
The two different Bridgestone carcasses were identifiable by the presence of 4 lines in the ring forming the shoulder in place of the usual 2. No less than 4 stffening layers had been applied. While proving to be very competitive, this feature also allowed us to easily identify the choices made by the various teams.

Into the last two events of the season Bridgestone took a dramatic leap forward in their qualifying form, with Ferrari showing a huge superiority in qualifying yet they insist there was no tyre-related technical development behind this. "We brought familiar constructions and compounds," says Bridgestone's chief of track engineering Kees van de Grint. "We can only assume the conditions fitted perfectly for us and poorly for our competitor."

Changeable weather during the Chinese Grand Prix weekend gave an excellent insight into the relative Bridgestone and Michelin wet weather performances. In the heavy rain of Saturday practice it was apparent that the Bridgestone extreme wet was still quicker than the Michelin equivalent – just as it has traditionally been. A more traditional Bridgestone construction, its stiff sidewalls seem to allow better 'mechanical' grip, with more opposing rubber deformation of the tread to aid 'indentation' – a force opposing that of the cornering. But as the track began to dry it was clear that the Michelin intermediate was

usable much earlier than the Bridgestone equivalent. This gave Renault a huge advantage in the semi-dry conditions of qualifying, just as it had during the race in Hungary. But as it dried yet further, the Michelin inter would overheat in conditions where the Bridgestone inter was still working well. It was clear that each company had placed the weather window of their intermediate at different places. But the Bridgestone drivers had much the more comfortable changeover period from inters to dries because not only did the inters stay good into quite dry conditions, but their dry weather tyre was usable in damper conditions than the Michelin one. The Bridgestone drivers had a wider dry-inters changeover window, but the Michelin drivers enjoyed a wider inters-wet changeover period.

Such competitive variation made the tyre war an excellent mechanism for inducing a level of unpredictability in the sport, and there are those who feel that its ending and a single supply Bridgestone tyre for 2007 is a negative thing.

Mark Hughes

BRIDGESTONE

Race	Ferrari	Williams	Toyota	Midland	Super Aguri	Comments
Bahrain	**Ferrari**	**Williams**	**Toyota**	**Midland**	**Super Aguri**	Williams and Toyota had joined the Bridgestone squad. The 2006 Bridgestone front tyres looked squarer than the previous type externally but emphasis was put more into the construction. Bridgestone tested various co structions during winter to improve longitudinal grip. The concept behind the new construction change was to be able to use a softer compound with less graining. There were 3 compounds from the medium range and top 3 teams ended up using the same compound which was the softest available in Bahrain. The tyres that Massa and Michael Schumacher used were of the same compound but of different constructions. Although bo utilized the new construction, Massa used a more flexible one which warmed up more quickly. Williams and Toyota ended up using the same latest construction too, but Toyota suffered warm-up problems with its tyres could not get sufficient grip. In the end, two compounds were selected by all Bridgestone drivers, there was not much difference between them. Super Aguri used the tyres with the old standard construction due to thei lack of testing with the new one.
Prime	MSC	MW & NR	RSC & JT	?	TS & YI	
Option	Massa					
Malaysia	**Ferrari**	**Williams**	**Toyota**	**Midland**	**Super Aguri**	Bridgestone took 4 different compounds from their soft to medium range for its five teams in Malaysia. Just as in Bahrain, Ferrari opted to use the proven compounds matched with the 2006 construction while Williams Toyota went for the new generation of compounds for their two tyre options. Midland had what was believed to be the same compounds as Ferrari. These four teams all settled for the softer of the two compounds avail to each team. Super Aguri had the two specifications of tyres with the same compound which was from slightly harder end of the suitable range for Malaysia allied to the old and new constructions that the top three Bridgestone users had been running since the start of the season. In the end, they chose to run the one with new construction. On the race day, the ambient and track temperatures were cooler than anticipated and Bridgestone runners had a bit of trouble generating heat into the tyres, thus many drivers reported lack of grip. However, Hirohide Hamashima (Head of Tyre Development, Bridgestone Motorsport) hinted it was not total down to the cooler track temperature but the position of compounds might have shifted slightly by the introduction of the 2006 construction.
HARD					TS & YI	
SOFT	MSC & FM	MW & NR	RSC & JT	CA & TM		
Australia	**Ferrari**	**Williams**	**Toyota**	**Midland**	**Super Aguri**	Bridgestone introduced a new generation of compounds in Melbourne. There were a total of 4 compounds available in Albert Park, Williams and Toyota dutifully took the latest compound because it offered better warm and first lap performance which happened to be the key issue of the weekend. The race was held four weeks later than usual (autumn rather than late summer) due to the Commonwealth Games. The new compounds w effective in cool weather, Toyota who had been having tyre temperature problem in the first two races, was able to maximize its advantage. Ralf Schumacher finished third. Ferrari had a choice of the new compound but not even try it! Ross Brown explained the reason as 'the damp track condition of the Saturday morning prevented it.' They stayed with what they were familiar with for the race, and as it turned out, that was a wrong cal Although Michael Schumacher was quick once the tyres got up to working temperature, he struggled badly during the qualifying session and the race, especially right after each of the Safety Car periods.
HARD	MSC & FM			CA & TM		
SOFT		MW & NR	RSC & JT		TS & YI	
San Marino	**Ferrari**	**Williams**	**Toyota**	**Midland**	**Super Aguri**	Bridgestone provided 5 compounds for its teams which were further developed along the line of the latest family of compounds which had shown their effectiveness in Melbourne. Midland had joined the top three Brid stone teams by switching to the latest constructions, that left Super Aguri as the only team staying with the older construction. Ferrari chose the new generation of Bridgestone compounds which they did not race in Au tralia. The Italian team decided to run the softer of the two options. It offered first lap performance that the team was looking for, but when Ferrari put the new set onto M. Schumacher for his second stint during the rac mysteriously it lost the pace. It seemed that this compound suffered overheating during the race and it was later thought that the compound was better off to go through a heat-cycle before the race. Hence, After this ra this compound was available on some other occasions, but Ferrari avoided to use it unless they had no other choices.
HARD			RSC & JT			
SOFT	MSC & FM	MW & NR		CA & TM	TS & YI	
Europe	**Ferrari**	**Williams**	**Toyota**	**Midland**	**Super Aguri**	For its teams, the Japanese tyre manufacture came to Nurburgring with 3 compounds which were all used in Imola. Bridgestone's top three teams chose the same Hard compound for 2 consecutive races, in fact the Ha compounds were the same for every team. It is interesting to note that Ferrari avoided selecting the compound that M. Schumacher had lost pace with during the second stint of the race in Imola as their designated So and decided to try the Soft raced successfully by Williams's Mark Webber two weeks ago. Therefore, the 2 specifications that Ferrari had were exactly same as the ones that Williams and Toyota had in Imola. Coinciden ly, the specification combination that Ferrari had in Imola became that of Williams and Toyota in Nurburgring! As for the construction, Midland and Super Aguri had switched to the latest ones used previously by the top three teams. However, the Softs were too soft. The grip did not come back after an initial graining period. On the other hand, the Hard was fast enough and consistent, so everybody decided to qualify and race with the Hard except for Midland.
HARD	MSC & FM	MW & NR	RSC & JT		TS & FM	
SOFT				CA & TM		
Spain	**Ferrari**	**Williams**	**Toyota**	**Midland**	**Super Aguri**	There were 5 different compounds to choose from at the Circuit de Catalunya. The Softs had so much graining and looked too soft. Ferrari had 2 options of tyres from different family. Michael Schumacher stayed on the Soft most of the time during Saturday morning, just before the qualifying session, they chose the harder of the two, and the other Bridgestone runners chose the Hard as well except Midland. However Midland's Soft we comparable to the Hard use by the others anyway. Ferraris were quick and looked unbeatable on old tyres during Saturday morning but they struggled to keep up with Renault on the race day. After the race, Hirohide Hamashima thought the track was too rubbered-in for the Hards to bite into the surface.
HARD	MSC & FM	MW & NR	RSC & JT		TS & FM	
SOFT				CA & TM		
Monaco	**Ferrari**	**Williams**	**Toyota**	**Midland**	**Super Aguri**	Last time Bridgestone won in the Principality was in 2001. It looked as if the Japanese tyre manufacture and Ferrari was on their way to the top of the podium in 2006 until Saturday night. The number of the tyre compoun brought to Monaco was five. Ferrari, Toyota, and Williams had the Hard with the same compounds, and Ferrari and Toyota decided to use it for the race while Williams went for the Soft. Williams's Webber qualified 2nd wit and showed fantastic pace in the race before his cracked exhaust forced him to retire. It was interesting that Ferrari took some time to decide which specification to go with. M. Schumacher stayed with a used set of the S in Saturday morning session. He only tried a new set of the Hard at the end of session. Nevertheless, after starting from the pit-lane, M. Schumacher recovered to finish 5th while setting the fastest lap of the race.
HARD	MSC & FM		RSC & JT	CA & TM		
SOFT		MW & NR			TS & FM	
G. Britain	**Ferrari**	**Williams**	**Toyota**	**Midland**	**Super Aguri**	There were 6 compounds all together, 1 Hard and 5 different Softs. It was unusually warm in Silverstone, and the track temperature was well over 40 degrees. Sato was the only one to choose the Hard, and the rest of Bridgestone drivers opted for Soft. This was due to the fact there were not a great deal of difference between the respective Soft and Hard. The balance was fine and the performance drop-off was minimal for Ferrari du the race, but they could not match the pace of Renault who got their tyres spot on.
HARD					Sato	
SOFT	MSC & FM	MW & NR	RSC & JT	CA & TM	Montagny	
Canada	**Ferrari**	**Williams**	**Toyota**	**Midland**	**Super Aguri**	Bridgestone brought 6 compounds including new types. They were all from the softer end of the range. Ferrari selected the Hard (the hardest of all available in Montreal) which was the same specification used by M. Sc macher on his way to the victory in Nurburgring. The choices of Toyota drivers were split. Trulli opted to use the Hard which was the new compound and a little softer than the one used by Ferrari. Super Aguri drivers ch the same. Ralf Schumacher favored the Soft. The softest compound was chosen by both Williams and Midland. It was rather hot day in Montreal, and Williams' Mark Webber and Ralf Schumacher suffered tyre graining throughout the race and thus lack of grip. In contrast, Ferrari's choice was a little out of the operating temperature during the Qualifying session, but it provided speed and consistency in the race and Michael Schumach came home with 2nd. It should be noted that the track surface crumbled away from the forces which was exerted by soft rubbers. The track was covered by tyre marbles and stones at the end.
HARD	MSC & FM		Trulli		TS & FM	
SOFT		MW & NR	RSC	CA & TM		
USA	**Ferrari**	**Williams**	**Toyota**	**Midland**	**Super Aguri**	Bridgestone waited till Wednesday before the race to decide on the specifications for the Indianapolis. They brought tyres which comprised of 6 different compounds and 2 constructions. The Primes incorporated the la construction which had softer sidewall and the Options were with 2006 construction as back-ups. The Primes worked without any problems and eventually, all the teams chose to run the respective Primes. Ferrari's cho was a slightly softer compound than Toyota's or Williams's. Midland also took advantage of their Bridgestones in Indianapolis to qualify 14th and 15th but they could not convert that into a good finish in the race.
Prime	MSC & FM	MW & NR	RSC & JT	CA & TM	TS & FM	
Option						
France	**Ferrari**	**Williams**	**Toyota**	**Midland**	**Super Aguri**	There were 5 compounds available at Magny-Cours, they were from the medium-soft range and race proven. All the Softs that Bridgestone brought showed graining to certain extent, but to close the point deficit to Renault, Ferrari and Bridgestone had to go aggressive. In fact, Ferrari did not bother to try the Hard at all and they stayed with the Soft, anticipating that the track would be well rubbered-in during the race. Williams hac same idea as Ferrari. Toyota were more conservative and they went for the Hard which they thought would give them more consistency in the race. Local boy Montagny opted for the Soft with 3 stop strategy while his team mate Sato went for the Hard doing a 2 stopper. It was interesting to note how the Ferrari's softs performed during the second stint. M. Schumacher nursed his tyres at the beginning of the stint and he kept good p to the end while Massa's pace fell off after pushing hard at the beginning of the stint. Webber's left rear delaminated after overheating.
HARD			RSC & JT	CA & TM	Sato	
SOFT	MSC & FM	MW & NR			Montagny	
Germany	**Ferrari**	**Williams**	**Toyota**	**Midland**	**Super Aguri**	4 compounds were available from Bridgestone for Hockenheim. Although the drivers had to nurse the tyres carefully, Ferrari used the softer of their options because they thought that they needed to control the race fro the front. This was the softest compound that Bridgestone had at the German track. MF1's Monteiro and Super Aguri chose a touch harder compound than Ferrari. Williams decided to use the Hard after the Soft had shown signs of drop-off during free practice session. Toyota also went for the Hard that was the hardest available in Hockenheim. According to Hamashima, Toyota could have used the Soft but they chose the Hard for better durability and consistency. Ferrari's choice paid off in the race and they scored comfortable 1-2 finish.
HARD		MW & NR	RSC & JT	Albers		
SOFT	MSC & FM			Monteiro	TS & SY	
Hungary	**Ferrari**	**Williams**	**Toyota**	**Midland**	**Super Aguri**	Graining was the issue with the soft Bridgestones. Therefore every Bridgestone shod car opted to run the harder of the two they had. Among the top 3 Bridgestone runners, Toyota's hard was thought to be the hardest all, William's being in the middle, Ferrari's choice was the softest, but it did not really matter because it rained on the race day. Bridgestone's intermediates did not work as good as Michelin's in the early stage of the rac when the track was still very wet, but once the dry line started to appear, it began to perform. M. Schumacher kept the same set of intermediates at the final stop but the track became too dry toward the end. His intern diates became too bold to hold off the rivals who were on dry tyres. He retired with a bent track rod eventually.
HARD	MSC & FM	MW & NR	RSC & JT	CA & TM	TS & SY	
SOFT						
Turkey	**Ferrari**	**Williams**	**Toyota**	**Midland**	**Super Aguri**	Bridgestone came to Turkey with 7 compounds. Usually the compounds are closely matched within a working range, but 'some Softs were extremely soft and some Hards were really hard' according to Hisao Suganum Ferrari had Hockenheim Hard as the designated Soft here, but it proved to be too soft. Thus Ferrari went for the harder of the two, but their Hard was still the softest of all Bridgestone compounds raced. Graining appea first at the front, then at the rear, and it was obvious that the tyre needed nursing. But it was not graining that M. Schumacher suffered from after the first stop during the safety car period when he lost a position to Alon His rear tyres suffered blistering. MF1's Albers and Super Aguri shared the same compound. Williams, R. Schumacher, and Monteiro opted for the compounds from medium range. Trulli was the only one who selected t tyre from the hard range.
HARD	MSC & FM		Trulli	Monteiro		
SOFT		MW & NR	RSC	Albers	TS & SY	
Italy	**Ferrari**	**Williams**	**Toyota**	**Midland**	**Super Aguri**	Bridgestone took only 3 compounds for Monza. Those compounds were all previously used in racing conditions. The top three Bridgestone runners chose the same compounds for their 2 options but Williams and Toyota matched those compounds with the latest construction which was designed to suit the fastest track of the year. Midland and Super Aguri selected their 2 tyre options which were one step softer than the top three teams, meaning their Hard was identical to the Soft of the big teams. Again, Ferrari played conservative and did not bother to try the Soft at all, and they stayed with the Hard which proved to be quick during three days of testin previous week. Williams and Toyota opted for the Soft, Super Aguri selected the Hard, and MF1 went for the Soft, an adventurous choice. Although Michael Schumacher won the race comfortably, he reported to Bridgest that Ferrari should have chosen a compound which was one step softer than they actually used. He never forgets about racing even on the emotional day on which he announced his retirement at the end of the season.
HARD	MSC & FM	MW & NR		CA & TM	TS & SY	
SOFT			RSC & JT			
China	**Ferrari**	**Williams**	**Toyota**	**Midland**	**Super Aguri**	Bridgestone brought 5 compounds. It was a rather cooler weekend than anticipated and because of that, the Soft tyres were unsuitable due to excessive graining. Therefore, every driver opted to use the Hard. But it di not really matter as the sun did not appear from Saturday morning on. Bridgestone's intermediates incorporated hard compound with stiff construction. The reason was to have a smooth transition from wet to dry tyres damp to drying track condition. At the start of the race, the track was totally wet therefore the condition was not ideal for the Bridgestone shod cars. They were off the pace compared to their Michelin rivals. However, c the track started to dry out, the Bridgestone's intermediates were effective and the dry tyres provided more grip in drying conditions. The Bridgestone runners dominated the top 5 of the fastest lap list of the race.
HARD	MSC & FM	MW & NR	RSC & JT	CA & TM	TS & SY	
SOFT						
Japan	**Ferrari**	**Williams**	**Toyota**	**Midland**	**Super Aguri**	Technical Manager of Bridgestone, Hisao Suganuma said that there were 6 compounds available in Suzuka, but it was believed that Midland/Spyker was the only team who had the slightly softer Prime (Hard) tyre while rest of the teams had the same harder one and Toyota had the slightly harder Option (softer) than the others who selected the same compound. All were from the harder sector of the compound range and race-proven. weather was warmer on Saturday than forecasted, therefore Ferrari did not bother to try the Soft again. For the qualifying session and the race, everybody except for 2 Williams chose to run the Hard. Despite the select tyre performing so well in the qualifying session for Ferrari and Toyota (with lighter fuel-load though), who dominated the first two rows of the grid respectively, Bridgestone shod teams race pace was hampered by the c er weather than the previous day. Massa suffered a slow puncture on the right rear tyre due to a cut during the race which forced him to pit earlier than planned.
HARD	MSC & FM		RSC & JT	CA & TM	TS & SY	
SOFT		MW & NR				
Brazil	**Ferrari**	**Williams**	**Toyota**	**Midland**	**Super Aguri**	Bridgestone was very aggressive going into the last battle with Michelin. They brought 5 kinds of compound to Sao Paulo but only 2 were chosen to race. Ferrari and Williams chose the Soft, and Super Aguri and Mid-land/Spyker opted to use the same compound which was slightly harder than Ferrari chose. Surprisingly, Toyota went with an even harder one. Bridgestone had a big advantage with these tyres. Ferrari's Massa won the race comfortably and M. Schumacher recorded the fastest lap of the race. Emphasizing the Japanese tyre manufacture's advantage was the pace of Super Aguri. Sato clocked 9th fastest time while his team mate Yamamoto also placed himself 7th on the list although he used lightly scrubbed (almost new) set with light fuel load.
HARD			RSC & JT			
SOFT	MSC & FM	MW & NR		CA & TM	TS & SY	

MICHELIN

rain	McLaren	Renault	Honda	Redbull	BMW	Toro Rosso	2006 was the year that tyre change was reintroduced during the race. Michelin brought 8 specifications which comprised of 5 different compounds. McLaren, Renault, Redbull, and Toro Rosso used the same compound for their Prime (hard) specification and Honda, BMW chose the other compound as their Prime. Michelin claimed those 2 compounds were almost identical in performance levels. For the Option (Soft) tyres, there were 3 choices of compound available and all the teams had the same compound available except for McLaren and the Honda. McLaren's option tyre was softer than the one that Honda chose. The tyre choices were divided among Michelin runners as Nick Shorrock, Michelin Formula One director stated "Our partner teams would use six different types of tyre in the race." Honda opted to run the Option tyre against the advice from Michelin but it proved to be a wrong choice. Also McLaren admitted that Montoya chose the incorrect tyre. In fact, all the runners who settled on the Option seemed to suffer lack of pace during the race.
e	Raikkonen	GF & FA		Coulthard		Speed	
ion	Montoya		JB & RB	Klien	NH & JV	Liuzzi	
aysia	McLaren	Renault	Honda	Redbull	BMW	Toro Rosso	There were 4 different dry-weather compounds for Sepang. Except for Honda, all Michelin runners chose the same compounds and the construction for their respective Prime and Option. Their Option compound was the one all the teams (except for Honda and BMW) had run as the Prime in Bahrain. Honda again chose a slightly different combination of compounds and rear tyre construction to the others. Their compound choices were more suitable for a relatively lower temperature range than the tyres used by everyone else. This was due to Honda's poor characteristic to warm up tyres. Everybody settled for the Option (soft) tyres at the end. Although the ambient temperature for the race day was 10 degrees lower than Saturday, it did not change the overall pictures among Michelin runners.
e							
on	KR & JPM	GF & FA	JB & RB	CK & DC	NH & JV	VL & SS	
tralia	McLaren	Renault	Honda	Redbull	BMW	Toro Rosso	Michelin had 8 specifications of tyres available for its 6 teams in Melbourne. Renault and McLaren chose the new rear casings which helped the compounds to warm up quicker. Those two teams had exactly the same tyre options, but Renault went for the Soft while McLaren opted for the Hard. Honda and BMW chose the old type of front/rear constructions, but BMW's specification adopted the same two compounds as Renault and McLaren. Honda again asked for different compounds to the others. The track temperatures were well below 30 degrees centigrade throughout the weekend. Jenson Button sat on the pole, but every time the Safety Car was deployed (4 times in total), he lost track positions due to a severe problem of getting heat into the tyres. He eventually finished disappointing 9th. On the other hand, Renault was able to generate enough heat much quicker than any other of the Michelin runners. This helped Alonso to win the race easily.
D	KR & JPM						
T		GF & FA	JB & RB	CK & DC	NH & JV	VL & SS	
Marino	McLaren	Renault	Honda	Redbull	BMW	Toro Rosso	Michelin Provided 5 different specifications for the race in Ferrari's home territory. The Prime (Hard) specifications were for lower temperatures, and the Option (Soft) ones were for higher temperatures. The forecast for Sunday was relatively warm, therefore all the teams settled for the Options except for Redbull's Klien who was the only one to go with the Prime. McLaren and BMW's Option compound was slightly different from the one that Renault or Honda selected although they were all in a similar range. That Option specification was believed to be one step softer than the one the other teams used. Although the Bridgestone shod Michael Schumacher won the race, the Michelin shod Alonso clearly had better race pace.
e				CK			
on	KR & JPM	GF & FA	JB & RB	DC	NH & JV	VL & SS	
ope	McLaren	Renault	Honda	Redbull	BMW	Toro Rosso	Michelin brought 4 compounds – 2 types of Prime (hard) compound and 2 types of Option (soft) compound – and several constructions which led to a total of 7 different specifications covering a wider temperature range due to the difficulties of forecasting weather in Nurburgring. McLaren, Renault, and Honda had the one step harder Primes and Options than 3 other teams. Actually their tyre options in Nurburgring were exactly same as what Renault and Honda had 2 weeks ago. All the teams opted to use the Option (softer of the two) except for Redbull. Although Alonso, who put his Renault on the Pole position, originally planed to stop 3 times, when he and Renault crew found that M. Schumacher was on 2 stop strategy, he had to switch to the same strategy. But the higher degradation rate of his Michelins did not allow the reigning champion to keep the Ferrari behind. As Nick Shorrock admitted "It looks as though the compounds we selected were probably too hard for the prevailing conditions, those choices were too conservative." That's how most teams felt after the race as well.
e				CK & DC			
on	KR & JPM	GF & FA	JB & RB		NH & JV	VL & SS	
n	McLaren	Renault	Honda	Redbull	BMW	Toro Rosso	The abrasive track surface of Barcelona became gentler on tyres after resurfacing at the end of 2004. The French tyre manufacture brought 4 compounds which included the latest compounds, which were designed after evaluating the data acquired in the previous races. Those tyres were from a rather 'aggressive range of tyre compounds' according to Renault's Pat Symmonds. Renault and Honda used the same compound combinations but both teams decided to use the Hard as they found that the Soft was too soft. McLaren opted to use the Hard as well but theirs were of a slightly different compound. Renault showed good first lap speed and consistency over a race stint while McLaren were nowhere near the front.
D	KR & JPM	GF & FA	JB & RB	CK & DC	NH & JV	VL & SS	
T							
aco	McLaren	Renault	Honda	Redbull	BMW	Toro Rosso	Although Michelin claimed that they brought 6 compounds to Monaco, there were in fact, just three compounds and various constructions. The Soft compound was prepared in a hurry after Michelin's teams tested at Paul Richard the previous week and found the original Soft compound was too hard and requested Michelin to provide something softer. The original Soft subsequently became the Hard. The only team to race the original Soft was BMW. The other teams opted to use the Softs with respective construction. Although Renault reckoned that they would have more problems with the rear tyres than the other Michelin runners, just like last year, they went for the Soft and this time around Alonso nursed the tyres perfectly once he was in the lead. He was also helped by the Safety Car, he won the race easily.
D							
T	KR & JPM	GF & FA	JB & RB	CK & DC	NH & JV	VL & SS	
ritain	McLaren	Renault	Honda	Redbull	BMW	Toro Rosso	Michelin came to Silverstone with 6 compounds. After Monaco, the Michelin teams went to Barcelona to test. The harder Prime tyres all the top Michelin runners chose after the test were more suited to lower tyre temperature whereas the Options were for higher temperatures – which are more dependant on track characteristics and not the actual track temperature, which is only a secondary consideration. All the teams opted for the Option tyres, but the one that Renault and BMW were on had a even higher working temperature range than the other Michelin runners while expecting unusually warm weather. Renault only changed the Option compound in the last minute after seeing the weather forecast prior to the Grand Prix. This was a gamble to certain degree, but paid dividends in the race, especially for Renault.
D							
T	KR & JPM	GF & FA	JB & RB	CK & DC	NH & JV	VL & SS	
ada	McLaren	Renault	Honda	Redbull	BMW	Toro Rosso	Michelin's Formula One director, Nick Shorrock was quoted as saying "This year we brought four different types of tyre to Montreal and two are totally new products," he was believed to be referring to four different compounds. Actually Michelin had 10 specifications with various construction/compound combinations. All the users opted for the Softs in the end. It was believed that Renault, McLaren, Honda, and BMW had the same compound, and Redbull and Toro Rosso chose the other compound which was very similar to the one that the top four teams used. Michelin dominated the qualifying session. Alonso scored his fifth consecutive Pole position with it, but suffered with rear end grip problems in the race. However, he won the race because Raikkonen had problematic pit-stops. It was Michelin's 100th Grand Prix victory.
D							
T	KR & JPM	GF & FA	JB & RB	CK & DC	NH & JV	VL & SS	
	McLaren	Renault	Honda	Redbull	BMW	Toro Rosso	Michelin's preparations and approach for Indy were very cautious. The Primes for all the teams had a slightly flexible construction. The Option had a very stiff construction so as not to repeat the embarrassment of 2005. The Prime specifications that Honda's Davidson and Redbull's Doornbos used showed signs of delamination, which brought back memorys of the previous year's "Indy-gate." Immediately the teams who had the same construction/compound combination were advised not to use them. However, a McLaren and Renaults used the Primes but the tyres were still too conservative and could not match the pace of Ferrari.
e	Montoya	GF & FA					
on	Raikkonen		JB & RB	CK & DC	NH & JV	VL & SS	
ce	McLaren	Renault	Honda	Redbull	BMW	Toro Rosso	There were, amazingly, 10 specifications from Michelin for their home race. Renault and Honda had the same compounds for their two options while McLaren and BMW shared the identical compounds for theirs. McLaren used the latest construction for the front and rear. It rained heavily on Friday night; therefore the track was still green on Saturday. The conditions made all the drivers settle for the Hard except Villeneuve. The wear rate and the degradation rate were thought to be too big for the Options. Against all odds, Villeneuve made the right choice because he was the 4th quickest Michelin driver while on a 2 stop strategy – the same strategy as Alonso who's fastest time was only 0.12 secs quicker than the Canadian.
D	KR & PDR	GF & FA	JB & RB	CK & DC	Heidfeld	VL & SS	
T					Villeneuve		
nany	McLaren	Renault	Honda	Redbull	BMW	Toro Rosso	The French tyre company brought 8 specifications to Hockenheim for its 6 teams. They consisted of one Prime compound and two Option compounds with various constructions. McLaren's Option compound was the softest available. Renault tried the new rear construction to compensate for the loss of its mass damper system. Renault and Honda decided to use the Soft which was of the same compound. The track temperatures went up well above 45 degrees centigrade on race day, the consequence was that almost every Michelin runner suffered blistering of the rear tyres.
D	KR & PDR	GF & FA		CK & DC	NH & RK	VL & SS	
T			JB & RB				
gary	McLaren	Renault	Honda	Redbull	BMW	Toro Rosso	Michelin reviewed their compounds and compound/construction combinations after their products suffered blistering in the previous race. The teams chose those tyres that were optimized to suit the high track temperatures of Hungary as the Option (Soft), but the weekend turned out to be cooler than anticipated. Hence most teams chose to run the harder Prime tyres except for Honda. Honda who had been suffering from inability to generate enough heat quickly enough opted to go for the softer Option against Michelin's advice. Honda knew that the tyres they chose would give them an advantage in the qualifying session but also knew that the tyres would suffer severe graining and wear during the race. Their gamble paid dividends on Sunday, because it was wet! Every Michelin runner chose to start with the intermediate (standard wet tyre) except for Barrichello who was on the extreme wet-weather tyre. The intermediates were very effective in the early stage of the race when the track was still wet.
D	KR & PDR	GF & FA		CK & DC	NH & RK	VL & SS	
T			JB & RB				
ey	McLaren	Renault	Honda	Redbull	BMW	Toro Rosso	For the second Grand Prix at the Istanbul Park, Michelin brought 9 compound/construction combinations, meaning almost every team had its tyres tailor-made. All compounds came from the medium to medium-hard range. However, Renault gave up on using the Soft after finding out it showed excessive graining and the rest of the Michelin runners followed the same route. The Hard option every team used had the same compound with construction of its choice. BMW's Kubica was the only driver to opt for the Soft. Alonso started the race with fresh tyres which grained slightly, but he used the scrubbed set for rest of the race, and they worked fine to fend off the charge of M. Schumacher.
D	KR & PDR	GF & FA	JB & RB	CK & DC	Heidfeld	VL & SS	
T					Kubica		
	McLaren	Renault	Honda	Redbull	BMW	Toro Rosso	Michelin decided to bring slightly softer compounds after three days of testing in the previous week in Monza. It was possible to use softer compounds because one third of the track was resurfaced and less strain was put on the tyres by switching to less powerful V8. There were 10 specifications available. In the end, 6 specifications were chosen for the race that included 6 different constructions and 4 different compounds. Renault selected the hardest specification but it showed improved performance during qualifying session and consistency in the race. However, it was the weekend to forget for Alonso. Not only did he suffer a puncture, which was suspected to have been caused by debris on the track, on his left rear during the final qualifying session, he was relegated to 10th place on the grid by the stewards, and finally he had an engine failure in the race.
D		GF & FA			Kubica		
T	KR & PDR		JB & RB		Heidfeld		
a	McLaren	Renault	Honda	Redbull	BMW	Toro Rosso	There were total of 10 different specifications available with 4 kinds of compounds and various constructions from Michelin. Among those 4 compounds, three were totally new. All the teams including Renault decided to use the Prime (hard) after finding that the Option or the softer compound with harder construction had trouble getting up to the working temperature. The Primes were designed to work at a track temperature of 35 degrees and higher in Shanghai. The qualifying session turned out to be a wet affair, and thus a tyre affair as well. Michelin's intermediates that had a softer compound and more flexible construction than Bridgestone's worked perfectly under the mixed Chinese conditions. But once dry lines started to appear on the track, Michelins intermediates began to overheat and its wear rate increased dramatically, thus losing grip. Alonso only changed the worn front to the new intermediates and kept the same rear at the first stop. This messed up the car balance and the consequence was severe graining on the fronts.
e	KR & PDR	GF & FA	JB & RB	DC & RD	NH & RK	VL & SS	
on							
an	McLaren	Renault	Honda	Redbull	BMW	Toro Rosso	After three days of testing in Silverstone a week before the Chinese GP, Michelin brought 10 specifications with 3 kinds of compounds which were newly developed, based on the compounds used during British GP weekend. The Primes which were suited to lower temperature were chosen by Renault, Honda, Redbull and BMW's Kubica. Renault and Honda opted for the same compound. The warmer weather did not favour Michelin runners, but all the selected tyres performed well during the race. Alonso ran away after Michael Schumacher hit engine problems.
e		GF & FA	JB & RB	DC & RD	Kubica	VL & SS	
on	KR & PDR				Heidfeld		
il	McLaren	Renault	Honda	Redbull	BMW	Toro Rosso	For their last F1 race, the French tyre manufacture had 10 specifications of tyres. Every car fitted with Michelin tyres went for the Option, but there were still 5 specifications with 3 compound variations. More specifically, Honda, McLaren and BMW chose the same compound and Renault ended up using the one which was more suited to lower temperature. Michelin runners were edged out by a large margin during the qualifying session. Renault's choice was forced to work out of its optimum temperature range on Sunday, but it performed consistent enough during the race for Alonso. Michelin won the driver's title for the fifth time.
D				Coulthard			
T	KR & PDR	GF & FA	JB & RB	Doornbos	NH & RK	VL & SS	

BRAKES

In the field of brakes too the introduction of 8-cylinder engines and the 400 cc reduction in displacement had consequences associated with the reduced traction out of corners and a reduction in the maximum speeds achieved by the cars. Then again, feverish tyre development provoked by the competition between the two suppliers Bridgestone and Michelin created an increase in both longitudinal and lateral grip, increasing corning speeds and reducing braking distances. If on the one hand the energy to be dissipated under braking was reduced as a function of the reduction of the difference in speed into corners, on the other the greater deceleration forces permitted by the tyres ensured that the braking power levels remained similar to those of the 2005 season with the 3000 cc 10-cylinder engines. The lower straight-line speed also had a slight effect on the cooling of brake discs and calipers.

However, it should be pointed out that tyre efficiency varied between the two axles: the front tyres guaranteed more grip for a greater number of laps, a factor which conditioned braking balance, necessarily adjusted in favour of the front axle, reaching values of up to 60% (brake bias = front pressure/(front pressure + rear pressure).

Having made these observations we shall now concentrate on Brembo's development of its 2006 braking system that principally focussed on the improvement of cooling, especially of the calipers. The previous season had seen the introduction of an air intake integrated with the caliper body and the new 2006 calipers produced by the Italian manufacturer saw further improvements made in this area.

While in the case of the 2005 caliper the air flow was channelled to the rear of the caliper alone via conduits cut into the caliper body and delimited by a carbonfibre ventilation shroud, in the 2006 calipers the air flow was conducted through openings over the top and back of the pistons and the back of the pads so as to improve cooling of the brake fluid. This ventilation system was shared by all the brake calipers supplied to the Brembo users, clearly integrated with the specific air intakes designed by the individual teams.

As it had to integrate with the air intake, the carbonfibre ventilation shroud was designed jointly by Brembo and the various teams in order to optimize its shape and size. A number of teams split the brake air intake at the mouth, others instead had an internal division channelling part of the cooling air directly to the caliper shroud.

Note that the surfaces in contact with the cooling air feature special ridges designed to optimize thermal exchange and therefore the ability to disperse heat.

The flow of air entering the intake is chan-

nelled within the upright, cooling the bearing. From here, part of the flow is directed towards the vents on the disc and part to the friction surfaces of the disc itself (face cooling). Moreover, in many cases, part of the cooling flow is directed towards the brake caliper, the air intake being linked to the caliper ventilation shroud by a dedicated passage, as described above.

With regards to the type of calipers used, the two HD (Heavy Duty) and LD (Light Duty) specifications were carried over from the 2005 season.

One of the novelties seen in 2006 was the appearance of the fourth caliper manufacturer joining the established pair of Brembo and A+P, which had shared the field through to the 2003 season. 2004 saw the debut of a third manufacturer, the British firm Alcon, exclusively supplying BAR (Honda from 2006). The new Japanese manufacturer Akebono (an industrial satellite of Toyota) was surprisingly installed as a supplier to McLaren from the Chinese GP. The surprise derives from the fact that in the 2005 Japanese GP these calipers had been fitted to the BAR Honda and no one expected to see them return on the McLaren,

The supply of calipers for the 2006 season was subdivided as follows:
Brembo: Ferrari, BMW, Toyota, Red Bull, Toro Rosso.
A+P: McLaren (through to the Italian GP), Williams, Renault, Spyker and Super Aguri.
Alcon: Honda.
Akebono: McLaren from the GP of China.

CANADA

The Montreal track is the hardest on braking systems and as usual we describe the strategies adopted by the various teams to deal with component wear. Larger cooling intakes with respects to the other circuits, albeit without the extremes seen in the past, largely because in the 2006 season the brake air intakes became an integral part of the search for maximum aerodynamic efficiency, with carefully designed shapes and reduced sections. The most eye-catching features were those seen on the Toyotas, Hondas and Williams, even though all the other cars had larger intakes. With regards to the supply of carbon brakes discs, the situation among the leading teams was as follows: HITCO: Renault, Toyota, Red Bull, Midland, Toro Rosso and Super Aguri.
BREMBO: BMW (with a new type of CCR disc already seen at Imola) and BAR Honda.
CARBON INDUSTRIE: the usual McLarens and Williams, with the addition of Ferrari, with a choice of three different materials and new flattened apertures as highlighted in the McLaren drawing.

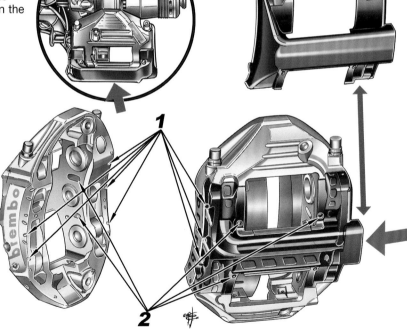

BREMBO CALIPER SHROUD

In 2006 Brembo paid great attention to the cooling of the calipers, equipping them with a carbonfibre shroud that directed the air through apertures (1) towards the back of the pistons (6 as required by the regulations) and exit vents (2) for the hot air behind the pads. The drawing depicts a front caliper, while the detail shows the rear caliper of the Ferrari 248 F1.

Toyota 2005

F2005

248 F1

FERRARI

After having introduced shrouds on the outsides of the discs too in 2002 and having retained them through to the 2005 season, Ferrari abandoned them on the front axle only in favour of shrouds that were closed above the discs but completely open towards the outside so as to channel all the hot air in that direction thus cleaning up the flow in the internal area between the wheels and the chassis.

RENAULT

The Renault was the only car not to do without external shrouds both front and rear. The drawings show the front air intakes with the Hitco discs and A+P calipers.

FERRARI

The famous Ferrari rear wheel that generated so much interest and controversy can be seen almost every chapter of this book. On their debut in Bahrain they featured a slim ring that was gradually expanded until it covered almost the whole of the wheel, leaving only space fir the insertion of the wheel changing gun. This fairing had a purely aerodynamic function: it was designed to clean up the external area of the rear wheel and expel hot air towards the inside so as to increase the downforce generated by the lateral diffusers.

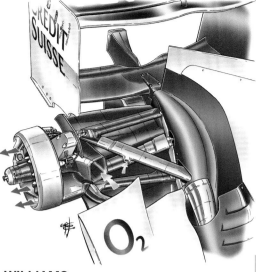

O_2

WILLIAMS

The Williams brake air intakes were very sophisticated, albeit less complex than those introduced at the Turkish Grand Prix in 2005 (with a dual external shroud (above). The shrouds used in 2006 closed around the full diameter of the discs but were partially open towards the outside. Above all, great attention was paid to the caliper cooling duct that took air from the internal part of the intake.

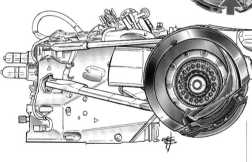

Imola

SAUBER

Sauber was fairly progressive in its use of brake air intakes carefully designed in the wind tunnel. Both front and rear the shrouds enclosed the disc but were completely open towards the outside, again to prevent the hot air from interfering with the tyre temperatures. Considerable work went into the design of the internal airflows, with a banana-shaped profile protruding in the lower section to better channel the air towards the rear.

AKEBONO

From the Chinese Grand Prix, McLaren brought in a fourth caliper manufacturer to join Brembo, A+P and Alcon (used by BAR-Honda only): the Japanese firm Akebono had made a fleeting appearance in the 2005 Japanese Grand Prix on the BAR Hondas. The firm's relationship with McLaren should instead be longer-lasting.

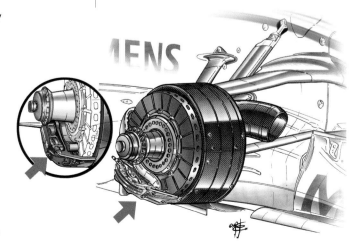

COCKPITS, PEDALS AND STEERING WHEELS

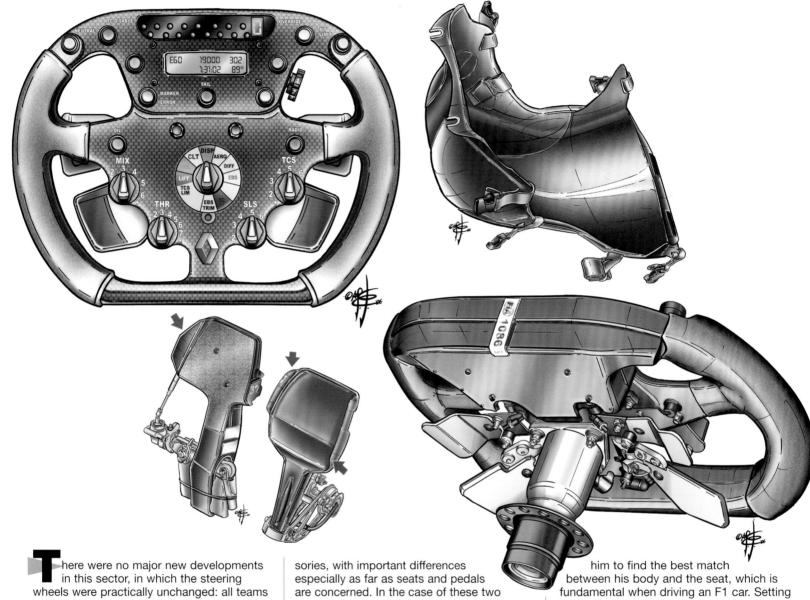

There were no major new developments in this sector, in which the steering wheels were practically unchanged: all teams and all drivers used the two pedals, made in carbon fibre. In a season that focused on the clash between Michael Schumacher and Fernando Alonso, it was decided to take a close look at the cockpits of these two great champions: in this specific sector, those of the Ferrari 248 F1 and the Renault R26 were at two different ends of the scale for various reasons. The difference between the two protagonists of the world championship were not limited to purely technical aspects but encroached on each other in almost all their details – even those that were hidden – such as, indeed, the cockpits. As is known, all drivers have completely personalised acces-

sories, with important differences especially as far as seats and pedals are concerned. In the case of these two great rivals, the differences are, to say the least, macroscopic. The cockpit of Alonso's Renault was more spartan and classical, while that of Schumacher's Ferrari was hypersophisticated and highly personalised. In this sector, too, the German champion has always distinguished himself from all the other drivers: the cockpit of the 248 F1 had inherited a detail from way back in 1997, which was never conceded to the second driver of the Maranello team and which, therefore, we shall no longer see. It is the seat with a special system of inflatable air bags in place of traditional inserts of the sponge rubber used by all the other drivers. The Schumi version enabled

him to find the best match between his body and the seat, which is fundamental when driving an F1 car. Setting up the seat is one of the most delicate operations, which takes place as soon as the chassis of a new car has been determined, so much so that sometimes it requires a number of fittings before arriving at the right level of comfort. Schumacher achieved this delicate equilibrium by inflating the various bags using an ordinary bulb, like a doctor uses when measuring blood pressure. An operation that the German carried out personally before every test session. Both seats have a series of straps as well as the traditional six-point safety belt system fixed to the chassis. The former was a sort of harness with fixed straps of pre-established colours imposed by the

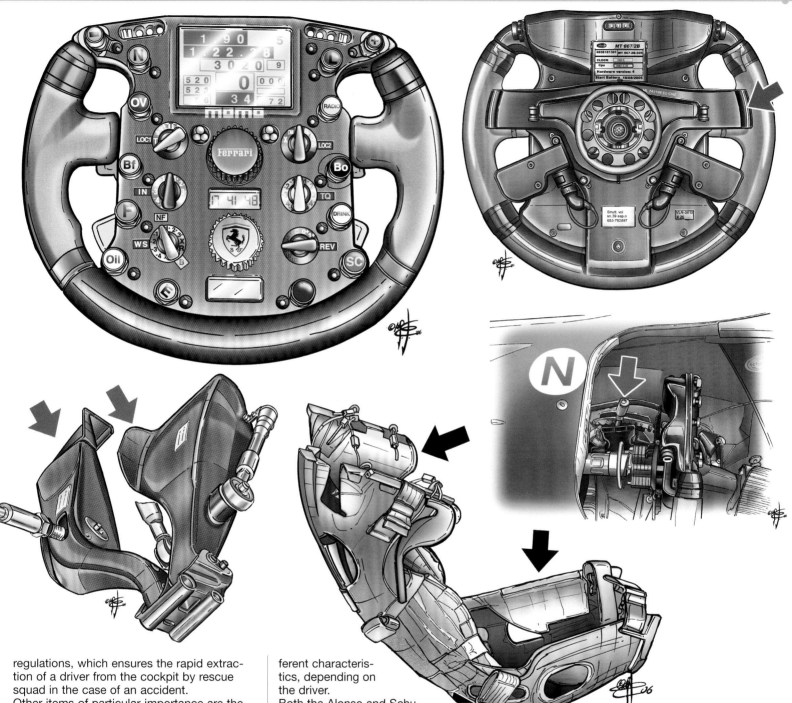

regulations, which ensures the rapid extraction of a driver from the cockpit by rescue squad in the case of an accident.

Other items of particular importance are the pedals, which change from driver to driver in their diversity, which is sometimes considerable. A user of the left foot braking technique, Schumacher was the first to request the introduction of a separator between the two pedals to stop movement from one pedal to the other, which meant the famous heel-and-toe technique of the days of the manual gear change disappeared. In that case, too, the German's pedal set-up was much different from Alonso's, mainly because those of the Renault were of two distinctly different elements installed separately, while those of the Ferrari were formed by a single block with dif-

ferent characteristics, depending on the driver.

Both the Alonso and Schumacher steering wheels were very sophisticated, as they are drivers who like to exploit the various available paddles, which were numerous and personalised in both cases. The two cars' steering wheels have retained the same existing shape and layout for many seasons, as have the positions of the different functions they control, which even vary from circuit to circuit. The Renault wheel had fewer paddles, even if it did have a large central one with which to select the various management programmes. But while Alonso retained the split levers for changing gear (top, in blue, while

those below in yellow operate the clutch) and must use both hands – the right to change up and the left to change down – Schumacher could use only one hand to change up and down with the single rocker, shown in yellow, which controlled the gears: the clutch levers were split, as on the Renault. In this way, he could entertain himself by playing with the brakes balance lever , which was separated from the steering wheel inside the cockpit and could only be manoeuvred with the right hand.

BMW-SAUBER AND WILLIAMS

The BMW-Sauber steering wheels were much different from each other. Heidfeld used a smaller one that was closer to the Sauber wheel of the previous season, while Villeneuve's wheel was bigger, more directly inspired by that of Williams. The British team's wheel was the same as a previous one fitted to the cars back in 2004.

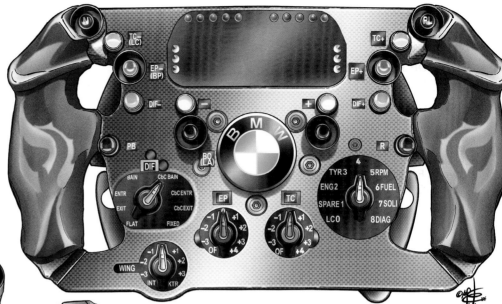

Heidfeld

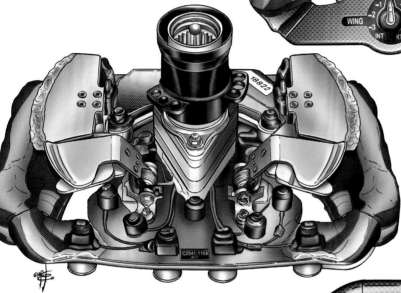

2004

Williams 2006

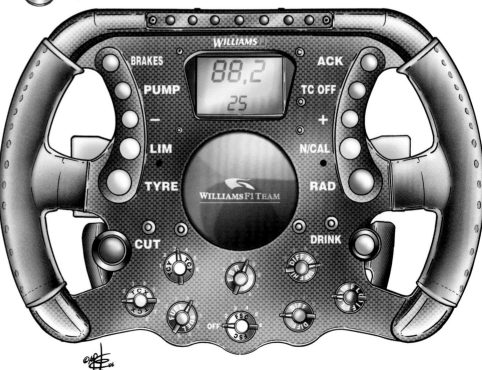

THE RETURN OF ZANARDI

Another interesting development was the BMW-Sauber steering wheel that was not Villeneuve's, but the one the team prepared to enable Alessandro Zanardi to drive a Formula One car once more. An undertaking which, even if it took place when the season had ended, needed to be featured here for the joy it gave all F1 enthusiasts as well as Alessandro.

The team started with the wheel used by Jacques Villeneuve for the simple reason that, from his world championship days with Williams, the Canadian has always wanted to change gear by operating only one lever with his right hand. That is contrary to all the other drivers except Schumacher, who use two levers, the right to change up and the left to change down. Like Villeneuve, Zanardi changes gear with his right hand, pulling the large lever towards him to change up and pushing it forward to change down. Underneath there was a single lever of the clutch (all the other drivers had two) used to manage the start and in the case of a spin.

The big difference can be found on the left hand side of the wheel, where there were no longer the double levers but a single, very large one decidedly distanced from the steering wheel as seen in the illustration above, to provide good dosage modularity of the accelerator (the task of that lever is to simulate the travel of the accelerator pedal). Alessandro Zanardi, therefore, controlled the power of the eight cylinder BMW with his left hand. Obviously, one of the pedals was replaced with a fixed footrest on the left, and the right (brake) was made to combine in the best possible way with a special prosthesis made for the occasion (cut high to ensure easier entry). The problems when driving on the limit did not originate from the management of these controls, but from the impossibility of concluding a complete rotation of the steering wheel. Zanardi actually drove the 2005 B car built on a chassis used by Felipe Massa, which was much lower. In that way, the knees were more bent and hit the steering wheel, which put a stop to the indispensible opposite locking in slow corners. But despite that, those who saw Zanardi's test at Valencia were able to enjoy one of the finest moments of the 2006 season.

UP
DOWN

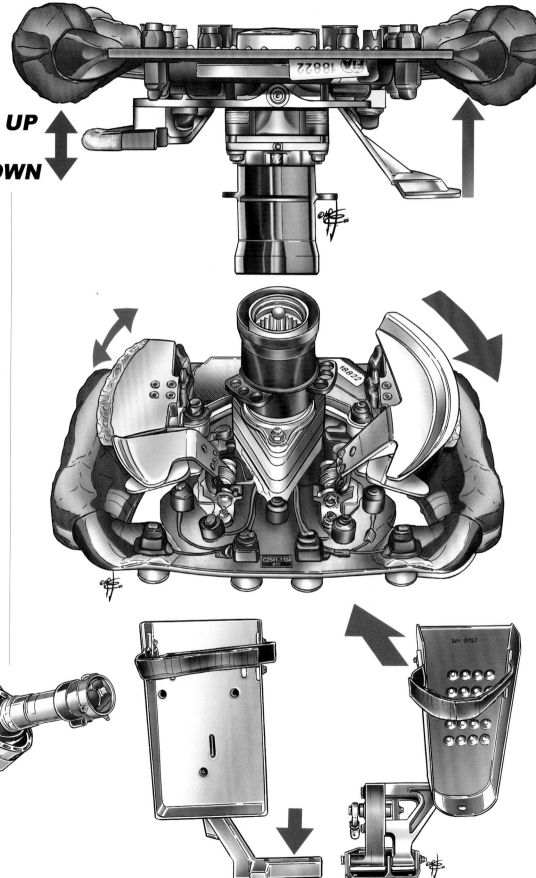

This was a season full of controversies and disputes stemming from the teams' introduction of new solutions considered at the limit of the regulations. In the annals of Formula One, 2006 will be long remembered for the constantly revived topic of the mass damper, which dominated the summer months and was resolved by forbidding the teams to use the device. The mass damper was introduced by Renault during the 2005 Grand Prix of Italy and it was no coincidence that it had already been illustrated in last year's F1 Analysis. But the component really came to light just before the Grand Prix of Monaco and then became a subject of real controversy at the German GP. And it developed into an affair that had severe repercussions on the result of the 2006 world championship.

THE MASS DAMPER

The case of the mass damper came to a head in the pits at Hockenheim. Despite the fact that it had been banned on the eve of the Grand Prix of Germany, Renault still presented its cars at scrutineering with the system fitted to its spare. Ferrari, Red Bull, Toro Rosso and Midland had used it in races and others, such as McLaren and Honda, only tried it out during private testing but did not have the unit. In Germany, Pat Symmonds' line of defence was centred on the fact that the device was to be considered an integral part of the car's suspension system. During its defence in Paris, Renault submitted to the Federation the entire suspension layout, accompanied by a document written by Symmonds of no fewer than 60 pages. The device is an inertial damper, a unit weighing about 7 kg which, combined with a system of springs, generates a vertical oscillation of the suspended mass with a frequency that interferes with that of the tyres in contact with the roughness of the asphalt and the kerbs. The brusque oscillations of the car – for example those provoked by the kerbs – are damped. The biggest advantages can be obtained by using the device at the front end where, due to the mass damper, it is possible to develop much more rigid car set-ups, still being able to reduce the hopping phenom-enon by using that device, which produces an advantage in the order of three tenths of a second per lap. Ferrari, who introduced the mass damper at Monaco, used the system to advantage at the Nürburgring, gaining particular benefit in slow corners even if afterwards the device was no longer used on the Scuderia's cars. It should be said that, for Ferrari and the other teams that used the mass damper, it revealed itself to be an adaptation of previous car designs. In the case of the Renault R26, the car was designed around the mass damper, which was fitted to the rear end, inside the gearbox casting. The absurd thing about this whole matter is that it blew up in Germany, but the mass damper was not definitively banned until the subsequent race in Hungary – 15 Grands Prix after the device was first used, initially by Renault and then by many other teams. It would have been better to outlaw that component on its first appearance at Monza or declare it irregular at the end of the 2005 season, to avoid teams possibly going to the absolute extreme, as has happened in the past with other items introduced by various teams.

R25

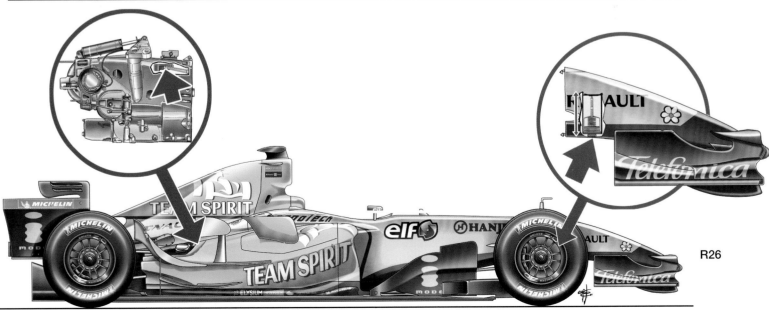

R26

RENAULT MASS DAMPER

The detail shows the layout of the front and rear mass dampers of the Renault. The system is much more evident at the front, where the mass (1) of about 7 kg is, in practice, suspended between two springs (2-3) of different pitch and rigidity, contained just like a damper in a shell (4) with a rod that anchors it inside the deformable structure of the nose. This supplementary damper monitored the variation in height from the ground, while the mass damper inside the gearbox of about 3.5 kg connected to the anti-roll bar reduced the car's hopping.

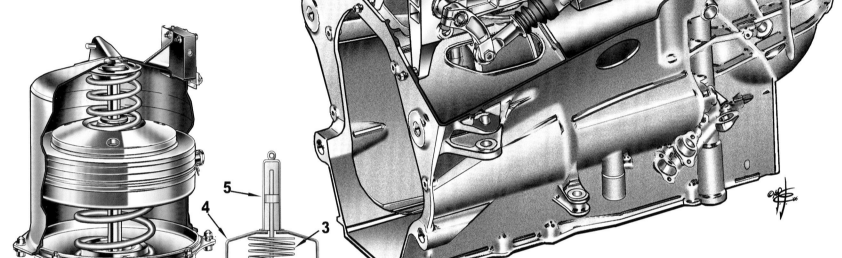

RIM FAIRING

The first controversy had already surfaced during the opening Grand Prix of the season in Bahrain. Attention in the paddock at Sakhir was concentrated on the Ferraris' rear wheels, which had a carbon fibre ring of about 4/5 cm placed at L on the external edge of the wheel, with the purpose of increasing the hot air extraction effect of the brakes and reducing the vortices generated by the wheels themselves. A development considered a sort of mobile aerodynamic appendage, and as such irregular; presented for examination by the Federation, it was nevertheless judged to be regular. During the previous season (see the 2005 Technical Analysis) after discontent at the interpretation of the shape of the brake cooling intakes and the wing fins that proliferated in that area of the car, a meeting of the technical group of the Federation took place immediately after the Grand Prix of Canada. Following that discussion, a new and more permissive form of definition of the brake cooling intake was devised, marking the boundary of the volume that started flush with the external rim. Ferrari was, therefore, to be considered absolutely compliant with the regulations. With that controversy resolved, Toyota then introduced a similar feature as early as Imola, to be followed by Toro Rosso from the Grand Prix of France and an even more extreme evolution of the same system by Ferrari for the Grand Prix of Turkey.

Another controversy exploded violently at the opening race at Bahrain, when Ferrari appeared with this fixed ring on the external edge of their rims. About 4/5 cm wide, that feature sparked off protests from Renault, who considered them a mobile aerodynamic device. But the Federation accepted Ferrari's point and declared that the devices were to be considered integral parts of the brake cooling intake.

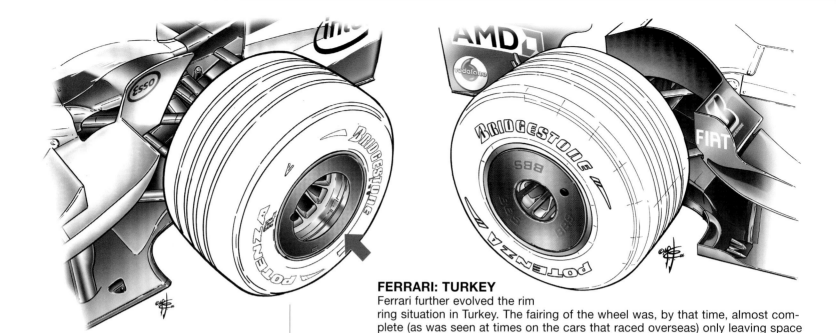

FERRARI: TURKEY
Ferrari further evolved the rim
ring situation in Turkey. The fairing of the wheel was, by that time, almost complete (as was seen at times on the cars that raced overseas) only leaving space for the insertion of the gun during tyre changes.

TOYOTA
The diatribe continued at Imola with Toyota, who took the Ferrari line with a ring that was slightly bigger. There was a further small escalation of the matter by Toro Rosso in Great Britain.

FERRARI FLAP: MALAYSIA
Second race, second controversy. On the spot this time were the Ferrari flaps which showed lateral movement in television pictures, brought out the fixing pin in the nose attachment point. The situation was verified by the Federation and it passed all the established tests. For that reason, it was considered legal. At the following Grand Prix of Australia, Ferrari had simply applied a small fairing unit that covered the gap between the anchorage point of the flap and the nose. Accusations saying the whole front nose group flexed were rejected as being responsible for the origin of the transverse movement shown in the illustration (7).

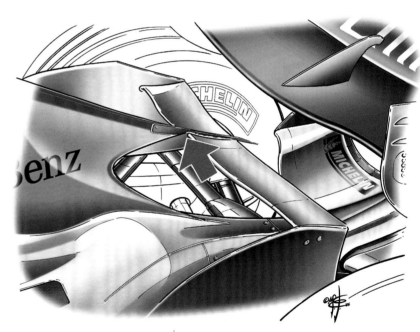

McLAREN: MALAYSIA
There were another two cases of wings being considered too flexible in Malaysia: the one above the rear axle of the McLaren and the end plates of the rear wing of the BMW Sauber. The former had already been stiffened at its anchorage point with the engine cover at Sepang.
In a pre-Imola meeting, the introduction of regulations for the 2007 season were discussed, which would limit the wing flexibility phenomenon.

FERRARI: SPAIN

The object of attention from rival teams in Spain was the new Ferrari rear end, which was considered too flexible despite having passed the FIA examination. The flap of the 248 F1's rear wing, which had a wider chord in its central area, was to partly hide a slot with the principal plane. At a determined speed, the flap flexed downwards and closed the passage of air, stalling the wing. That produced a drop in negative lift and a consequent increase in speed. The means of fixing the flap to the end plate with just two anchorage points left quite a substantial part of the plane's chord free. In addition, the two fixings were not blocked in a single opening, but in a housing that permitted a millimetric variation of the slot between the plane and the flap, depending on the circuit. In the end, Ferrari, like Renault and Honda, opted for central support of the rear wing. In that way, the two large central pillars "linked" only the main plane, while the lower unit, the end plates and the diffuser remained free. That way, it was possible to register millimetric variations: at a certain speed, the principal plane of the rear wing could be subjected to a small amount

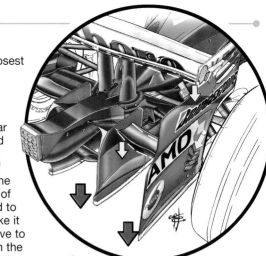

of flexing in the area closest to the end plates. As a consequence, both the end plates and diffuser would descend. In that case, the loss of the rear wing's downforce would be compensated for by the greater efficiency of the diffuser closest to the ground. The illustration of the latter was subjected to micro-evolutions to make it increasingly less sensitive to variations in height from the ground. To all effects and purposes, the Ferrari's rear end always turned out to be perfectly in line with the regulations at scrutineering.

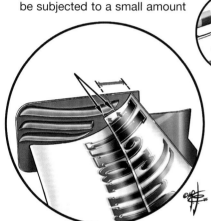

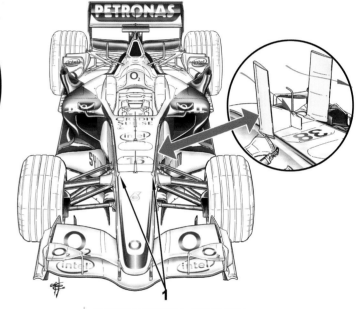

BMW-SAUBER: CANADA

A great deal of controversy was stirred up at Montreal by BMW's new rear wing, which allowed a certain flexibility due to the stiffening element between the principal plane and the flap, as confirmed by a number of photographs taken at the circuit and revealed on the Saturday on a British web site. After careful verification by the Federation's scrutineer, a check which was repeated on the Sunday morning when the car came out of parc fermé, the feature was declared acceptable. Nevertheless, at the subsequent Grand Prix of the United States a fixing of the wing's flap was imposed.

BMW SAUBER: FRANCE

There was still uncertainty within the Federation at the Grand Prix of France. Initially, the two large vertical fins (Tower fins) on the upper part of the BMW's nose were considered legal. An extreme solution that could have reduced visibility – Villeneuve had expressed doubts before track testing, asking if they could be made of transparent plastic, as with Red Bull and its new Renault-style fins on Coulthard's car, although Klien's had the normal units. Their purpose was to stabilise the air flow, especially when the car was slipstreaming, and improve the quality of flow towards the central and rear areas of the BMW, where McLaren-type "horns" had been added for the same purpose. In a surprise move, however, these strange appendages were banned before official testing.

RENAULT

It was not easy to do better than in 2005, when Renault won the world championship not just as an engine supplier to the likes of Williams and Benetton, but as a team in its own right. Yet they did so with the R26, which was an almost perfect car. As well as an increased number of points, other results that speak for themselves should be taken into account: Renault scored seven victories in the first nine races and were in the points in 17 Grands Prix out of 18. Only once did the two cars retire. It was at the Grand Prix of Hungary, where Alonso was afflicted by a badly fixed wheel during a pit stop, while the only break-down of the new eight cylinder happened to the Spaniard at the Italian Grand Prix. The new engine was one of the strong points of the French car, although it was designed and built at the team's Enstone headquarters in Great Britain. Its track debut took place with the new car without going through a series of test drives installed in a laboratory car, as did those of all the other teams. Yet as early as the first race of the season in Bahrain the Renault R26 scored its first victory.

The reduction in cubic capacity imposed by the regulations enabled the team to further refine the basic R25 project, of which the new R26 was a direct descendent. The minor need to dissipate heat favourably influenced the car's aerodynamics, which were also one of the French constructor's strong points in 2005: smaller radiant masses enabled the team to design even more tapered and lower sidepods, but especially to eliminate that series of louvers which characterised the previous model on the one hand, but were responsible for a slight loss of aerodynamic efficiency on the other, even though they were the best compromise in heat dissipation and aerodynamic efficiency during the 2005 season. The new engine also conditioned another technical choice connected with the switch to a seven speed gearbox in place of the traditional six, considered by Pat Symmonds to be faster. The need to be able to exploit the new engine that was always "pulling" was at the bottom of this decision, linked, obviously, to a tighter power curve and regulations that prohibited the use of variable height trumpets. The gearbox, of course, remained in cast titanium as did the reinforcing link between the 'box and the monocoque. In terms of suspension, the R26 was designed with the mass damper in mind, not just at the front, as was the case from the Grand Prix of Italy, but also the rear, even if with more limited benefits. The other teams that attempted to follow the Renault path simply adapted existing projects, while only the R26 was created with the objective of obtaining the perfect integration of the two elements with an improvement estimated at 3/10

Renault R25
Sao Paolo

Renault R26
Presentation

Renault R26
Montreal

Renault R26
Sao Paolo

PRESENTATION

The R26 was a logical evolution of the 2005 car. At the launch, its nose and front wing were those used in the second part of the previous season. The differences were in the details of all sectors, starting with the front suspension, which retained the central mount with its new V structure. The upper wishbone had more extended fairing (1). The twin barge boards behind the front wheels (2) were also new and were higher in the area near the chassis. The chassis was slightly higher and had a further divided (3) intake entrance for the radiators, which were smaller. In the circle are the sidepods of the old R25. The increase in the step in the lower area was to energise the air that flows in this zone and was directed towards the rear of the car, the Coca Cola narrowing of which was more accentuated, in part due to the considerable reduction in the bulk of the radiators. Even the location of the rear view mirrors (4) was different. The engine air intake (5) of the new eight cylinder was almost triangular in shape and was narrower. The complex disposition (6) of the chimney group, lateral flaps and screening of the rear wheels was practically unchanged and had the clear task of improving the air flow to the rear wing. The wing itself had curled planes that were different from those used on the R25, and also had ample horizontal louvers of the Toyota school in the end plates.

of a second per lap. And in consideration of that reason the severe imbalance affecting Flavio Briatore's team at the moment of the definitive banning of the mass damper on the eve of the Grand Prix of Germany, made the race one of the French constructor's worst. The R26 did, however, hark back to the of the R25 project, starting with the V-Keel for the front suspension and ending with the layout of the suspension itself with the bulky but profitable installation of the rear. The development of the car was continued and based not only on small details. Nothing was overlooked, not even the exploitation of features introduced previously by other teams, like BAR's vertical fins on the flanks of the sidepods from the Grand Prix of Canada, where the team fielded a B version of the R26. That continued right up to a Ferrari-type full width flap for the front wing at the German Grand Prix. In a chronological analysis, it was possible to note five rear wings and four fronts as well as those at the launch and the first tests, which were still of the old R25.

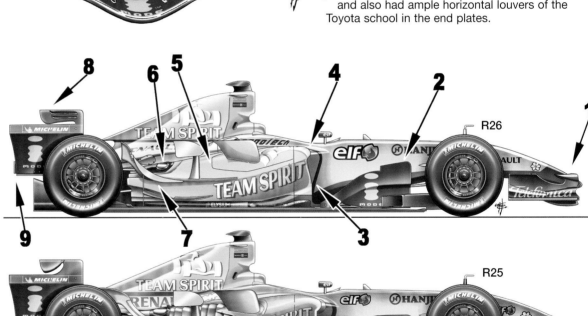

ENGINE

The new eight cylinder Renault RS 26, designed and built under the direction of Rob White, was one of the strong points of the French car. It was only at the Grand Prix of Italy that it broke down.

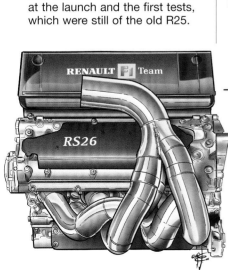

SIDE VIEWS

The R26 was a refined version of the R25, as can be seen by this side view comparison. (1) At the presentation, the front wing was the same, but already the barge boards behind the wheels (2) were higher. (3) The lower area of the sidepods were more tapered, while the chassis' belt line was slightly higher (4). Numerous louvers (5) had disappeared from the 'pods, while the exhausts were lower (6). The fins (7) in front of the rear wheels were new, as was the rear wing group. The section of the flap (8) was especially different as it was separated from the rest of the end plate. (9) The deformable structure was 10 cm longer, as required by the regulations.

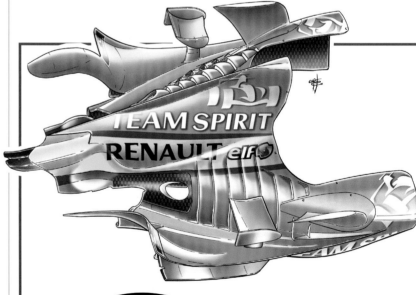

DIFFUSER

In pre-season testing, a diffuser was used that was derived from that of the R26 (opposite, circle). Note the substantial fairing in the area near the wheels that covers the suspension and increases the air extraction effect from the lower part of the car.

FRONT SUSPENSION

The R26 retained the unique front suspension mount, which was introduced on the R25. It was not the classic central bulb that created harmful turbulence in the air flow passing under the car. The highly permeable V-structure in carbon fibre guaranteed the aerodynamic advantages of the twin keel, which was abandoned by all teams with the exception of Ferrari during the 2006 season without the chassis and suspension structural and weight problems that it entailed. This feature was copied by the Red Bull RB02. Note the fins in the upper part of the chassis, which first appeared at the 2005 Grand Prix of Spain.

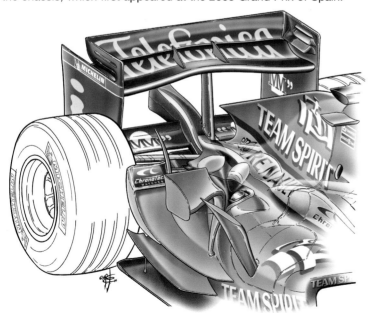

REAR WING

A new rear wing appeared from the moment of the car's presentation. It had new end plates with a different flap separation in relation to the end plate itself, but especially a new principal plane curved towards the upper area of its central section.

LOUVERS

The greatest difference between the R25 and the R26 was the disappearance of the series of louvers in the upper zone of the engine cover, in part due to the diminished necessity for heat dissipation generated by the 2400 cc eight cylinder compared to the 10 cylinder 3000 cc. The engine cover of the R26 is the one used at Monza.

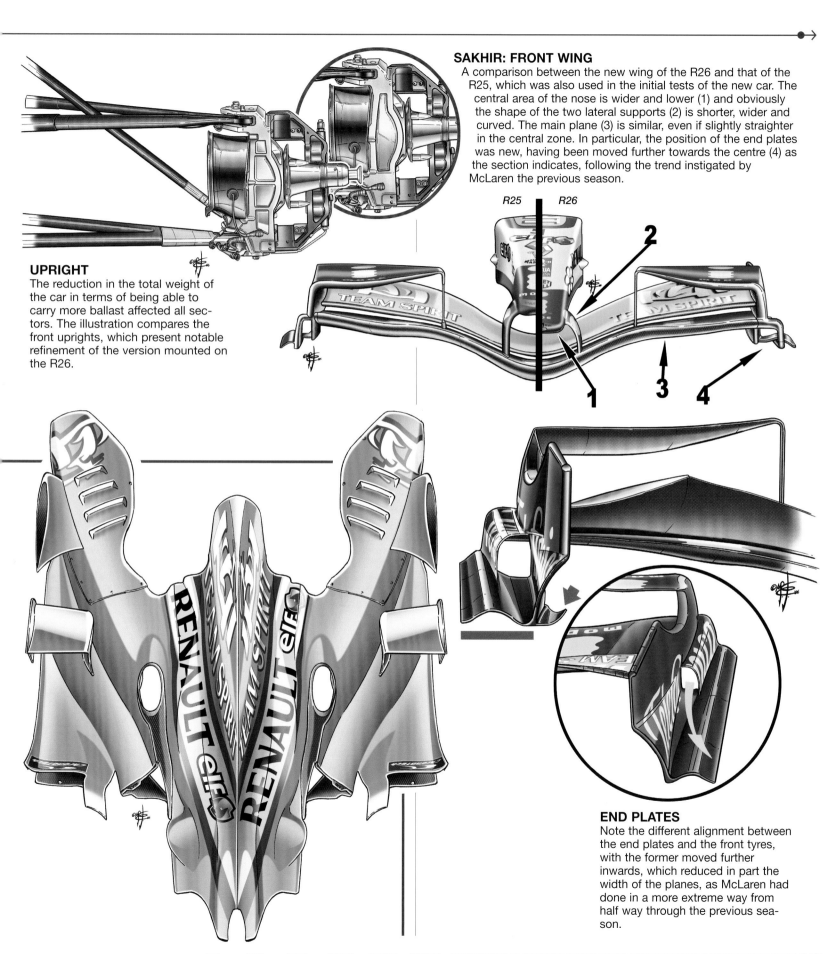

SAKHIR: FRONT WING

A comparison between the new wing of the R26 and that of the R25, which was also used in the initial tests of the new car. The central area of the nose is wider and lower (1) and obviously the shape of the two lateral supports (2) is shorter, wider and curved. The main plane (3) is similar, even if slightly straighter in the central zone. In particular, the position of the end plates was new, having been moved further towards the centre (4) as the section indicates, following the trend instigated by McLaren the previous season.

R25   R26

2

1

3

4

UPRIGHT

The reduction in the total weight of the car in terms of being able to carry more ballast affected all sectors. The illustration compares the front uprights, which present notable refinement of the version mounted on the R26.

END PLATES

Note the different alignment between the end plates and the front tyres, with the former moved further inwards, which reduced in part the width of the planes, as McLaren had done in a more extreme way from half way through the previous season.

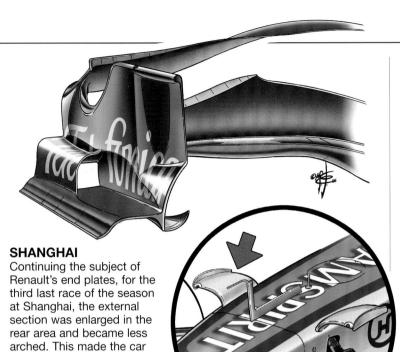

SHANGHAI

Continuing the subject of Renault's end plates, for the third last race of the season at Shanghai, the external section was enlarged in the rear area and became less arched. This made the car easier to drive, according to Pat Symmonds.

FINS

These aerodynamic appendages introduced at the 2005 Grand Prix of Spain and used for just three races, were recovered again from the depths of the Renault warehouse. They were identical to those of the R25 and their purpose was to re-stabilise the air flow that "shoots" upwards following the front flap incidence and guarantee a better flow of air towards the rear wing.

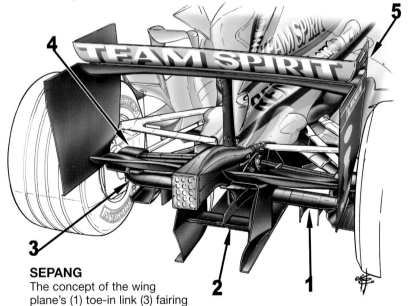

SEPANG

The concept of the wing plane's (1) toe-in link (3) fairing was extreme and had already been seen on the R25, with the evident task of extracting air from the lateral channels, which cannot be seen in the illustration. The small flap (2) in the central channel was also on the R25, as was the substantial fairing (4) in the area of the drive shaft mount, which was as wide as the permitted limit imposed by the regulations for fairing with aerodynamic flow. Note the strange mount (5) of the flap, introduced two years ago and retained in an even more accentuated manner on the R26.

MELBOURNE

In Australia, Renault used two rear wings: the one already seen in the first two races with planes that were curved upwards in the central area (see oval) and the one that ensured greater load with straight planes. In the end, the latter was selected.

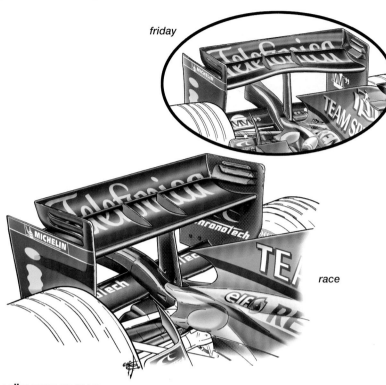

friday

race

NÜRBURGRING

Renault took a direction diametrically opposed to that of McLaren, widening the dimensions of the front wing to the detriment of the external part of the end plates, while with the MP4-21 the width of the plane was greatly penalised, creating a different alignment with the front wheels with which these end plates had to work. In effect, the plane itself was more efficient on the R26, while the MP4-21 made the end plates work harder.

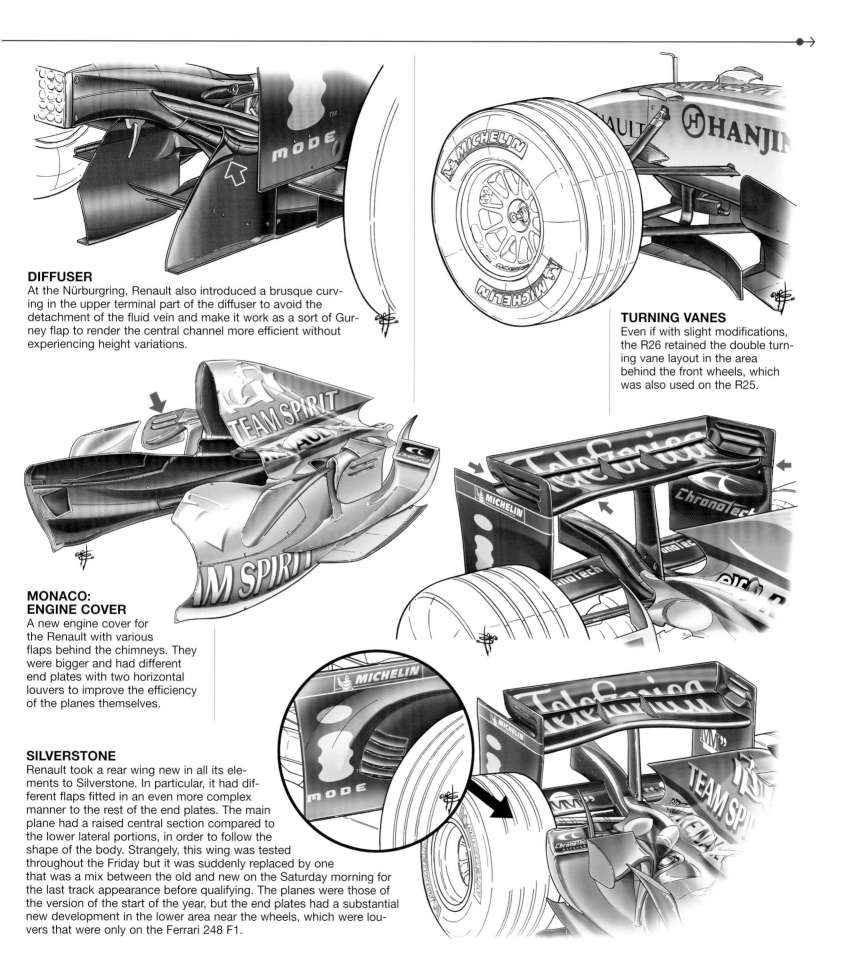

DIFFUSER

At the Nürburgring, Renault also introduced a brusque curving in the upper terminal part of the diffuser to avoid the detachment of the fluid vein and make it work as a sort of Gurney flap to render the central channel more efficient without experiencing height variations.

TURNING VANES

Even if with slight modifications, the R26 retained the double turning vane layout in the area behind the front wheels, which was also used on the R25.

MONACO: ENGINE COVER

A new engine cover for the Renault with various flaps behind the chimneys. They were bigger and had different end plates with two horizontal louvers to improve the efficiency of the planes themselves.

SILVERSTONE

Renault took a rear wing new in all its elements to Silverstone. In particular, it had different flaps fitted in an even more complex manner to the rest of the end plates. The main plane had a raised central section compared to the lower lateral portions, in order to follow the shape of the body. Strangely, this wing was tested throughout the Friday but it was suddenly replaced by one that was a mix between the old and new on the Saturday morning for the last track appearance before qualifying. The planes were those of the version of the start of the year, but the end plates had a substantial new development in the lower area near the wheels, which were louvers that were only on the Ferrari 248 F1.

MONTREAL

The new aerodynamics tested at Monza made their debut in Canada with a doubling of the length of the "horns" in the upper area of the nose in order to improve the quality of the air flow towards the central and rear parts of the car.

INDIANAPOLIS: REAR WING

At Indianapolis, Renault retained the wings that first appeared in Montreal: the front was inspired by the one used at Monza in 2005, while the rear had straight planes with a reduced chord and end plates without a separate element for the flap mount. The two horizontal louvers in the upper part of the barge boards were also different.

HOCKENHEIM

There was a new front wing for Renault in Germany. It was much inspired by one introduced by Ferrari from the debut of the 248 F1. The central part of the wide flap was fairly curled and inclined downwards to feed the lower area at the front of the car. Only the section near the barge boards had a negative lift function. The principal plane was also new, and had a wider spooned central section. The end plates were practically unchanged, except that they were slightly more closed in the rear area ahead of the front wheels.

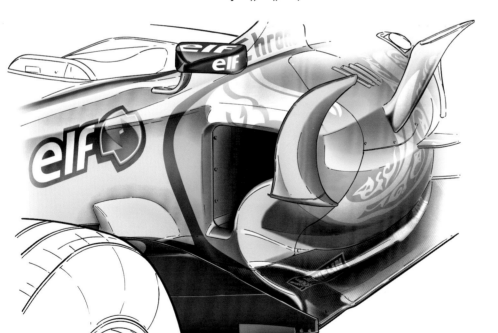

MONTREAL

The introduction of these deflectors in the upper area of the sidepods was curious. It was a reasonably logical solution on the Honda, which was the first to bring them in, Toyota and Midland, which did not have an evident device in the lower area to feed the air flow towards the so-called Coca Cola zone. Apparently, this technique enabled Renault to improve its car's efficiency.

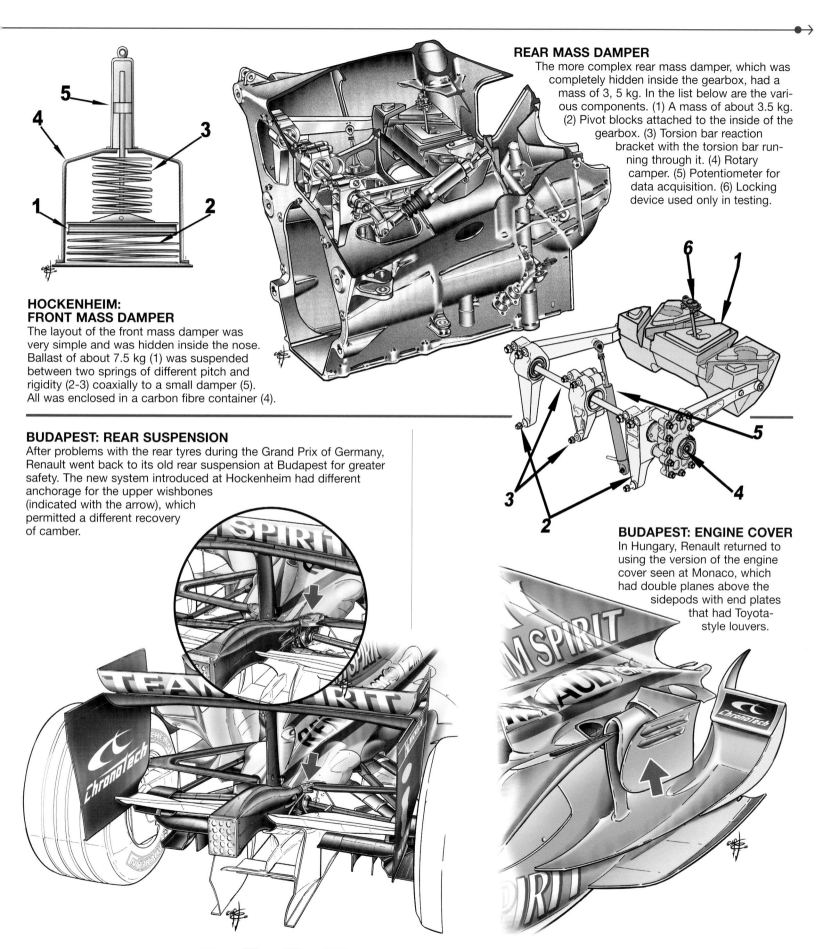

REAR MASS DAMPER

The more complex rear mass damper, which was completely hidden inside the gearbox, had a mass of 3, 5 kg. In the list below are the various components. (1) A mass of about 3.5 kg. (2) Pivot blocks attached to the inside of the gearbox. (3) Torsion bar reaction bracket with the torsion bar running through it. (4) Rotary camper. (5) Potentiometer for data acquisition. (6) Locking device used only in testing.

HOCKENHEIM: FRONT MASS DAMPER

The layout of the front mass damper was very simple and was hidden inside the nose. Ballast of about 7.5 kg (1) was suspended between two springs of different pitch and rigidity (2-3) coaxially to a small damper (5). All was enclosed in a carbon fibre container (4).

BUDAPEST: REAR SUSPENSION

After problems with the rear tyres during the Grand Prix of Germany, Renault went back to its old rear suspension at Budapest for greater safety. The new system introduced at Hockenheim had different anchorage for the upper wishbones (indicated with the arrow), which permitted a different recovery of camber.

BUDAPEST: ENGINE COVER

In Hungary, Renault returned to using the version of the engine cover seen at Monaco, which had double planes above the sidepods with end plates that had Toyota-style louvers.

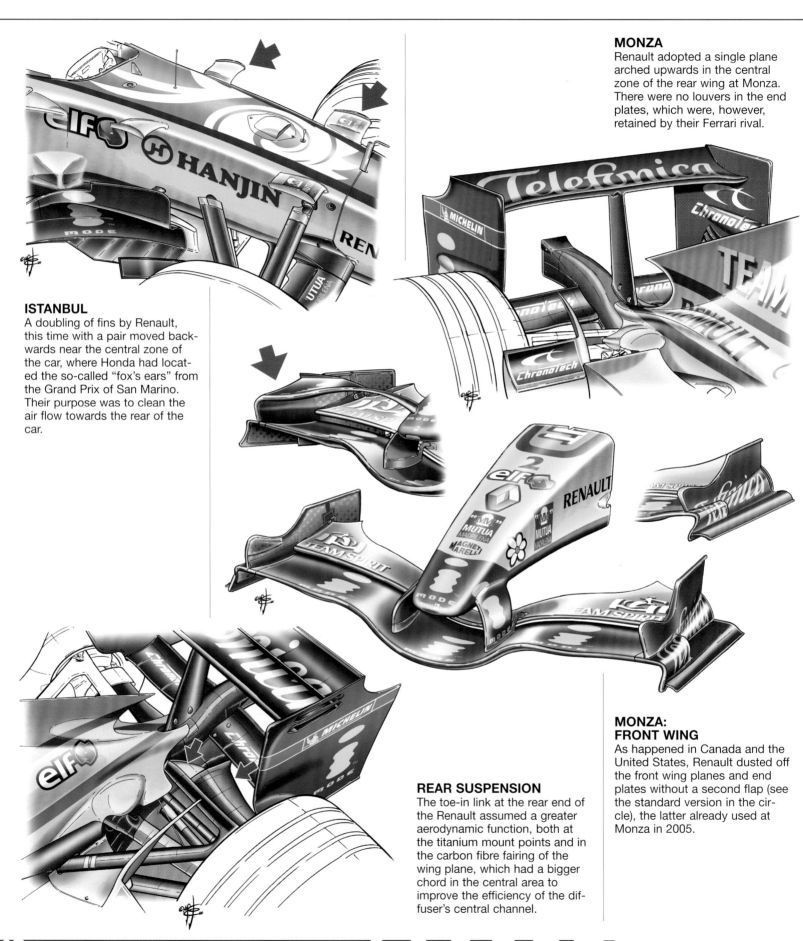

MONZA

Renault adopted a single plane arched upwards in the central zone of the rear wing at Monza. There were no louvers in the end plates, which were, however, retained by their Ferrari rival.

ISTANBUL

A doubling of fins by Renault, this time with a pair moved backwards near the central zone of the car, where Honda had located the so-called "fox's ears" from the Grand Prix of San Marino. Their purpose was to clean the air flow towards the rear of the car.

REAR SUSPENSION

The toe-in link at the rear end of the Renault assumed a greater aerodynamic function, both at the titanium mount points and in the carbon fibre fairing of the wing plane, which had a bigger chord in the central area to improve the efficiency of the diffuser's central channel.

MONZA: FRONT WING

As happened in Canada and the United States, Renault dusted off the front wing planes and end plates without a second flap (see the standard version in the circle), the latter already used at Monza in 2005.

SHANGHAI

Renault retained the fins in front of the sidepods, which were introduced in Canada and copied by Ferrari for China. On the R26, they were combined with slightly modified barge boards in the area of the triangular fin. For that reason, a new, flat bottom was produced with modifications in the front area that satisfied the drivers.

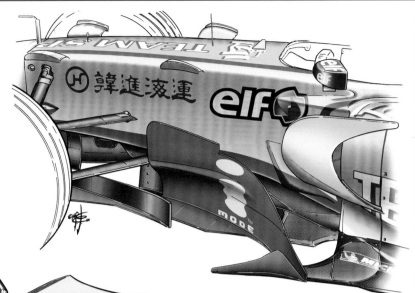

SHANGHAI

In China, the Renault had new end plates with the external zone less curved and slightly wider in the rear area to give better alignment with the front wheels.

SAO PAOLO

Renault was one of the few teams that did not use double drums in the brake air intakes; the possible loss in terms of aerodynamic efficiency was partly compensated for by the much reduced bulk of the real cooling intakes, which did not have entry mouths more or less large. In compensation, a small horizontal fin was used and integrated with a very thin cooling louver

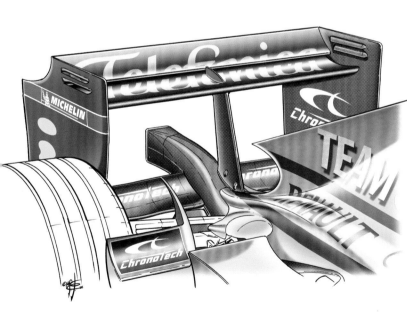

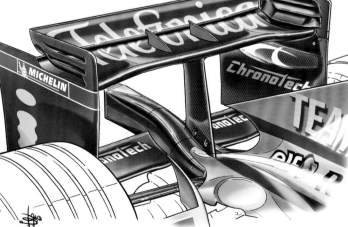

SAO PAOLO: REAR WING

The French team started Friday testing with a rear wing of medium-low load: in practice, it was the one from Montreal, but with greater incidence on the planes. Note the monolithic end plates (different from the solution adopted on the Saturday and the race, which was based on the Silverstone wing that had a detached flap mount). This medium-low load wing was used with less incidence of the planes and without louvers in the low part of the end plates.

GEARBOX COMPARISON

In practice, the R26 retained the same gearbox and rear suspension layout with three dampers positioned longitudinally above the 'box itself. The cast gearbox was longer (1) so as not to change the wheelbase despite the use of the shorter eight cylinder engine. The new power unit also required the adoption of seven speeds (against the six for the 10 cylinder). (2) The torsion bar was no longer external. (3) The position of the caliper was slightly modified (less horizontal). (4) The rigidity between the gearbox and chassis, which was introduced at the time of the 111° "flat" engine, was maintained. (5) As required by the regulations, the deformable structure was 10 cm longer.

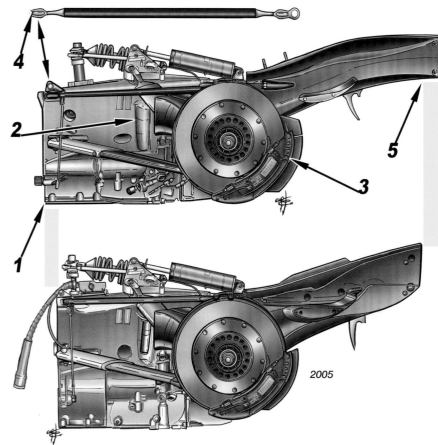

2005

SAKHIR

The R26 was the direct descendent of the car that earned Renault its first world championship and its aerodynamics were substantially evolved. The new nose with a wider central area was only brought in for the first race: the biggest difference compared to the R25 was the more fully fashioned shape of the entry to the sidepods and the absence of the numerous louvers in the upper area of the engine cover.

Imola

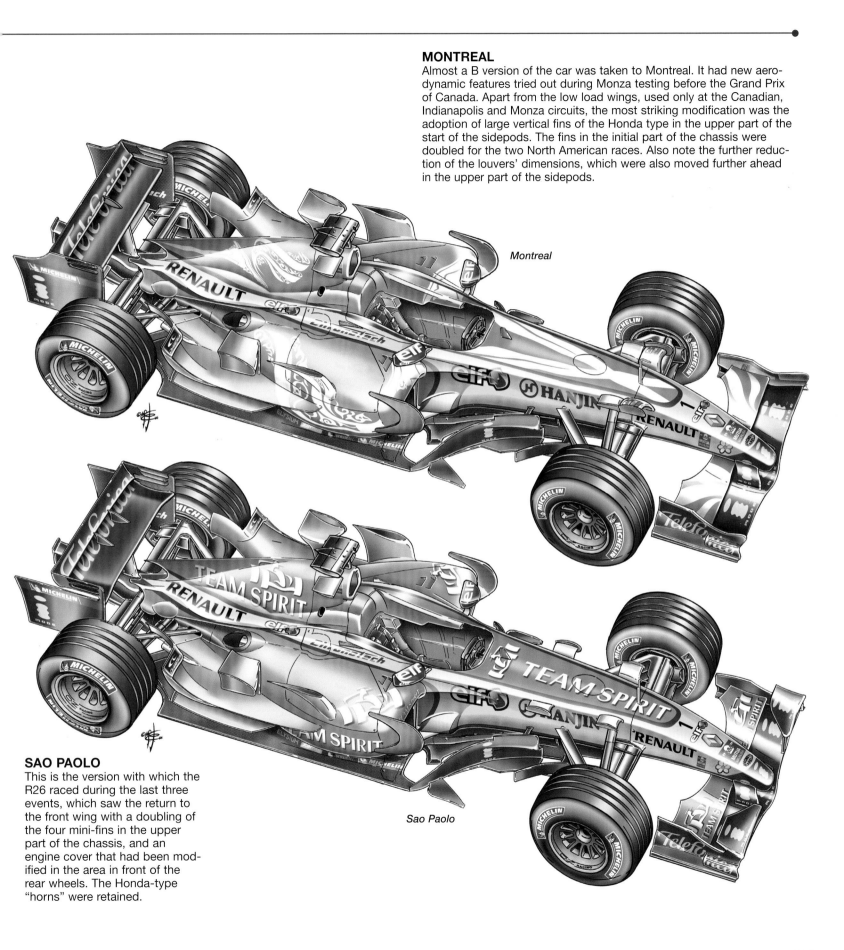

MONTREAL

Almost a B version of the car was taken to Montreal. It had new aerodynamic features tried out during Monza testing before the Grand Prix of Canada. Apart from the low load wings, used only at the Canadian, Indianapolis and Monza circuits, the most striking modification was the adoption of large vertical fins of the Honda type in the upper part of the start of the sidepods. The fins in the initial part of the chassis were doubled for the two North American races. Also note the further reduction of the louvers' dimensions, which were also moved further ahead in the upper part of the sidepods.

Montreal

SAO PAOLO

This is the version with which the R26 raced during the last three events, which saw the return to the front wing with a doubling of the four mini-fins in the upper part of the chassis, and an engine cover that had been modified in the area in front of the rear wheels. The Honda-type "horns" were retained.

Sao Paolo

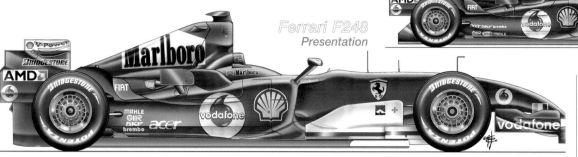

Ferrari F2005 Sao Paolo

Ferrari F248
Presentation

Ferrari F248
Sakhir

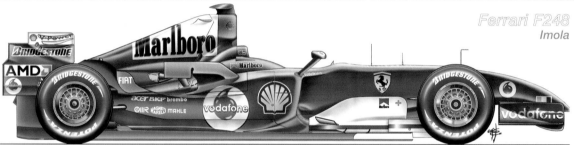

Ferrari F248
Imola

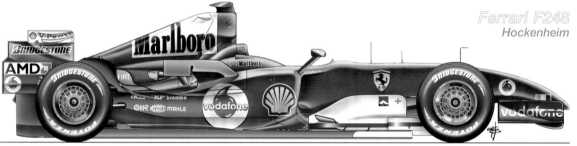

Ferrari F248
Hockenheim

Ferrari F248
Istanbul

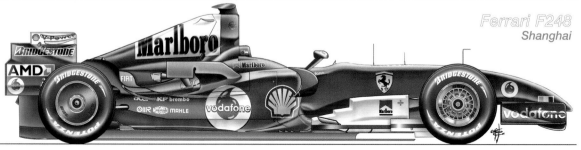

Ferrari F248
Shanghai

CONSTRUCTORS' CLASSIFICATION			
	2005	2006	
Position	3°	2°	+1 ▲
Points	100	201	+101 ▲

Even if it appeared camouflaged by the wings of the F2005 at the official presentation, the F248 immediately showed its greater connection with the previous, more competitive F2004, with which all the comparative winter tests were conducted. That was justified by the fact that the F2005 was the result of the severe aerodynamic limitations imposed by the Federation for that season and emerged from a compromise that was too unbalanced on the recovery of lost load, with the front wing raised and the limitation of just two elements in the rear wing. With the 248, Maranello went back in search of maximum efficiency to the detriment of pure downforce . The lower power output of the eight cylinder 2400 cc engine in respect of the old 10 cylinder 3000 cc impeded the waste of more with aerodynamics with greater load but with less efficiency. All of the work carried out in the design headquarters by the group directed by Aldo Costa and Nicholas Tombazis was aimed at developing a car of little resistance, effective in all conditions and little pitch sensitive. To that should be added that the monopoly situation with Bridgestone, a company that had been at the basis of many Ferrari successes, was at a distance a source of partial technical isolation. The arrival of Williams and Toyota in the Japanese tyre manufacturer's field in 2006 led to an incoming of information and experience that showed itself to be very useful and that enabled the modification of the typology of simulation work in the wind tunnel. Here's just one example: in producing the scale models for wind tunnel tests, Ferrari has always used wheels made of metal materials with characteristics of rigidity and deformability a long way from real rubber. The arrival of the two teams of the Michelin school brought confirmation that the tests conducted by Michelin were carried out with rubber tyres of reduced scale made by the French manufacturer itself. The first concrete result of this new methodology was the aerodynamic package that made its debut on the 248 at the Grand Prix of Bahrain. There was no longer a wing with a "moving ground" but another more efficient and sophisticated one with a full width raised flap. The basic theme of the design and enormous development that took place during the course of the season was that of a constant aerodynamic micro-improvements to always obtain the best possible efficiency on all types of circuit. Take the case of the mirrors, for instance, and their unusual location, becoming the first element of the chimneys and flaps combination with an aerodynamic function to direct air in the most efficient way possible towards the rear end. That is the light in which the considerable amount of work on the brake cooling intakes should be seen in that, due to regulation concessions, they became increasingly proper aerodynamic devices. Ferrari were back at top the level, but especially became an example to follow for the other teams, due to the new aerodynamic features it introduced, like the full width flap linked to the central part of the nose, the fairing of the rear rims, the steps in the turning vanes that had "curls", the louvers in the lower area of the rear wing's end plates. All new developments that were subjected to constant evolution and that, bit by bit, eventually appeared on all the other cars. Even the much contested fairing of the rear wheels made its converts. The team's development work with Bridgestone and the continual presence of new technical solutions at every race permitted Ferrari to zero the points gap between them and Renault in the third last race of the season which, with the turning point of the Grand Prix of Canada, was quite an achievement: Michael Schumacher had no fewer than

25 points less than Alonso. A number of technical problems too many had their negative influence on Maranello's battle for the world championship, culminating in the broken engine in Japan at a crucial point in the title chase, when Schumacher was in the lead and on his way to certain win. Another, however, was his fuel pump failure when qualifying for the Brazilian Grand Prix.
As far as the 248 was concerned,

this son of the F2004 kept its mentor's wheelbase dimensions despite the shorter new engine, the disposition of the mechanics, its radiators without the double inclination of the F2005, but in particular ballast sufficient to more freely adapt weight distribution to the various circuits. A great deal of work was also done on a number of occasions on the suspension for the Nürburgring,

Imola and Silverstone, the basic layout of which was unchanged in relation to the F2004. The ban of the mass damper worked in Ferrari's favour in its fight with Renault, but it should still be emphasised that the 248 F1 was the only rival car to exploit this device well, coming second in its race debut at Monaco and winning in France – the other race in which the mass damper was used – before it was banned in Germany.

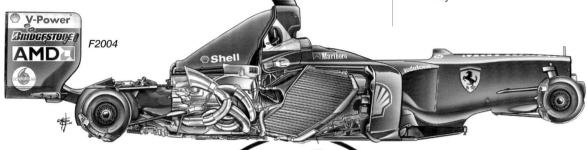

F2004

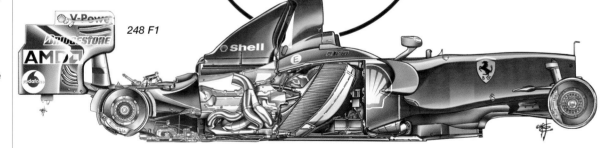

F2005

The 248 F1 had close links to the F2004 rather than the more recent F2005: it was certainly no coincidence that the winter comparison tests were always carried out with the two year old car. Therefore, the double

inclination radiators characteristic of the F2005 were dropped. The front drum brake air intakes were very different, partially closed on the F2004 and drum but open at the sides on the F248.

248 F1

FRONT VIEW
The 248 F1 was the only 2006 car to retain the mono-keel mount for its front suspension. Note the position of the rear view mirrors, which became the first element of the turning vane-chimney group, applied in the upper part of the sidepods.

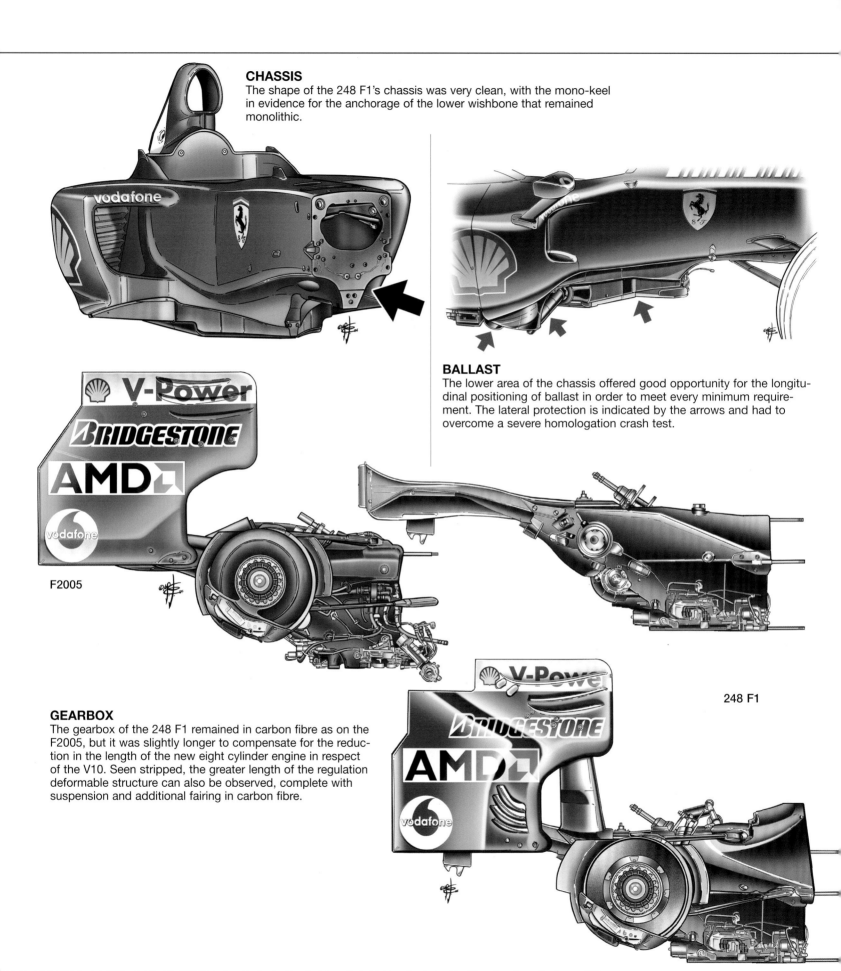

CHASSIS
The shape of the 248 F1's chassis was very clean, with the mono-keel in evidence for the anchorage of the lower wishbone that remained monolithic.

BALLAST
The lower area of the chassis offered good opportunity for the longitudinal positioning of ballast in order to meet every minimum requirement. The lateral protection is indicated by the arrows and had to overcome a severe homologation crash test.

F2005

248 F1

GEARBOX
The gearbox of the 248 F1 remained in carbon fibre as on the F2005, but it was slightly longer to compensate for the reduction in the length of the new eight cylinder engine in respect of the V10. Seen stripped, the greater length of the regulation deformable structure can also be observed, complete with suspension and additional fairing in carbon fibre.

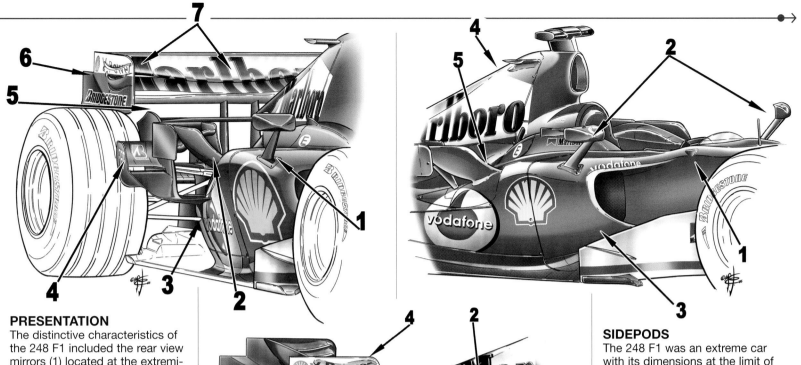

PRESENTATION

The distinctive characteristics of the 248 F1 included the rear view mirrors (1) located at the extremity of the sidepods. The position (2) of the chimneys was new and they constituted a single entity with the lateral flaps. The rear of the car was much more tapered, both below (3) and in the zone in front of the rear wheels. (4) The rear wing group was new, with its planes forward (5) and, in particular, with new concave end plates (6) and a flap with an inconstant chord with the central part curved downwards (7).

SIDEPODS

The 248 F1 was an extreme car with its dimensions at the limit of the regulations, as is shown by this small protrusion (1) to respect the regulations in that area of the chassis. The position of the rear view mirrors (2) was new, their supports that becoming real mini-turning vanes. The entire lower area of the sidepods (3) was very narrow and the engine cover was rather tapered (4). The chimneys were closed and they also became aerodynamic devices.

REAR WING

The exhausts were very low and advanced (1), inserted in a rather tapered engine cover (2). Vertical fins (3) at the sides of the body in front of the rear wheels. The rear wing had large louvers of the Toyota school (4) and its end plates were very complex and concave (5). The diffuser had a very high central channel that was curved upwards in the lower area (6).

DIFFUSER

The 248 F1 had the extreme lower rear aerodynamics already seen on the F2005. The central channel was even higher (1) and retained the flap at mid-height to better manage the air flow that arrived from the rear of the car. It also retained the two lateral mini-channels (2) that were already on the F2005 and are shown in the circle. The runner in the lower area of the central channels had an upwards progression (3). The sealed zone of the rear wheels (4) was very elaborate, with a rounded vertical end plate (5).

FRONT WING

Ferrari abandoned the front wing with the central "step" (1) used in 2005 and which was on the presentation car. This feature ensured good downforce, but it was too pitch sensitive to variations in height with a net loss of braking efficiency. The new wing had a heavily spooned progression (2) with passages among the diverse heights that were less brusque and produced a more homogeneous handling of the car. New, although not for Ferrari who used them in 2001, was the doubling of the flaps (3) located in the central area like a conveyor of air flow, in unison with the small neutral fins in the upper area (4). This plane at the sides in the area close to the end plates had a more downforce progression. The external part (5) of the end plates was also new and had returned to being curved, as on the F2004 of two years earlier.

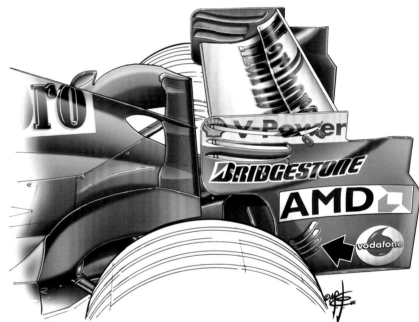

SAKHIR

After four years of double drums around the brake discs, Ferrari dropped them. This was a move dictated by needing to blow all the hot air towards the external part of the rims, following the development carried out by other teams over the last two seasons. In particular, the new air intake was very similar to that on the rear of the Toyota, starting from the Grand Prix of Japan and the B version of the car.

REAR WING

The Ferrari rear wing with the double vertical pillar destined to be the single support of the principal plane created controversy, while the lower one was split in two parts, fixed at the sides of the central channel of the diffuser. The end plates were new and had a series of added louvers in the area above the wheels to reduce turbulence.

SEPANG

More controversy in Malaysia due to the lateral movement of the raised flap at the anchorage point with the nose, shown in television pictures. The Federation judged the flap to be legal and Ferrari covered the movement with the addition of a small piece of fairing around the plane.

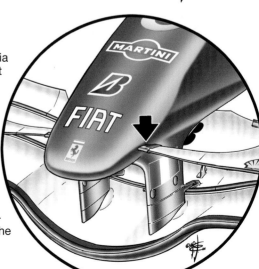

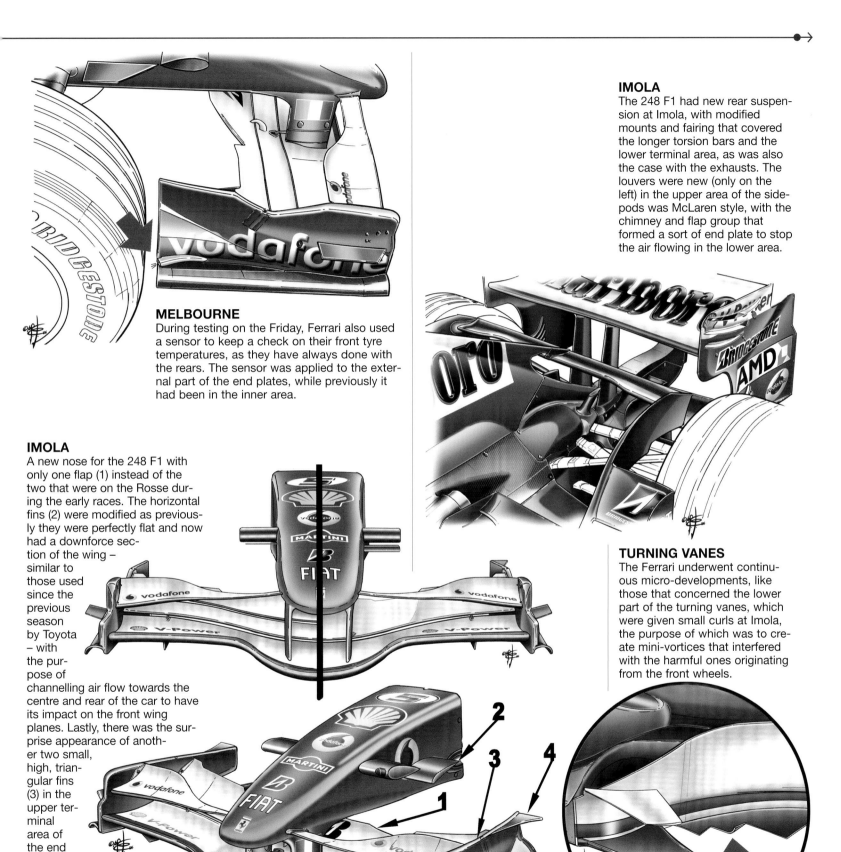

MELBOURNE

During testing on the Friday, Ferrari also used a sensor to keep a check on their front tyre temperatures, as they have always done with the rears. The sensor was applied to the external part of the end plates, while previously it had been in the inner area.

IMOLA

The 248 F1 had new rear suspension at Imola, with modified mounts and fairing that covered the longer torsion bars and the lower terminal area, as was also the case with the exhausts. The louvers were new (only on the left) in the upper area of the sidepods was McLaren style, with the chimney and flap group that formed a sort of end plate to stop the air flowing in the lower area.

IMOLA

A new nose for the 248 F1 with only one flap (1) instead of the two that were on the Rosse during the early races. The horizontal fins (2) were modified as previously they were perfectly flat and now had a downforce section of the wing – similar to those used since the previous season by Toyota – with the purpose of channelling air flow towards the centre and rear of the car to have its impact on the front wing planes. Lastly, there was the surprise appearance of another two small, high, triangular fins (3) in the upper terminal area of the end plates (their design was unchanged) and their task was to better control the harmful vortices in the area of the front wheels.

TURNING VANES

The Ferrari underwent continuous micro-developments, like those that concerned the lower part of the turning vanes, which were given small curls at Imola, the purpose of which was to create mini-vortices that interfered with the harmful ones originating from the front wheels.

LOUVERS

The 248 F1 had been given new hot air louvers in the upper part of the sidepods, which had been moved further back than those at Imola, both in the Friday version, which had less need to dissipate heat, and the one used on the Saturday and Sunday.

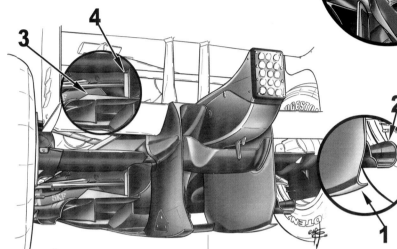

NÜRBURGRING

Further modifications to the 248 F1's diffuser were seen at the 'Ring. The illustration shows the solution used until Melbourne; on the right are the modifications introduced at Imola and retained at the Nürburgring. They were a curving of the knife edge zone (1) at the base of the central channel and a greater height of the curved end plate (2) in an area that sealed the wheels. In addition, the dimensions of the triangular Gurney flap on the lateral (3) channels were reduced, while the vertical Gurney flap (4) near the central channel was bigger to augment its efficiency.

TAIL

The new rear suspension brought with it further refinement of the body, with two small V-shaped fairing elements to cover the bulk of the longer torsion bars.

FINS

There were also modifications in the area in front of the rear wheels with a greater separation between the body and the flap to avoid the detachment of the fluid vein and gain almost 10 kg of load in a rather easy manner, without penalty in terms of penetration resistance. This was a technique that had already been adopted by McLaren and Renault.

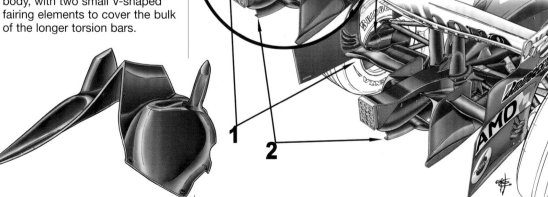

BARCELONA: DIFFUSER

The illustration shows the Imola diffuser, with the modifications brought in at the Nürburgring on the right, which was a rounded low terminal of the central channel (2) so that it was less pitch sensitive to variations in height. The lower plane (1) was also new and on the Ferrari had no structural function, the wing being supported by two vertical pillars. The twisted shape of the plane was developed in relation to the closed brake air intake (3): the task of air extraction in this area wielded great influence.

REAR WING

There was nothing new about the rear wing, which was used with a greater angle of incidence of the flap and, as a result, with a different position of the main plane, as can be seen in the comparison with the broken line showing the position of the plane used in Spain.

BRAKE AIR INTAKES

Another fin (2) added to the front brake air intakes in the search for a few more kilos of downforce on the unsuspended mass, which would be extremely useful in relation to analogous solutions applied to the body of the car. The upper one (2) was introduced the previous year at Monaco and, after a period of problematic discussion, was approved before the Grand Prix of the United States.

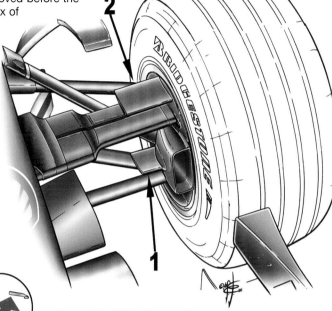

MONACO: FRONT WING

At Monaco, there was a new flap on the front wing with a bigger chord and a Gurney flap in the central zone, as indicated by the arrow. After Thursday testing, a small portion of the horizontal fins was cut in the terminal area of the end plates that touched the tyres on full lock, which was taken to 22° for Monaco.

SILVERSTONE

There was new front suspension with a different steering geometry and a diverse angle to ensure greater contact with the ground in medium-fast corners. This also meant the use of different suspension wishbones and a wheelbase shortened by a few millimetres.

ASYMMETRIC LOUVERS

Asymmetric louvers were often used where the oil radiator was housed, with the number of apertures greater on the left side.

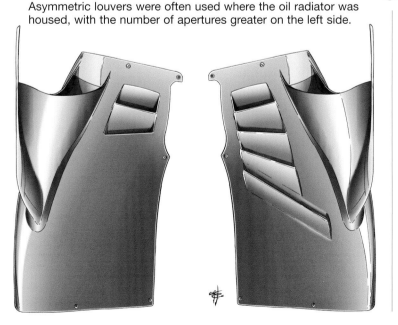

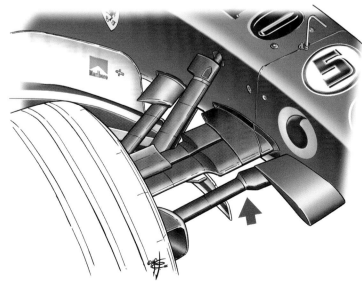

REAR WING

The rear wing was new in all its elements. A stiffening device was added between the principal plane and the C-shaped flap (1) to provide greater efficiency in the area near the slot between the two planes. The shape of the main plane was new and in some ways brought to mind that of Renault, with the central part slightly raised to better follow the progression of the air flow coming from the car's body. The end plates were also new, with only two horizontal louvers in the upper part instead of the habitual three.

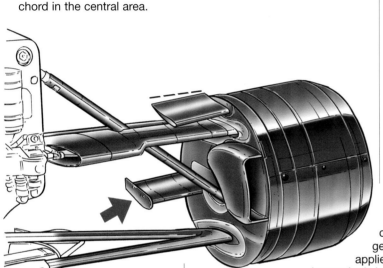

MONTREAL

In Canada, Ferrari had three different front wing flaps and opted to use the one with less chord in qualifying and the race, as can be seen in the illustration's broken line, and without the increased amount of chord in the central area.

BRAKE AIR INTAKE

The continuous evolution of the car by Maranello was most intelligent, with the use of small winglets applied to the brake air intakes. They increasingly became generators of vertical load on the wheels that ensured, perhaps, only a little more than about 10 kilos but it helped produce the tyres' greater adhesion to the ground without costing anything in forward progression. Now, these winglets also have screening applied to the lower elements.

MAGNY COURS

Ferrari had a new engine cover for the French circuit with an even more tapered Coca Cola zone, plus different internal fluid dynamics and hot air vent. There were also two different openings under the closed chimneys.

INDIANAPOLIS

Indy is a track which is not very hard on the brakes and certainly does not need large air intakes like for Montreal. Once again, Ferrari used the small plane with negative lift linked to the little intake. The team also went back to its usual Brembo discs, as did BMW-Sauber, while Renault, Toyota and Rubens Barrichello's Honda had Hitco but McLaren and Williams fitted those of Carbon Industrie.

Montreal

Indianapolis

ISTANBUL

Four rectangular apertures were made in the rear of the Ferrari's circular intakes, which completely covered the front discs from the start of the season, to improve disc cooling. The arrows also indicate the small wing planes applied to the brake air intakes.

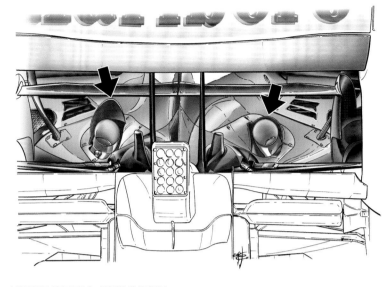

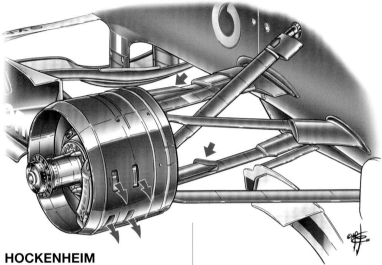

HOCKENHEIM

There was a further modification of the engine cover with a reduction in height of the vertical end plates in front of the rear wheels and introducing a second fin, as on the Renault, located slightly lower to make the so-called Coca Cola zone work better. The old technique is shown in the circle.

ASYMMETRIC CHIMNEYS

Ferrari used the maximum number of apertures in the upper area of the sidepods for especially hot circuits and, as from the Grand Prix of France, the chimneys of the asymmetric exhausts to improve the evacuation of hot air from the left sidepod.

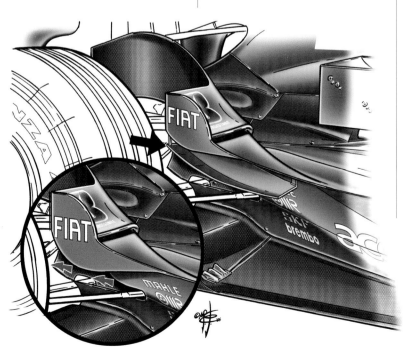

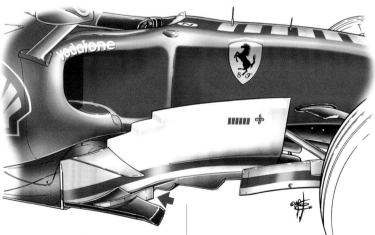

BARGE BOARDS

These barge boards appeared in Turkey for the first time, having previously been used only in private tests. Apart from the stepping in the upper area to create vortices in a controlled manner and, therefore, positive to the progress of the flow in this area of the car, there was a small vertical end plate in the horizontal fin to increase its efficiency.

FAIRED WHEELS

Ferrari took to Turkey the latest examples of their fairing to the external part of the rims, which Maranello introduced at the season's first race at Bahrain. At the time, the approximately 4 cm carbon fibre ring, which had become almost 5 cm on the Toyota –the first to copy that feature for the Nürburgring – reached about 6.5 cm on the Toro Rosso from the Grand Prix of France. The 248 F1 ring increased to over 15 cm with a hole that only allowed the gun to get through during tyre changes.

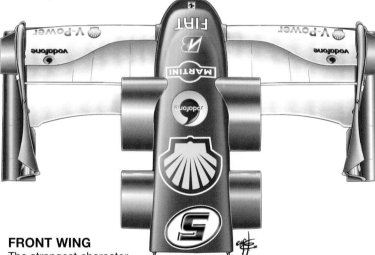

FRONT WING

The strangest characteristic of Ferrari's aerodynamic package for Monza was the doubling of the air flow stabiliser fins at the sides of the nose, combined with a flap with a much reduced chord with the purpose of improving aerodynamic efficiency, which is extremely important at the fast Monza circuit.

MONZA: FRONT WING

At Monza, Ferrari used a front wing that was almost completely different in all its elements, while retaining the raised flap. The principal plane was new and notably less spooned (see the comparison below) linked to a flap with a reduced chord. In particular, two large fins with positive planes were added to avoid the separation of the fluid vein and direct it towards the central part of the car and the rear wing.

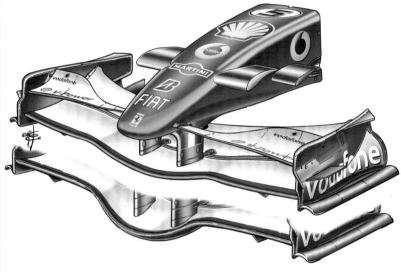

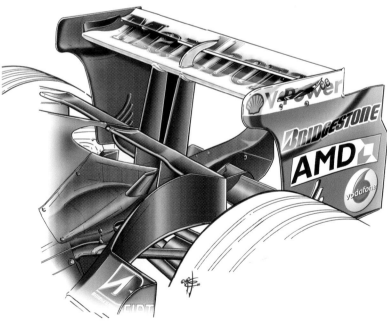

REAR WING

Ferrari made the classic choice for Monza: the main plane with a reduced chord combined with a very small flap. Note the cut end plates with a Toyota-style single louver.

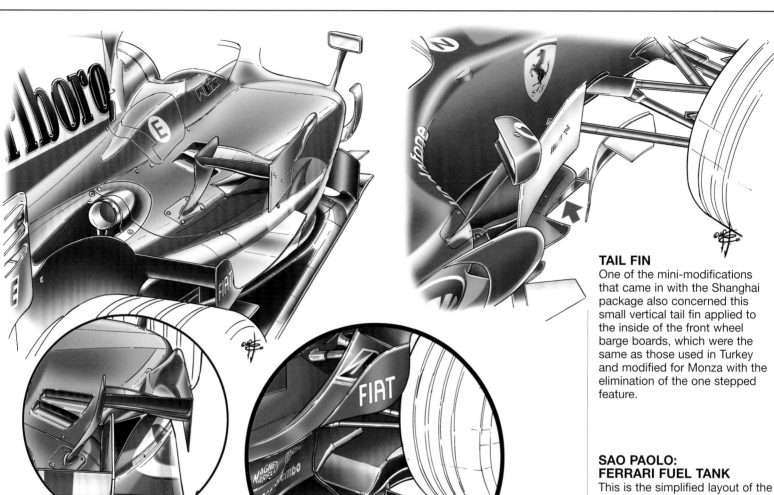

TAIL FIN

One of the mini-modifications that came in with the Shanghai package also concerned this small vertical tail fin applied to the inside of the front wheel barge boards, which were the same as those used in Turkey and modified for Monza with the elimination of the one stepped feature.

SAO PAOLO: FERRARI FUEL TANK

This is the simplified layout of the fuel feed system inside the petrol tank that betrayed Michael Schumacher in qualifying. (1) There were at least four electric pumps in the low peripheral zones that ensured the acquisition of fuel, even during assorted jerking. The petrol is sent at high pressure into a tank (four top-ups) and from there via a mechanical pump (2) to the flutes and then to the injectors. It is this pump that broke down on Schumacher's car, which cannot be explained because it passed the delicate initial phase of test driving. (3) Shows the return of the petrol from the engine to the fuel tank.

SHANGHAI

Ferrari came up with a really new aerodynamic package for China with Renault-style fins, which were the same as the 2005 BAR. They were the most striking elements and were combined with new stepped barge boards similar to those used at Monza (with only two steps) but had a fin fitted with greater incidence. The first illustration shows the new solution, which is compared with the barge boards that appeared for the first time at the Grand Prix of Turkey, where they had three steps and the fin of more horizontal shape. The new fins were combined with further tapering of the engine cover, which was easier to dismantle to meet the various heat dissipation requirements. In the low temperatures in which both qualifying and the race were run, Ferrari opted for a new solution with a semi-vertical louver that was very narrow and is compared in the circle with a larger version used when temperatures were higher.

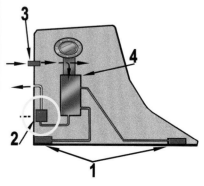

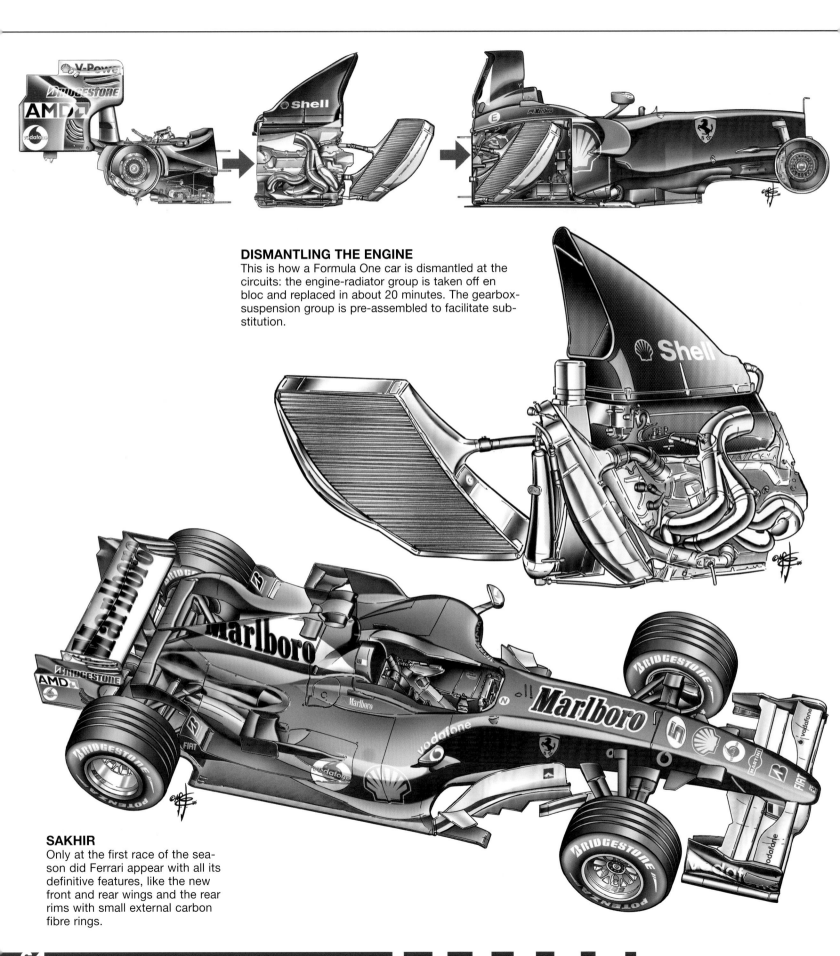

DISMANTLING THE ENGINE

This is how a Formula One car is dismantled at the circuits: the engine-radiator group is taken off en bloc and replaced in about 20 minutes. The gearbox-suspension group is pre-assembled to facilitate substitution.

SAKHIR

Only at the first race of the season did Ferrari appear with all its definitive features, like the new front and rear wings and the rear rims with small external carbon fibre rings.

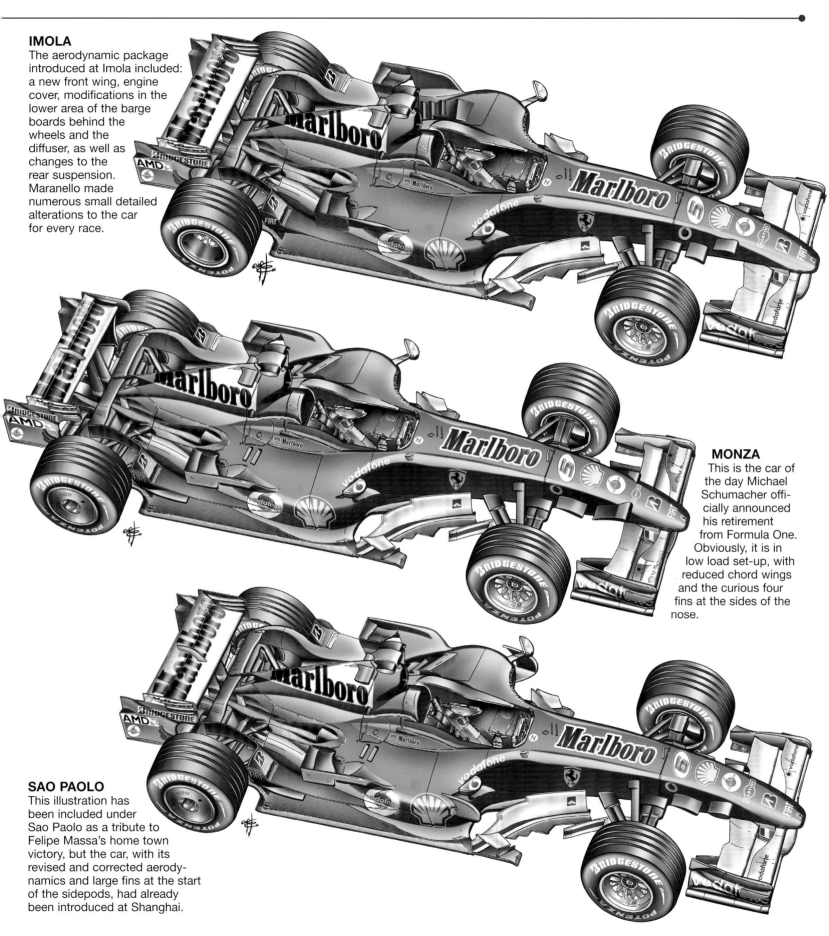

IMOLA

The aerodynamic package introduced at Imola included: a new front wing, engine cover, modifications in the lower area of the barge boards behind the wheels and the diffuser, as well as changes to the rear suspension. Maranello made numerous small detailed alterations to the car for every race.

MONZA

This is the car of the day Michael Schumacher officially announced his retirement from Formula One. Obviously, it is in low load set-up, with reduced chord wings and the curious four fins at the sides of the nose.

SAO PAOLO

This illustration has been included under Sao Paolo as a tribute to Felipe Massa's home town victory, but the car, with its revised and corrected aerodynamics and large fins at the start of the sidepods, had already been introduced at Shanghai.

McLAREN

McLaren MP4-20
Sao Paolo

McLaren MP4-21
Presentation

McLaren MP4-21
Nürburgring

McLaren MP4-21
Indianapolis

McLaren MP4-21
Sao Paolo

The McLaren-Mercedes MP4-21 certainly inherited both the beauty of its lines and sophisticated technical features from the previous model, but also the MP4-20's reliability which, unfortunately, was not exceptional. The result: not a single victory during the whole season and the departure of Kimi Raikkonen for Maranello, as well as a sharp drop in the world championship with no fewer than 72 points less in the constructors' classification. The team ended up one place behind Ferrari, which, as the championship progressed, assumed the leading role as Renault's main rival in their quest for the world title.

The MP4-21 was no jump into the dark unknown, but a logical refinement of concepts expressed by the MP4-20 and still was created under Adrian Newey's direction. Apart from that, the MP4-21 duplicated the layouts of the previous car, of which it retained the wheelbase dimensions, the architecture of the suspension and the carbon fibre gearbox. The departure of the British genius was felt even more because Peter Prodomou, who has had great experience of McLaren aerodynamics, also joined Red Bull. And it was the aerodynamics that were the main inspiring force behind the new model, with even more extreme solutions, which clashed with the unexpected thermal dissipation requirements of the new eight cylinder Mercedes-Benz engine. The unit appeared more fragile and in difficulty at maximum revs in relation to its direct competitors. For races that were to take place in torrid heat, louvers often appeared on the splendid body of the MP4-22 and they partially reduced the car's aerodynamic efficiency. A B version of the MP4-21 was taken to Monaco. Not only were the front and rear wing completely new, so was the entire central area of the body. The shape of the engine air intake was of slightly bigger section to enable the eight cylinder Mercedes-Benz power unit to breathe better: that was combined with an engine cover which was decidedly narrower and wrapped itself around the mechanics like a second skin. The area around the exhausts and gearbox was also new. Paradoxically, it was precisely this extreme slimming cure that caused Raikkonen the noted problems in both Thursday testing and the Sunday race. In both situations, the anti-heat screening around the exhausts caught fire. Developed to withstand over 400°C, the material was modified after the testing problem and even a different light grey paint was used instead of the usual black in an effort to better expel heat. The problem presented itself again due to low speed and consequent lower intake of air into the radiator mouths, but only on the Finn's car, as he exploits his engine in an extreme manner. The cooling louvers in the upper area of the sidepods were also new and contained no fewer than six apertures each. They were symmetric, as were the chimneys, although these were asymmetric in Spain and at the Nürburgring. When the "circus" returned to Europe after the North American races, McLaren immediately took measures to introduce a version of its car in France with bigger sidepod entry intakes, even if their shape was almost unaltered. Much work was done on the front wing planes and the end plates, which progressively increased their alignment towards the interior of the front wheels, with an external section that was notably bigger in relation to their competitors. Towards the end of the season, a new brake system supplier made its debut. The traditional A+P calipers were replaced by those of Japan's Akebono, a Toyota satellite. These were calipers that had appeared on

the BAR-Honda during the last three races of the 2005 season. McLaren showed it was in some difficulty in relation to Renault in the exploitation of Michelin's ultra-high performance tyres, which, as required by the regulations, were no longer fitted for the whole race and, in particular, were prepared in a climate of total competition with their rival Bridgestone. The decision taken by the Federation to re-introduce tyre changing during races after the events at Indianapolis in 2005 caught McLaren off guard, as they had almost finalised the design of their new car at the time the revolutionary measure had been taken.

FRONT VIEW

A clear derivation of the MP4-20, the shape of the MP4-21's chassis and the whole front area, with the zero keel well in evidence. (1) The lower wishbone mount was, in fact, slightly further down and the shape of the chassis was more arched (2). Much work had been carried out on the turning vanes (3), which were more or less similar to those of the MP4-20. The greatest difference compared to the 2005 car (above) was concentrated on the sidepods, which were more tapered and had an almost triangular mouth.

FRONT SUSPENSION

The front suspension layout was unchanged, although the chassis of the MP4-21 was slightly higher and there was no longer the protrusion to accommodate the suspension rockers (see circle). Unlike all the other cars, the torsion bars did not pass through the front of the chassis but the upper zone at an angle of about 20°.

"VIKING HORNS"

The original "Viking horns" were retained, including the version sent to Monza, although they were taken off at the Italian circuit in 2005. Their task was to improve air flow efficiency towards the rear wing.

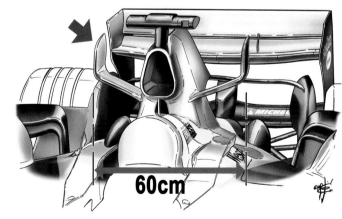

60cm

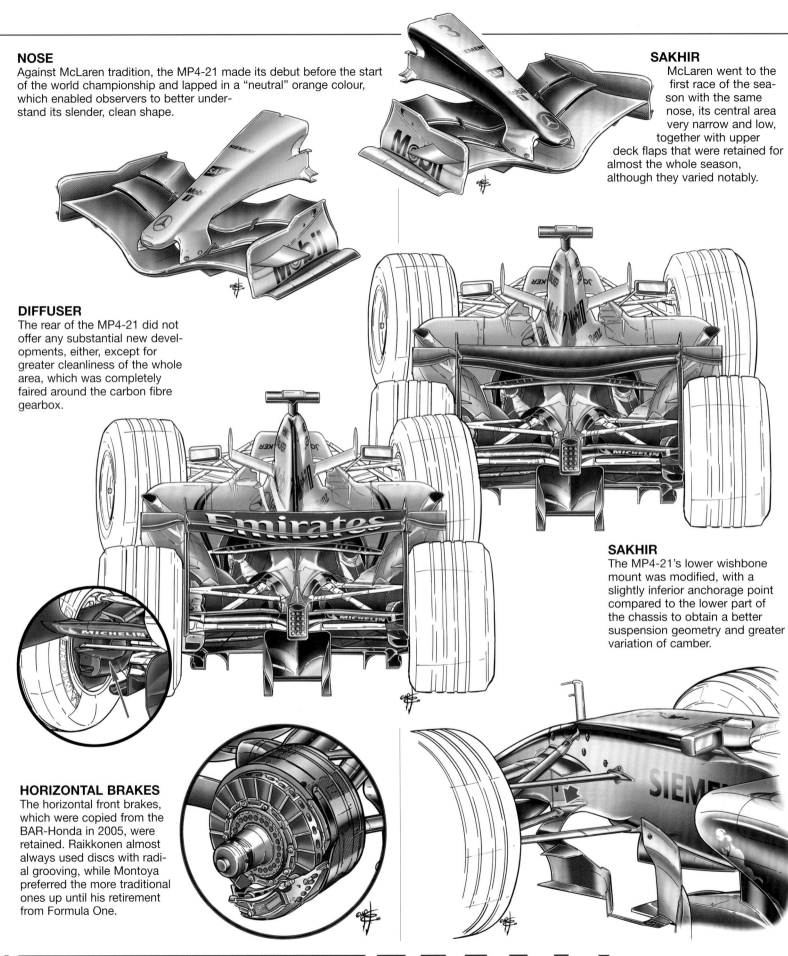

NOSE

Against McLaren tradition, the MP4-21 made its debut before the start of the world championship and lapped in a "neutral" orange colour, which enabled observers to better understand its slender, clean shape.

SAKHIR

McLaren went to the first race of the season with the same nose, its central area very narrow and low, together with upper deck flaps that were retained for almost the whole season, although they varied notably.

DIFFUSER

The rear of the MP4-21 did not offer any substantial new developments, either, except for greater cleanliness of the whole area, which was completely faired around the carbon fibre gearbox.

SAKHIR

The MP4-21's lower wishbone mount was modified, with a slightly inferior anchorage point compared to the lower part of the chassis to obtain a better suspension geometry and greater variation of camber.

HORIZONTAL BRAKES

The horizontal front brakes, which were copied from the BAR-Honda in 2005, were retained. Raikkonen almost always used discs with radial grooving, while Montoya preferred the more traditional ones up until his retirement from Formula One.

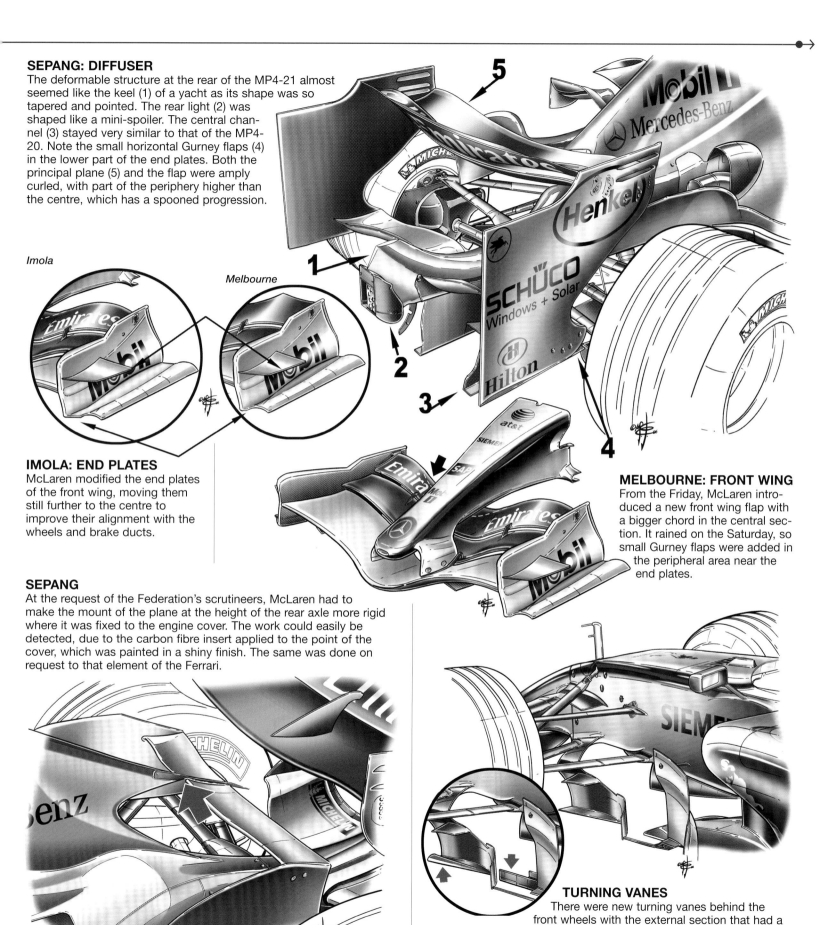

SEPANG: DIFFUSER

The deformable structure at the rear of the MP4-21 almost seemed like the keel (1) of a yacht as its shape was so tapered and pointed. The rear light (2) was shaped like a mini-spoiler. The central channel (3) stayed very similar to that of the MP4-20. Note the small horizontal Gurney flaps (4) in the lower part of the end plates. Both the principal plane (5) and the flap were amply curled, with part of the periphery higher than the centre, which has a spooned progression.

Imola

Melbourne

IMOLA: END PLATES

McLaren modified the end plates of the front wing, moving them still further to the centre to improve their alignment with the wheels and brake ducts.

SEPANG

At the request of the Federation's scrutineers, McLaren had to make the mount of the plane at the height of the rear axle more rigid where it was fixed to the engine cover. The work could easily be detected, due to the carbon fibre insert applied to the point of the cover, which was painted in a shiny finish. The same was done on request to that element of the Ferrari.

MELBOURNE: FRONT WING

From the Friday, McLaren introduced a new front wing flap with a bigger chord in the central section. It rained on the Saturday, so small Gurney flaps were added in the peripheral area near the end plates.

TURNING VANES

There were new turning vanes behind the front wheels with the external section that had a further sleeve, part of which was only flat at first.

MONACO: FRONT WING

At Monaco, McLaren fielded almost a B version of the MP4-21. But only Montoya used the new front wing, which was of more sophisticated shape: its planes had been raised brusquely (1) in the area near the end plates, and there was a more sinuous progression both of the main plane and the first flaps (2). The middle plates in the lower area (3) were new, longer and bent forward. The trailing edge of the second flap was indented (4) while the support of the principal plane was also different as it, too, was connected to the initial flap for the first time.

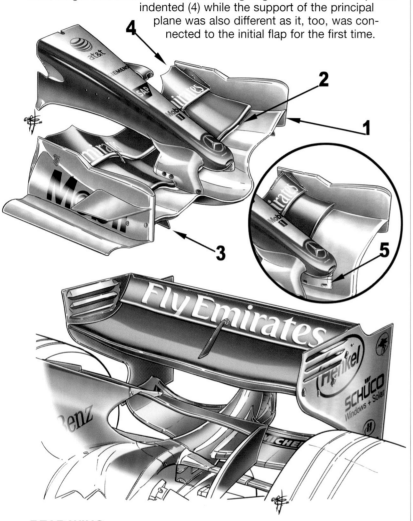

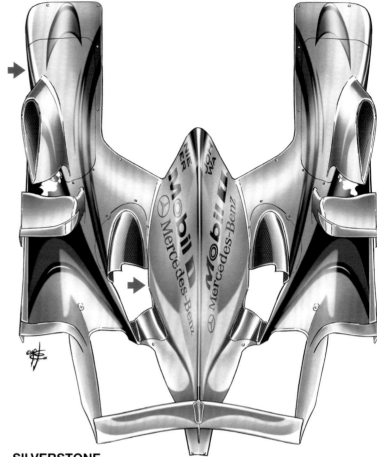

SILVERSTONE

Modifications were made to the B version of the MP4-20 to ensure greater reliability, despite the new version of the engine cover being much more tapered to the point that it formed a sort of second skin around the mechanics. Its shape is well displayed from above in the illustration. The team worked hard to ensure the screen in carbon fibre completely insulated the mechanics from the exhausts, which were even closer to the car's body, in that way avoiding the possibility of them going up in flames as happened twice at Monaco.

REAR WING

The rear wing was also new and was no longer spooned, but of the kind adopted the previous season. It provided more downforce and, at Monaco, was combined with end plates with horizontal louvers.

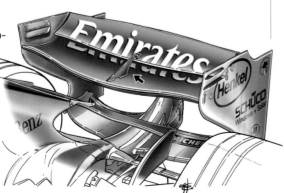

SILVERSTONE: REAR WING

On the Friday, Raikkonen always used the old rear wing together with the old front element, but then he moved on to the wing introduced at Monaco, only at the rear end though.

MONTREAL: REAR WING

McLaren dropped the spooned planes that were heavily curled and used until Canada. They were replaced with straight planes and flaps (1) for fast circuits and had a rigidity element similar to that of the other two versions of the rear wing. The two horizontal louvers (2) had a new shape, being longer and thinner than the previous version and were moved slightly upwards

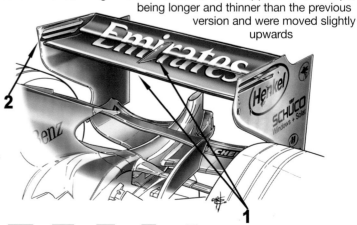

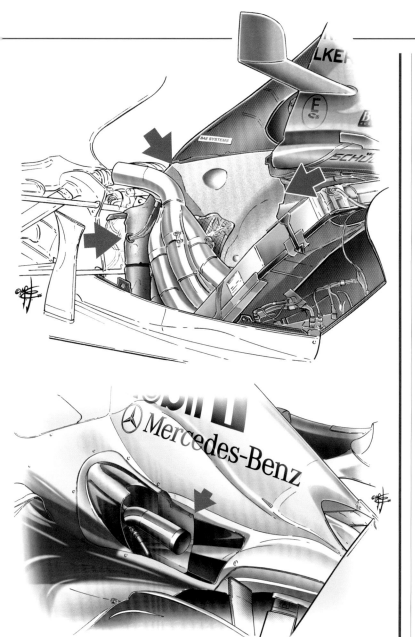

DISC BRAKE

McLaren used special brake discs made by Carbon Industrie, which were produced specifically for the Canadian race. They had closely ranged perforations that were flattened and close together to improve heat dissipation without the wear rate being penalised. Note the bigger intakes of the cooling system, with the marked alignment of the end plates, which were notably moved inwards.

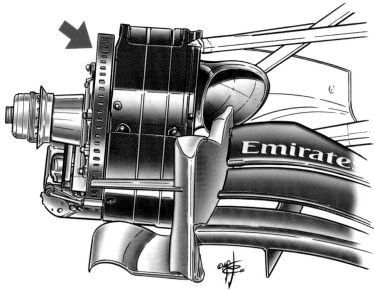

MAGNY COURS

McLaren carried out an important modification for the Grand Prix of France with the remaking of the initial area of the sidepods, which obliged the team to subject the chassis to a new crash test. While not wishing to alter the exit zone in the rear of the car, to improve cooling the constructor increased the capacity of the entry intake. The illustration shows the difference between the new and old sidepods in yellow, the latter on the spare car.

INDIANAPOLIS

Nobody took the extreme path opened up the previous year by McLaren with their movement of the end plates towards the centre of the car, having an external section that was increased from the 2006 Grand Prix of Europe. In that way, a different alignment was formed with the inner part of the tyres. The width of the planes (140 cm maximum) was reduced to little more than 110 cm, with the surface loss compensated for by the two flaps that helped provide a much more extended sum total of chord of the planes themselves.

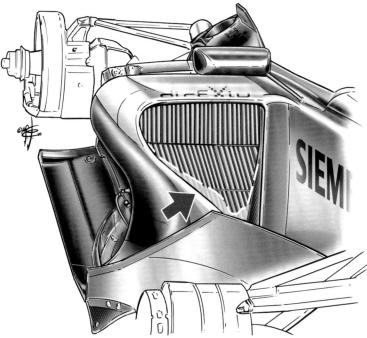

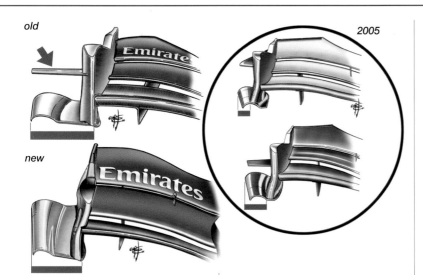

old

new

2005

MONZA: REAR WING

McLaren used a single plane (1) at Monza with one element of straight progression that was very simple: a feature that ensured less penetration resistance. The plane above the rear axle (2) had a greatly reduced chord.

1

2

HOCKENHEIM: FRONT WING

A completely new front wing was introduced by McLaren for the German weekend. The end plates were no longer straight but had a flared shape down below and no longer had the wide horizontal fin on the outside. The ratio between the three planes had changed altogether: the principal unit had a much reduced chord and a progression that ascended in the peripheral zone. The first flap had a more than ample chord, while that of the second was slightly inferior. On the MP4-21 there were various extreme revivals of the concept of the end plates aligned towards the internal area, which first came in during the 2005 season (see circle).

FRONT WING

In the view from above, note the single flap in place of the usual two on the front wing, which was also taken to Monza for the first time. It was a precise calculation of how much the external parts of the end plates reduced the width of the planes.

STABILISER FIN

There was a new horizontal stabiliser fin in the front suspension area. Its purpose was similar to the bigger version used by Renault, Ferrari, Red Bull and Midland: to improve efficiency in the central zone of the car and the rear wing.

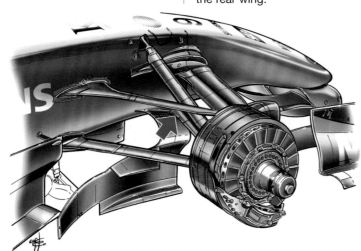

MONZA

The new horizontal fin seen on the start line of the Grand Prix of Turkey was retained, located inside the front suspension with the task of cleaning the air flow towards the central area of the car.

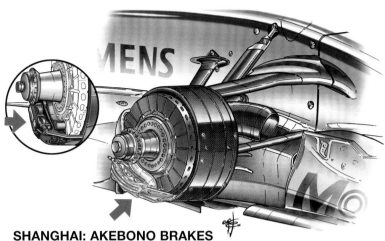

SHANGHAI: AKEBONO BRAKES
Surprisingly, McLaren switched to new brake calipers on the two cars for this race, adopting those of Japan's Akebono, which were easily recognisable by their light colour in relation to those of the usual A+P. Note the channelling that carries air to the calipers, starting from the rear of the drum intake, a technique adopted by Red Bull from last year. Akebono calipers were seen the previous year on the BAR-Honda at the Grand Prix of Japan, an arrangement that was not continued because Akebono is a Toyota satellite company.

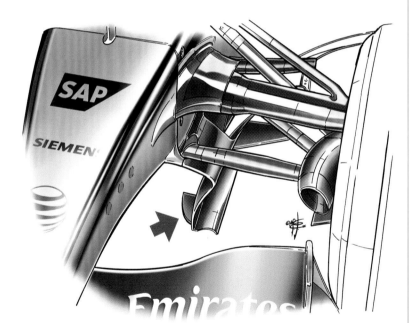

SUZUKA
A notable volume of micro-developments were seen on the 2006 McLaren, although the team was already concentrating on the development of the car for the following season. At Suzuka, McLaren had modified the large twin barge boards in the front suspension area: they had new appendages, like this small section that was almost triangular internally, combined with a double sleeve in the upper area.

BRAKE AIR INTAKES
The continuation of the constructional philosophy of the MP4-21 in respect of the previous 19-20 can also be noted from the drum brake air intakes. They were open towards the exterior so as to expel hot air in that direction and not against the internal part of the rims, with the negative influence that would have on the temperature of the tyres. Note the new Akebono callipers, which were easily distinguishable from those of A+P by their much lighter colour.

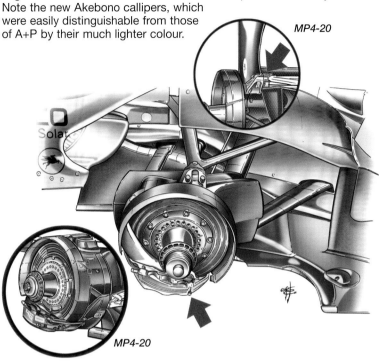

MP4-20

MP4-20

SAO PAOLO: WINGS
McLaren was the only team to keep the medium-low load Montreal wings even if, naturally, the planes at the rear were fitted with greater incidence. That could be seen from the more significant distance of the principal plane in relation to the lateral louvers, as shown in the circle, in which there is the comparison with the Montreal version. There were three different wings for the front, but the one used at Montreal was selected here, too, with a second flap fitted with more incidence.

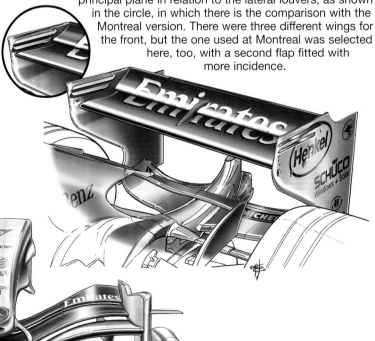

HONDA

CONSTRUCTORS' CLASSIFICATION			
	2005	2006	
Position	6°	4°	+2 ▲
Points	38	86	+48 ▲

BAR 007
Suzuka

Honda RA 106
Presentation

Honda RA 106
Imola

The BAR Honda was a logical evolution of the 2005 car from which it inherited its general shape, even though it boasted a few new features. Among the most important was the disappearance of the single keel in favour of the split anchorage of the lower wishbones in the lower area of the chassis, as with the previous year's McLaren. Next was the adoption of a new front suspension layout with horizontal brake calipers as on the MP4-20 and 21, which required a great deal of work to ensure good overall torsional rigidity. Another unique characteristic was the steering link half way along the upright and not in line with the upper wishbone, as on all the other cars. Initially, the

Honda's wheelbase was unchanged despite the less bulky new eight-cylinder engine, which was compensated for by the slight increase in the length of the carbon fibre gearbox (see the Suspension chapter) and the increased capacity fuel tank. BAR Honda used a quick shift gearbox based on a project carried out with the Japanese manufacturer. During the season, though, the car's wheelbase was lengthened by 50 mm, inclining the front suspension wishbones forward, as was seen in Turkey. However, the 2006 season was a very strange one for BAR Honda, which was fully acquired by the Japanese car maker. Looking at the Constructors' classification, the team's 2006 result cannot be

considered anything other than positive, with Honda in fourth place immediately behind the top three teams and Jenson Button's first F1 victory in the Grand Prix of Hungary. However, it must be said that the yield of the 007 was not constant, as it was competitive at the beginning of the season but then less incisive as the championship progressed. Technical development was not consistent and some new features were dropped after a single test race. Certainly, insurgent problems with the calibration of the wind tunnel and the departure of Wilheim Toet, head of that sector, had their negative influence, as did the other departure of the project's boss Geoff Willis. The team's only victory by Jen-

son Button in Hungary was achieved with a car that constituted a mix between new and old features. Rubens Barrichello, who was often considered ill at ease in his new team, was the key individual who convinced the Honda technicians to put more effort into a number of sectors in which the team wrongly believed it was already among the best. That especially included the car's traction control, one of the disappointing elements to the Brazilian driver, who was used to the hyper-sophisticated Ferrari system. Button adapted himself – perhaps too well – to the shortcomings of the car as, unlike Barrichello, he had no direct point of reference. At the height of the summer, the Japanese racing department's best brains were applied to resolving the traction control problems, rightly considered significantly connected to the frequent cyclical breakdowns of the Honda engine. The same can be said for the modularity of the braking system, which was another thorn in Barrichello's side.

As far as the specifics of the car are concerned, many new features were introduced during the later races; not all of them worked and those that did not were dropped before Hungary, where Honda fielded two cars with the following characteristics: Nose - having abandoned the previous three developments, the team went back to the Imola version, with a spoon shaped section that was not extreme in the central area. Suspension - the faired version brought in at Imola remained, but with new geometry. Sidepods - the new fins first seen at Monte Carlo were confirmed, together with the "fox ears" (Imola) at the sides of the cockpit, while the hammer planes behind the anti-roll bar that first appeared at Imola continued to be used, but the new rear body seen in France that was narrower in the lower area was dropped. The new end plates that were added to the rear wing in Canada were rejected in favour of a more classic derivative with an advanced plane above the rear axle. The rest resulted from the considerable amount of work invested in the suspension, weight distribution and tyre construction. At Budapest, Honda opted for soft tyres with a construction identical to those of Renault at the rear, and a number of different types at the front. Honda dared a little more on the rear wing flexibility, sufficient to generate perplexity among some of its direct rivals, but without them taking the matter as far as a real protest.

HONDA RA 106E

The new RA 106E had also abandoned the mono-keel, adopting a layout first used the previous year by the McLaren MP4-20, with split lower wishbones anchored to the inferior area of the chassis (1); it is interesting to note that the car, designed by Geoff Willis, was the only one not to have its steering link at the same height on the upper wishbone, but recessed into the upright (2) at half distance to give more precision. The aerodynamic solutions of the old BAR remained, even if in evolved shape, both at the base of the sidepods (3) and the upper area where, however, they appeared much bigger (4). The position of the short (5) fin was almost unchanged under the larger one in front of the rear wheels. The chimneys (6) were completely new and of the Renault school, combined with double flaps. The position of the exhaust terminals (7) was very similar to the system adopted by the BAR of the previous season, as was the pentagonal shape of the engine air intake (8). The use of the miniplanes (9) behind the anti-roll bar was unvaried, as were the double supports of the rear wing, which had been present on the last BAR from the start of the 2005 season.

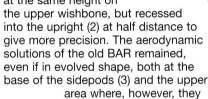

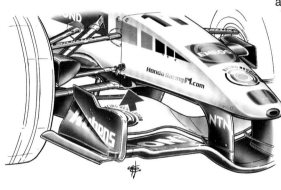

FRONT SUSPENSION

These two drawings show the split anchorage of the front suspension's lower wishbone with and without the nose; there were no great variations in shape or the chassis' height from the ground in relation to the old BAR- Honda.The lower wishbone is fixed under the real structure. Also note the steering link in a central position in relation to the wheel and not aligned above with the upper wishbone, as on all the other cars.

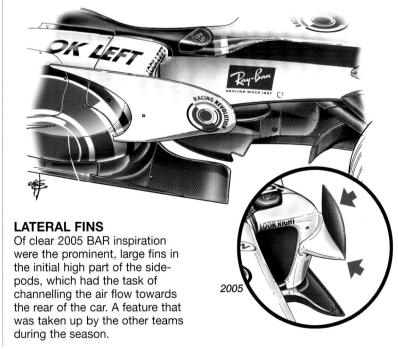

LATERAL FINS

Of clear 2005 BAR inspiration were the prominent, large fins in the initial high part of the sidepods, which had the task of channelling the air flow towards the rear of the car. A feature that was taken up by the other teams during the season.

2005

HORIZONTAL CALIPERS

Honda followed McLaren's example, not only in the way it anchored the lower triangles of its suspension, but also in positioning its brake calipers horizontally, obviously in an attempt to reduce the centre of gravity of the unsuspended mass. That technique was only used by those two teams.

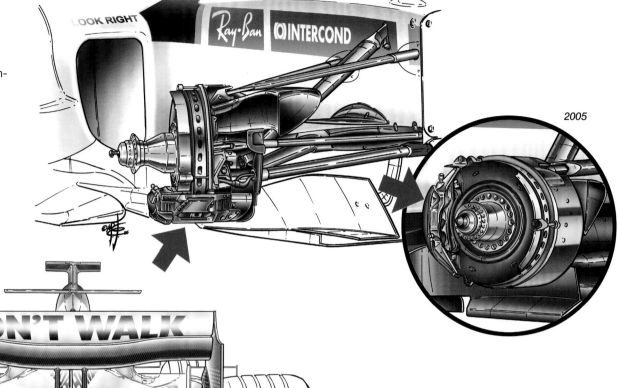

2005

DIFFUSER

The Honda had mini-channels (1) at the sides of the central section of the diffuser, first used by the Ferrari F 2005 the previous year. The central channel was very high and square, with a second vertical end plate (2) that increased the section of the central channel in the area above the lateral sections. The knife edge zone (3) was very flat and wide at the sides of the rear wheels. Honda also kept the two central vertical supports to sustain the rear wing group, which were already present on the previous year's BAR.

MELBOURNE: REAR WINGS

BAR Honda tried two rear wings in Melbourne. In the end, they opted for the one fitted to the car with a straight plane, combined with one of short chord above the rear axle.

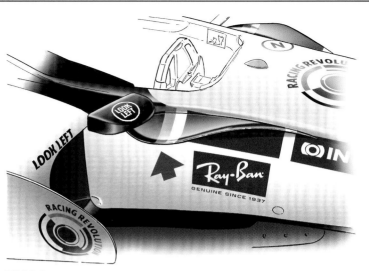

IMOLA

A new aerodynamic package was introduced at Imola, which included these odd looking fins nick-named fox ears. Their purpose was to clean the area of vortices that disturbed the air flow towards sidepod intakes and the rear of the car.

IMOLA

Another new detail that appeared at Imola concerned the shape of the double T of the first straight planes in the area immediately above the engine air intake.

IMOLA AND THE NÜRBURGRING

A comparison between the new wing brought in at Imola (left) and the one used at the Nürburgring (right), which seemed to reduce the brusque transverse air flow in the lower area, even if to the detriment of a slightly reduced aerodynamic load.

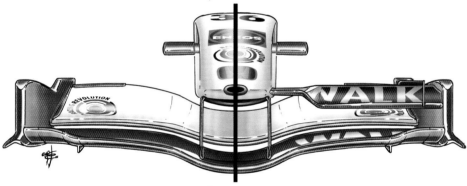

IMOLA

There was new and very special fairing of a unique arrow shape for the upper wishbone of the front suspension.

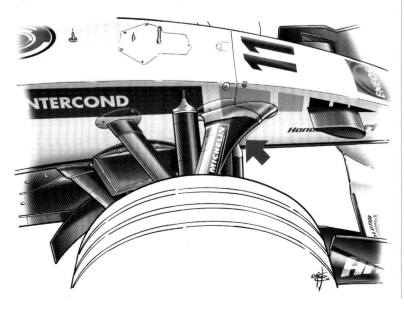

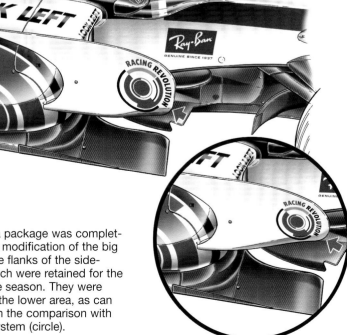

IMOLA

The Imola package was completed by the modification of the big fins on the flanks of the sidepods, which were retained for the rest of the season. They were bigger in the lower area, as can be seen in the comparison with the old system (circle).

MONTREAL

Two new rear wings were introduced by Honda, both of them with Renault-type detached flaps and a well executed feature in the connecting area with the rear end plate. After having been tested at Monza, the flap was given two stiffeners in the central area in order to respect the new norms introduced by the Federation in Canada. Barrichello went out briefly with the main plane of his car heavily arched upwards in the centre, but the feature was immediately dropped in favour of one with a straight plane. The terminal area of the engine cover was also different (pointed in the stepped version), while the gills in the high initial zone of the end plates were the same, even if they were modified in relation to the standard version.

MAGNY COURS

A new front wing came in at Magny-Cours to provide greater load, in particular for the steered wheels. These Williams-style (2) appendages neutralised the negative effects of the interaction between the wing and the steered wheels. The main plane (1) was also new as was the flap (3), the previous version of which was of straight progression.

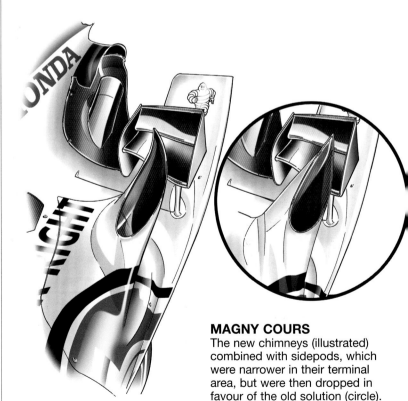

LONG WHEELBASE

At Monza, Honda had modified the geometry of the rear suspension and retained the lengthened wheelbase introduced in Turkey, with the front wishbones angled forward. This was a solution that also required a repeat of the front crash test in order to maintain the regulation distance in relation to the front axle.

MAGNY COURS

The new chimneys (illustrated) combined with sidepods, which were narrower in their terminal area, but were then dropped in favour of the old solution (circle).

BUDAPEST

Honda abandoned its latest aerodynamic features, such as the new Williams-style nose introduced in France, to return to the one used at Imola that had a spooned central zone.

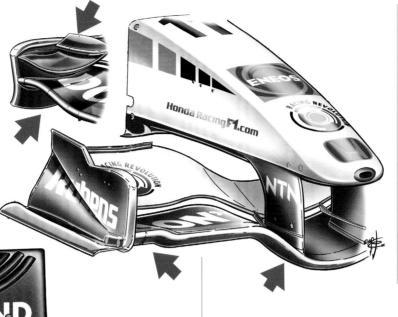

ISTANBUL

The aerodynamics of the Honda were decidedly simplified in Turkey, with an uncomplicated turning vane in the area behind the front wheels instead of the previous complex system. The front wing was also new.

2005

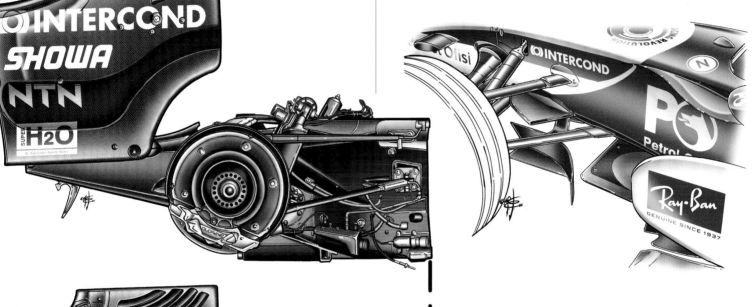

2006

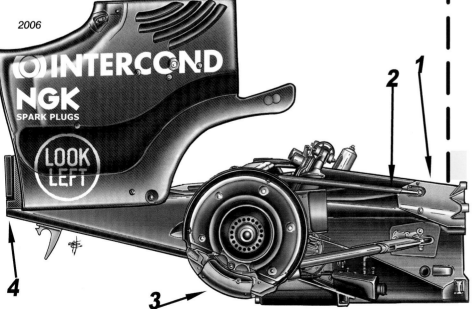

CARBONFIBRE GEARBOX

Honda retained the carbonfibre gearbox introduced in 2004, modifying it in accordance with the changing requirements. The longer carbonfibre casing (1) compensated for the shorter V8 engine compared with the V10 and kept the wheelbase unchanged. It was also slightly lower with different wishbone mounts (2). The brake calipers were again Alcon units but had a carbonfibre cooling shroud (3); lastly, the deformable structure was 10 cm longer to satisfy the stricter regulations and pass the new rear crash test.

BMW-SAUBER

CONSTRUCTORS' CLASSIFICATION	2005	2006	
Position	8°	5°	+3 ▲
Points	20	36	+16 ▲

Sauber C24
Silverstone

BMW-Sauber F1-06
Presentation

BMW-Sauber F1-06
Sakhir

BMW-Sauber F1-06
Magny Cours

BMW-Sauber F1-06
Hockenheim

The 2006 season ushered in a new era for Sauber, which had been transformed into BMW Sauber. Willy Rampf turned over a new leaf from the aerodynamics point of view, abandoning both the twin keel layout, which he introduced in 2000, and the single keel used by the Saubers for the last two seasons. The designer decided to follow in the footsteps of McLaren by eliminating the keel from his F1.06 car and, just like on the McLaren MP4-20, the lower wishbones went back to being split, anchored in the inferior area of the chassis which, for this reason, were in that position in order to ensure a more favourable suspension geometry. That decision conditioned all the aerodynamics of the new car: the nose had a progression that looked like an anteater, notably arching itself in the lower area to better exploit the greater amount of air under the car, which was no longer disturbed by the presence of the central bulb. The wing planes were new and inspired in one way or another by those of Williams rather than the stepped units on the old Sauber C24. The twin bargeboards were also of McLaren inspiration and began from inside the front wheels. For the remainder, the BMW Sauber F1.06 was a further and substantial development of the previous season's car starting with the shape of the chassis, which retained the characteristic sidepods but which were more concave in the lower area. All the aerodynamics to the back of the sidepods and the rear end were revised with the adoption of large fins in front of the wheels and horizontal openings in the upper area of the engine cover for good heat dissipation. The switch to the eight-cylinder engine coincided with the adoption of a new power unit by the team in place of the 10-cylinder Ferrari. The eight cylinder BMW was under constant development for almost all of the races before it arrived

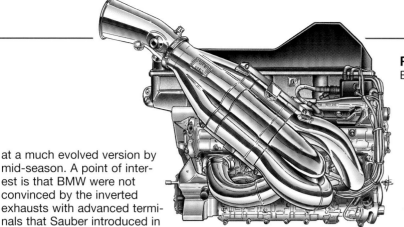

at a much evolved version by mid-season. A point of interest is that BMW were not convinced by the inverted exhausts with advanced terminals that Sauber introduced in 2005 when they were using the Ferrari engine. Immediately after the car's launch in Valencia, it was further refined in general, ending in the debut of the first definitive version in Bahrain. BMW Sauber was one of the most active teams in evolving its car, so much so that it has been necessary to move some of its features to other chapters of this book (see Aerodynamics and Brakes). Modifications were brought in at almost every race, but it was at Imola that the first new aerodynamic package appeared and comprised a new nose, a body modified with different chimneys, a new engine cover and diffuser. The aerodynamic package developed for tracks of high load appeared at Monaco and soon afterwards the medium load version competed in Canada. At Montreal, BMW Sauber were at the centre of controversy due to a new rear wing, which was suspected of being too flexible and which had already been modified to get past scrutineering for Indianapolis a week later.

Another important phase coincided with the Grand Prix of France, where the new front wing made its first appearance and was unmistakable due to its McLaren style Viking horn and especially the new, large vertical fins on the upper part of the chassis. This was a feature accepted by the Federation at first, but later prohibited together with further developments of it by other teams (see the Controversies chapter). More important modifications appeared at the subsequent Grand Prix of Germany with the adoption of fins at the front of the sidepods. Perhaps the season's best version of the car was taken to Monza with its low load aerodynamic package

that affected all sectors and worked especially well. The last evolution of the BMW Sauber appeared just before the transfer to China and Japan. In the comparison between the various side views used by the teams during the season, we have not included those for Monza because they represent an obligatory stage for all the squads and they are not indicative of the work carried out by the designers in the development of the car.

RADIATORS AND EXHAUST PIPES

BMW Sauber did away with its sophisticated split radiator layout with the double V-shaped forward inclination in the front and moved on to an installation with vertical open V radiator packs, but inclined inwards. The Ferrari-type inverted exhaust pipes were also dropped in favour of a more classical disposition with terminals turned backwards.

PRESENTATION

The F1.06 dropped the single keel feature and adopted a split mount (1) of the lower wishbones to improve the quality of the airflow under the car. The central bulb in the lower area of the chassis disappeared, as can be seen by the section shown in yellow (2). The front wing plane was of spoon progression and was considerably different from the usual unit on the C24, which had its well-known Ferrari type central "running board" (see the C24 plane). (3) The twin bargeboards inside the front wheels were very similar to those on the McLaren MP4-20. (4) The shape of the chassis and sidepods came from the 2005 Sauber and had an almost triangular entrance, the lower part deeply concave. (5) The long fins on the sidepods were new, as were the small curved middle wings plus the fins (6) in front of the rear wheels. (7) The exhaust pipes were set back and integrated into the rear of the rather streamlined body. (8) The entire rear wing assembly was new and had an added miniplane down low, above the rear light. The mini-planes behind the engine air intake had disappeared, while the endplates of the wing with Toyota-style gills remained, having been introduced during the second part of the season on the C24.

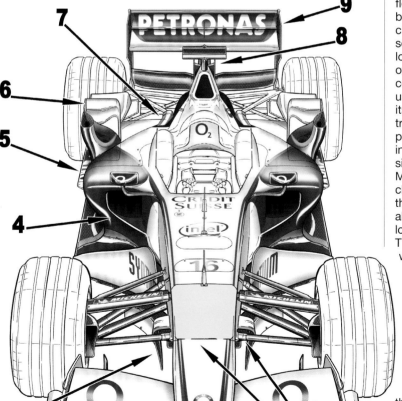

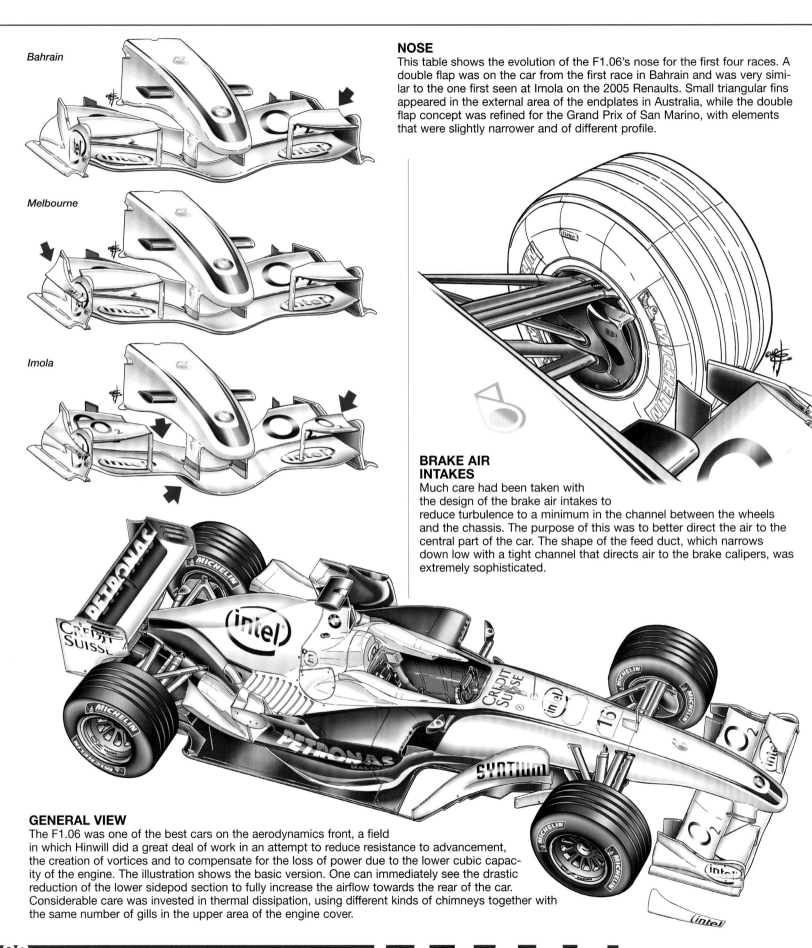

Bahrain

Melbourne

Imola

NOSE
This table shows the evolution of the F1.06's nose for the first four races. A double flap was on the car from the first race in Bahrain and was very similar to the one first seen at Imola on the 2005 Renaults. Small triangular fins appeared in the external area of the endplates in Australia, while the double flap concept was refined for the Grand Prix of San Marino, with elements that were slightly narrower and of different profile.

BRAKE AIR INTAKES
Much care had been taken with the design of the brake air intakes to reduce turbulence to a minimum in the channel between the wheels and the chassis. The purpose of this was to better direct the air to the central part of the car. The shape of the feed duct, which narrows down low with a tight channel that directs air to the brake calipers, was extremely sophisticated.

GENERAL VIEW
The F1.06 was one of the best cars on the aerodynamics front, a field in which Hinwill did a great deal of work in an attempt to reduce resistance to advancement, the creation of vortices and to compensate for the loss of power due to the lower cubic capacity of the engine. The illustration shows the basic version. One can immediately see the drastic reduction of the lower sidepod section to fully increase the airflow towards the rear of the car. Considerable care was invested in thermal dissipation, using different kinds of chimneys together with the same number of gills in the upper area of the engine cover.

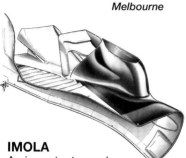

Melbourne

Imola

IMOLA

An important aerodynamics package affecting more or less most of the car's sectors came in at Imola: it included a new nose, diverse chimneys and an innovative engine cover with a vertical fin that was detachable so that new versions could be inserted. The chimneys were lower and tapered and were combined with flaps that had notably curled supports.

DIFFUSER

The rear end of the BMW Sauber was extremely sophisticated, with a body that closed around the gearbox plus faired suspension with large wing planes. The central channel of the diffuser, however, seemed penalised by the dimensions of the deformable structure, which blocked a substantial part of the hot air exit. The lateral channels had curious half moon-shaped Gurney flaps.

BARCELONA AND SILVERSTONE

The lower part of the bargeboards behind the front wheels had added horizontal appendages and were stepped in order to increase the efficiency of the initial lower area of the sidepods. There was also a low pressure zone extremely important to the management of airflow, which is then directed towards the rear of the car: the feature had been long used by Ferrari. By Silverstone, the initial part of the stepped area had been given a small upwards curvature to better channel air to behind the front wheels.

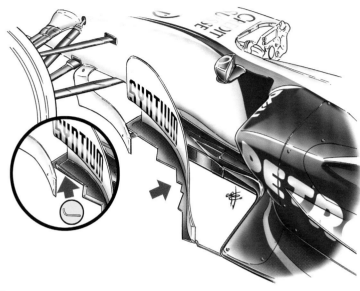

GEARBOX

The BMW Sauber's gearbox was very narrow and light, with torsion bars integrated into the casting. One of the new 2006 regulations dealt with the deformable structure, which was the object of an even more severe crash test that meant exceeding the traditional 100 mm overhang to arrive at a total of 600 mm.

MONACO

Obviously, wings of high aerodynamic load were taken to Monte Carlo. The front had much bigger flaps in the chord, while the rear boasted endplates with one more gills as well as planes of bigger section and incidence.

MONTREAL

The upper wishbone mount on the monocoque had elegant fairing, a feature seen for the first time on the McLaren at Imola during the 2005 season and used by many other teams in 2006.

MONTREAL: REAR WING

The BMW's new rear wing caused considerable controversy in Montreal. Despite the stiffening element between the main plane and flap, the component still permitted a certain flexibility, as shown in photographs taken on the track and carried by a British web site on the Saturday. After careful verification by the Federation's technical delegate, which was repeated on the Sunday morning when the cars had exited parc fermé, the wing was judged regular without showing any aspect that deliberately infringed the regulations.

MAGNY COURS

BMW Sauber brought in the most important new development of the season at the Grand Prix of France, comprising two large vertical fins mounted on the upper part of the car's nose. They were extreme features which, theoretically, should not have obtained the approval of the Federation's technical delegate, but which were fielded normally. Despite that fact, the development was then banned for fear of the proliferation of even more radical solutions at subsequent races. The task of the fins was to stabilise the air flow, especially during the delicate phase in which the car was slip streaming: the fins also produced an improvement in the air flow towards the central and rear parts of the car, where McLaren-type "horns" were added for the same purpose. BMW was the only team to copy that feature, which was introduced on the MP4-20 in 2005. The illustration also shows the small manifold.

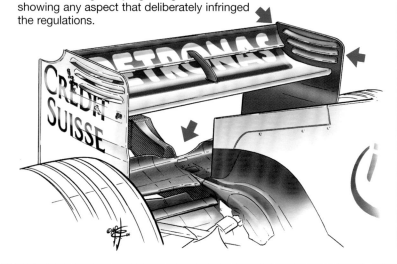

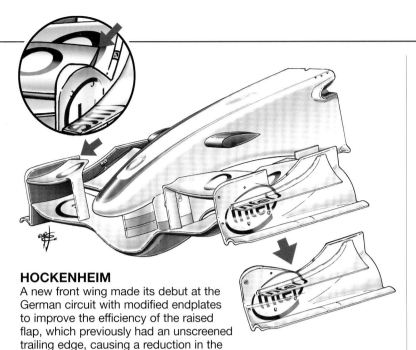

HOCKENHEIM

A new front wing made its debut at the German circuit with modified endplates to improve the efficiency of the raised flap, which previously had an unscreened trailing edge, causing a reduction in the negative lift effect and in the creation of small vortices harmful to the car.

HOCKENHEIM

BMW went along with the tendency towards high anchored fins at the front of the sidepods and a shadow plate in the bargeboard area. That was how to obtain aerodynamic benefits without losing efficiency in terms of blocking, as in the case of the entire sidepod lengthened forwards and, as such, closer to the front wheels.

COOLING

Cooling in line with the various environmental necessities and circuits was developed with great care. The large illustration shows a comparison between the two solutions of medium (right) and high thermal dissipation. The BMW Sauber had various combinations of chimney apertures (see circle), but the number and disposition of the vents in the central part of the sidepods also varied. At Monza, the low load configuration also included the elimination of the small flaps behind the chimneys.

MONZA

BMW Sauber took the prize for the most innovative rear wing, which was produced especially for Monza. The main plane not only had a rather reduced chord (2) but also a fairly curved progression with a higher central zone (3). The flap, used with little incidence, did not exploit all the height (1) permitted by the regulations. The little flap (4) fitted at the centre of the lower plane was eliminated. There was a curious small intake (5) to cool the carbon fibre arms of the rear suspension.

high

medium

TOYOTA

CONSTRUCTORS' CLASSIFICATION			
	2005	2006	
Position	4°	6°	-2 ▼
Points	88	35	-53 ▼

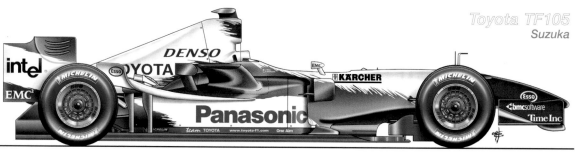

Toyota TF105
Suzuka

Toyota TF106
Presentation

Toyota TF106
Sakhir

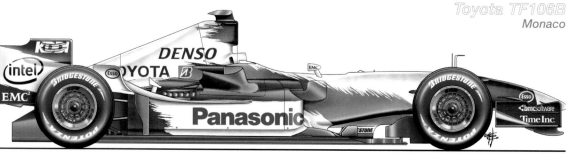

Toyota TF106B
Monaco

Toyota TF106B
Sao Paolo

The 2006 was a difficult season for Toyota, which dropped two places in the Constructors' Championship, which reflects the anomalous planning by the team's top management. There were three important stages in the season: the introduction of an almost laboratory version of the TF106 in early January, the debut of the car with the revised aerodynamics on the eve of the first world title race and, finally, the appearance of the "B" car at Monaco which was, to all intents and purposes, the one that competed throughout the rest of the 2006 season. An approach that was as laboured as it was strange, especially if one takes into account that Cologne had made lightening progress, deciding to field a laboratory car for the last two races of 2005. A "B" version appeared at the Grand Prix of Japan that had raised front suspension to free the lower part of the chassis. A move made possible by the then consolidated 4th place in the constructors' championship table, which was an exceptional result for the German-based Japanese company and a true revelation of the season. The decision to run the laboratory version would accelerate the realisation of the new car – or at least that was the intention – without the keel in the lower area of the chassis, in line with the McLaren MP4-20. So the decision to present the TF106 in January with a chassis that still had a central bulb in the lower zone was debatable, despite moving the suspension higher up; a decision that did not enable the team to free the lower area of the car or optimise the air flow to the rear, in particular towards the central channel of the diffuser, the downforce function of which had increased on the basis of the new regulation limitations for the lateral channels from the 2005 season. The only complete break with the past was the end of the

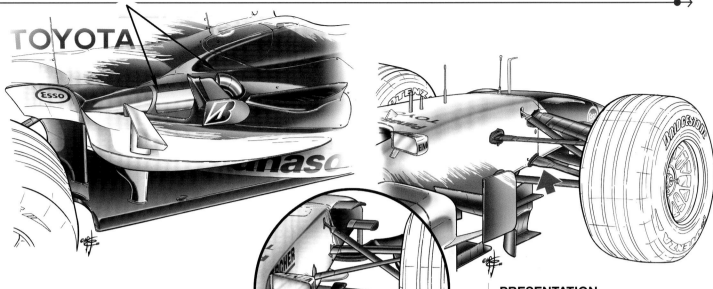

TOYOTA

rotary dampers in the rear suspension in favour of a development very similar to Renault's, with three dampers positioned horizontally in the upper part of the gearbox casting. After the presentation, a major development project was put in hand in two principal phases: the debut of the new aerodynamics at Vallelunga the week before the start of the world championship and the introduction of the B version of the car in definitive form, which appeared for the first time at Monaco. The new chassis minus the keel in its lower area also made its debut on that occasion, with the upper area boasting two large protrusions that ensured a more productive anchorage of the suspension push rods. This approach also meant the elimination of the 10 cm bell housing between the end of the chassis and the engine, as required by Mike Gascoyne, to ensure wheelbase values remained the same. It was a simple solution with which the team best adapted the new V8 engine to the monocoque, but one which did not provide great results in terms of rigidity. The new version retained the same wheelbase, and had a longer, lower fuel tank. As well as greater torsional rigidity, weight distribution was modified to produce a greater concentration on the front axle. In the meantime, technical direction passed from Gascoyne to Pascal Vasselon, the Michelin technician who joined Toyota at the end of the

2005 season. One of the features on which considerable work had to be carried out related to the greater wear of the Bridgestone tyres compared to that by the Ferraris. It was no coincidence that Toyota often found itself in difficulty in bringing the Japanese tyres to the right operating temperature: they had often shown evidence of graining, especially the fronts. Those preconditions forced Toyota to uselessly aim at goals they had achieved the year before, which enabled them to come fourth at the end of the world championship, behind Ferrari, Renault and McLaren. However, the Japanese constructor must be given the credit for devising gills in the rear wing endplates, which were introduced at the opening race in Australia in 2004 and then appeared on all the cars during the two subsequent seasons. Another feature brought in by the team at Suzuka in 2005 – as documented in the Brakes and Tyres chapter – was the drum ducts that entirely covered the discs and "shot" hot air into the lateral external zone, which was completely open. The feature was then copied from the first race by Ferrari for the 248 F1, but was only used at the front end. If the first part of the 2005 championship was the moment of maximum yield for Toyota, things did not work out like that in 2006, even if Ralf Schumacher did come third in Australia. The TF106 seemed to suffer consid-

erably from racing rhythm compared to qualifying. Development work was constant and based, in particular, on aerodynamics, with a series of small appendages making their appearance at almost every race. The new nose introduced in Canada was important and was taken there directly from the wind tunnel, then revised and corrected before being used again in Turkey. As with the 2005 season, Toyota took advantage of the last three races to bring in new features to be transferred to the 2007 car.

PRESENTATION

The TF106 was still a laboratory car at its launch, with many similarities to the model with which the team concluded the 2005 season. Points to note were the advancement of the exhausts by about 20 cm, the retention of the heavily inclined front suspension arms as on the TF105B, and especially the monocoque with a bulb in the lower area.

FRONT WING

The new front wing retained the basics of its predecessor with its heavily spooned planes. The new element was this mini-plane (1) connected to the endplate and almost hidden by a second flap (2) similar to the one used only at Monaco, but with a more heavily curled plane. (3) Another fin was sited on the exterior of the endplates. (4) At the sides of the central zone of the nose the planes were doubled compared to those of the TF105.

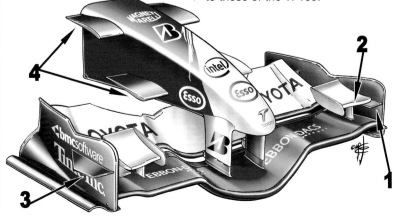

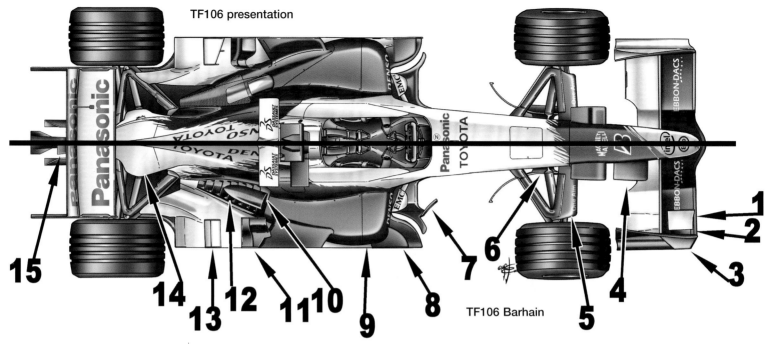

TF106 presentation

TF106 Barhain

15 14 13 12 11 10 9 8 7 6 5 4 3 2 1

SIDE VIEWS COMPARISON

The TF106's aerodynamic package for the start of the season concerned all sectors, starting with the nose. New developments included the external fins of the endplates (1). (2) The planes at the sides of the central part of the nose, which increased from two to four; the new turning vanes (3); the complex group of fins in front of the sidepods, which had small, vertical divergences (4). The most important new feature was the slot in the lower part to increase the airflow towards the rear. (6) The fins on the upper parts of the sidepods were also different. (7) The planes at the sides of the engine's air intake were doubled, and the positions of the exhaust terminals were lower, further advanced and surrounded by small apertures to dissipate heat. (9) The designers also attempted better integration between the chimneys and the lateral mini-flaps. (10) The body was modified in front of the rear wheels (11), while in the lower area in that position a single vertical fin was used in place of the two that appeared on the TF105 in Japan. (12) Shows a unique diffuser plane and (13) the new deformable structure with its mini-spoiler, which can be seen in the top view comparison.

TOP VIEW COMPARISON

In extremis, Toyota tested its new aerodynamics package announced at the presentation at Vallelunga just before the first race of the championship. There were new developments in all sectors, starting with a nose which had the added flap (1) that had only been used at Monaco the previous season, but with a new curled plane linked to a small fin (2) inside the endplates. There was another (3) shorter unit on the outside. (4) The planes at the sides of the central area of the nose were doubled in number from two to four. (5) The suspension wishbones had more fairing due to the adoption of a wing plane. (6) The turning vanes were also modified. (7) The fins in the front of the sidepods were different and had an added small vertical element (8), as was the shape of the aerodynamic appendages applied to the upper part of the sidepods. (9) The 'pods were more concave in the lower area. (10) The exhausts were in a new position and had small apertures at the sides (11) to help dissipate the sidepods' heat. (12) There was greater integration between the lateral planes and the chimneys, which were more outwardly inclined. (13) The position of the small wings, introduced last year on the TF105, was different. (14) The engine cover was better faired at the rear to where it linked up with the wing support. (15) The small spoiler on the deformable structure.

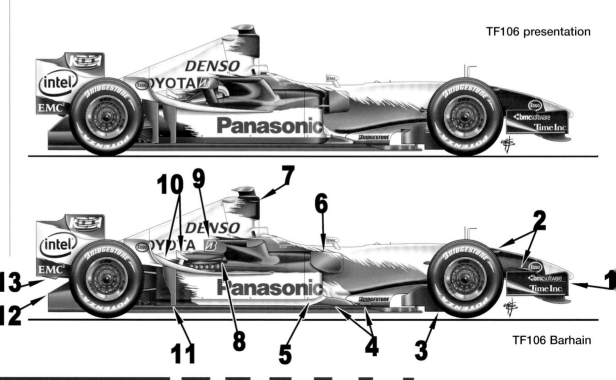

TF106 presentation

10 9 7 6 2

13 12 11 8 5 4 3 1

TF106 Barhain

REAR SUSPENSION

The TF106 no longer used rotary dampers (see the Suspensions chapter) but adopted a layout very similar to that of Renault with the dampers (1) fitted horizontally in V formation on top of the gearbox casting. (2) The torsion bars were vertical and external in relation to the casting. (3) The layout included a third central damper connected to the roll bar rockers. In addition, note the sensor for taking the rear tyres' temperature (4), the much curled part at the sides of the rear tyres to clear the lateral channels of turbulence created by the tyres (5), the wing plane fairing behind the drive shaft (6) and the spoiler integrated into the deformable structure (7)

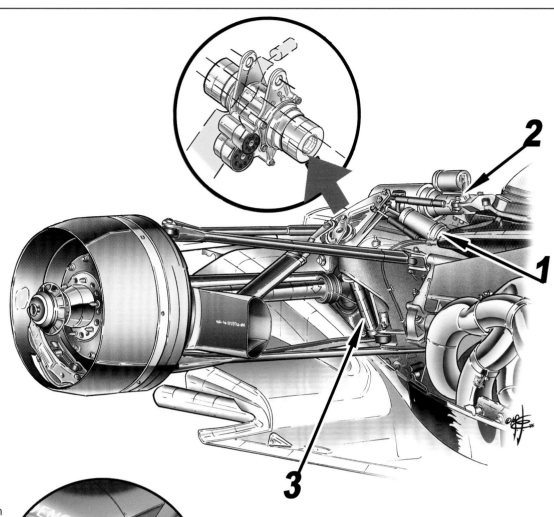

BUDAPEST

The new aerodynamic appendages (1) that appeared in Germany, with a doubling of the vertical fins in front of the sidepods, were combined with the old high load solution of the fins in the upper part of the 'pods (2), easily recognisable by the shape of the endplates (see the Hockenheim variant in the circle).

Hockenheim

FRONT SUSPENSION

In order to ensure an optimum angle of the pushrod, the TF106 B version chassis had an upward bulge in which there was the anchorage with the suspension rocker. That was how the team returned to suspension geometry values similar to those used for the old system, which was anchored at the central keel.

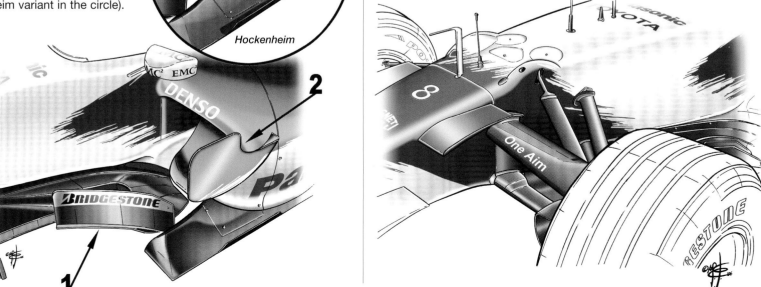

TF106 B MONACO

The TF106 venture began last year in Japan, where the team was the first to copy McLaren and bring in a car without a keel by positioning the front suspension up higher. Obviously, the keel remained because the monocoque of the previous car had to be retained. In the first comparison, we can see how all the suspension had been modified after considerable work that was to represent the first step towards fully exploiting the aerodynamic advantages the feature could bring. Oddly, a car was fielded in 2006 that retained that monocoque and, therefore, the central bulb, which was then eliminated on the B version (left), which was first taken to Monaco. The suspension geometry was also new and had a more opportune angle of the push rod, which required the adoption of these "ears" in the upper area of the chassis. The aerodynamics were also slightly modified.

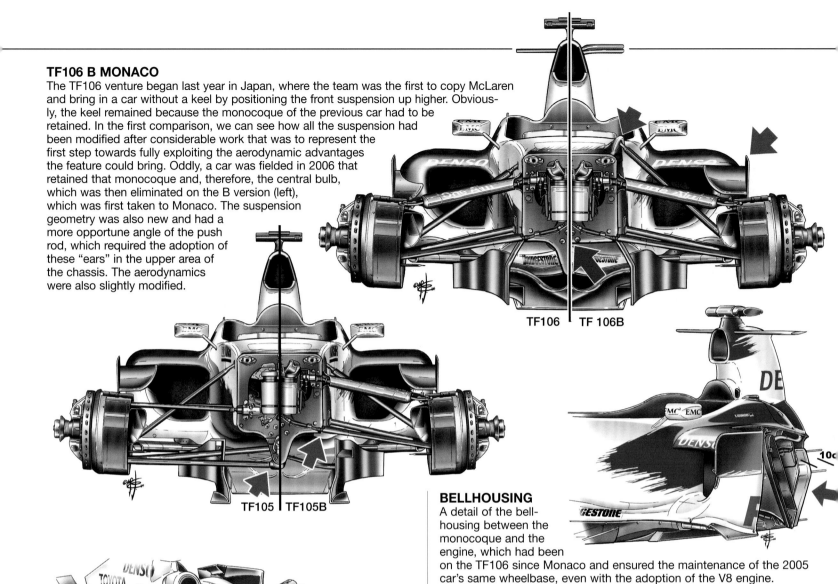

TF106 | TF 106B

TF105 | TF105B

BELLHOUSING

A detail of the bell-housing between the monocoque and the engine, which had been on the TF106 since Monaco and ensured the maintenance of the 2005 car's same wheelbase, even with the adoption of the V8 engine.

TF106B: MONACO

One of the congenital problems with the TF106 was eradicated on the B version of the car: the bellhousing (2) between the engine and the monocoque was brought in to ensure the wheelbase remained unaltered. That made the chassis longer (1) without needing to use a second small bell housing (2) between the engine and the gearbox. In that way, the torsional rigidity problems inherent in the car at the beginning of the season were eliminated. Weight distribution was also modified, with the greater load over the front end.

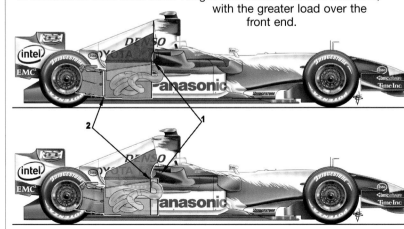

NEW SIDEPODS

Toyota's new aerodynamics package mainly concerned the central part of the car, with the lower area of the sidepods more concave (3) to improve the quality of the airflow towards the rear. In that context, the new, complex design of the fins (1) in front of the 'pods is shown, with added small (2) divergences; (4) the fin on the upper part of the sidepods was different and smaller. (5) The chimneys were more inclined towards the outside and integrated with wing planes applied to the sidepods.

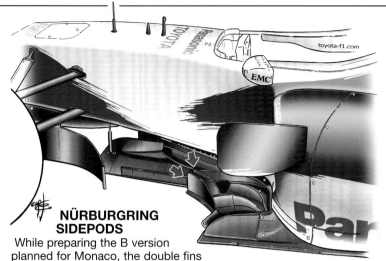

NÜRBURGRING SIDEPODS

While preparing the B version planned for Monaco, the double fins that came in at Imola were retained for the Nürburgring as they permitted the channelisation of the airflow in the low area in front of the sidepods.

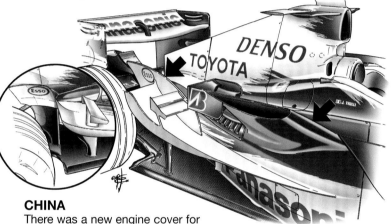

CHINA

There was a new engine cover for the Toyota, with a position for the exhausts that was more unified at the centre of the car, but in particular with large fins that started inside the rear wheels and where the small planes were connected in a more integrated manner to the diminutive planes, which were on the TF105B the previous year for the entire 2006 season.

SILVERSTONE

Refinement of the upper part of the Toyota's sidepods went on in Great Britain. The double fins used at Monaco had gone, but the surface of the lateral hinges had increased to the same extent as Honda at Monaco, with a notable increase in dimensions, as shown by the comparison with the old system in the circle. It is interesting to note that these two teams fielded cars with not very concave sidepods in the lower area, unlike almost all the other teams.

CANADA: FRONT WING

The new front wing – the old unit is shown in the circle – first appeared in Canada and was retained in the United States. It had a principal plane connected in a less brusque and clean manner in the spoon shaped central part. A solution that reduced sensitivity to ride height and the reaction of the tiresome transverse airflow, harmful to the exploitation of the lower aerodynamics, characteristic of the old feature.

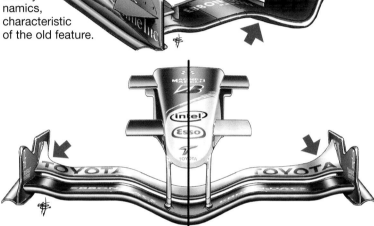

MONZA: FRONT WING

Toyota fielded two front wings at Monza that were designed around the main plane, which first came out in Canada and had two different types of flap. The version on the right was preferred for the race, the external section of the flap with a larger chord.

SUZUKA

Toyota was practically the only team to feature a new development at Suzuka compared to what was seen in the Shanghai paddock. It was these cooling intakes, the same as those used by the opposition. The section of the internal drum was new, as was the small cooling ear, similar to the one used by Ferrari. Note the adoption of the narrow Brembo calipers, which were also used by BMW Sauber.

SUZUKA

Together with the new drum ducts for the front brakes, Toyota also introduced new end plates at the penultimate race of the season. The vertical part was bent more towards the outside in order to better channel the air to the central and lower areas of the car.

RED BULL

Red Bull RB1
Sao Paolo

Red Bull RB2

CONSTRUCTORS' CLASSIFICATION			
	2005	*2006*	
Position	6°	7°	-1 ▼
Points	38	16	-22 ▼

concentrate on the future RB3 project. The only important development during the season appeared at Silverstone with the introduction of new front suspension geometry, which reduced the previous understeer.

The 2006 season was a difficult one for Red Bull, having dropped a position in the constructors' classification with no fewer than 22 points less than in 2005. The switch from the 10-cylinder Ford to the eight-cylinder Ferrari engine created quite a few installation problems, initially due in part to evaluation errors and the communication of the requirements of thermal dissipation between the two partners. All the pre-season tests were spent trying to improve cooling, which had immediately shown it was insufficient, so much so as to require a large aperture in the body to permit the car to be driven, despite relatively low ambient temperatures. Corrections that could not be transferred to the car to be raced during the new season, because that would have meant a 7% global loss of aerodynamic efficiency. Only a radical change of the radiators' installation resolved the problem, but that took attention away from the real development of the car. Before its debut in Bahrain, the entry mouths of the sidepods were completely modified with a slightly V progression when seen

from above to enable bigger and differently inclined radiators. The imposition of the RB2 was Renault influenced, given that the head of the project was Mark Smith, who had joined Red Bull from the French team. So it is no coincidence that the RB2 was the only car to have taken on the V-keel, introduced in 2005 by Renault, instead of the other technique that required the entire elimination of the keel, as begun by McLaren in the same season, an example that was followed by a large number of other teams. However, the Red Bull appeared to be an important development of the previous year's car: it retained the gearbox and rear suspension layout, into which were integrated some Renault elements such as the shape of the sidepods and the reinforcement between the gearbox and the monocoque to stiffen the rear end. The team suffered greatly from hydraulic and gearbox reliability problems, but more than anything else it paid the price for the stop in development of the RB2 imposed by the new technical director Adrian Newey after the Grand Prix of France, RB2 to

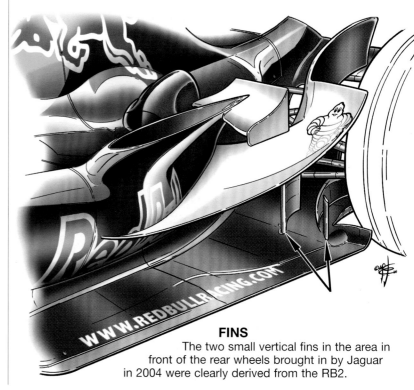

FINS
The two small vertical fins in the area in front of the rear wheels brought in by Jaguar in 2004 were clearly derived from the RB2.

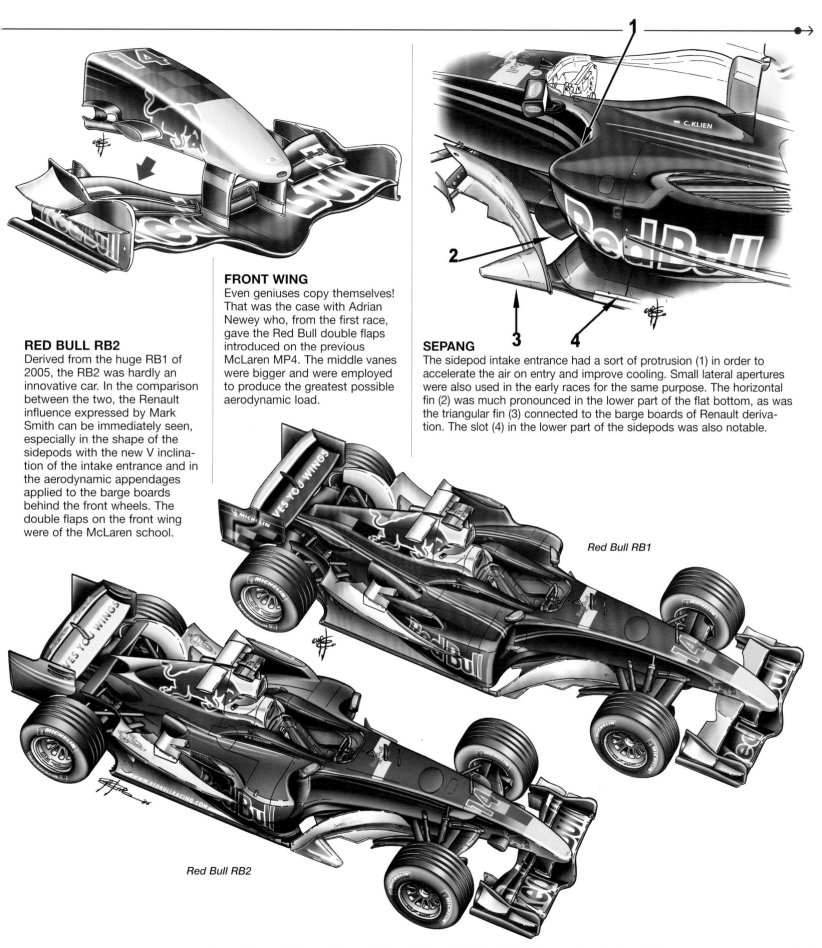

FRONT WING

Even geniuses copy themselves! That was the case with Adrian Newey who, from the first race, gave the Red Bull double flaps introduced on the previous McLaren MP4. The middle vanes were bigger and were employed to produce the greatest possible aerodynamic load.

RED BULL RB2

Derived from the huge RB1 of 2005, the RB2 was hardly an innovative car. In the comparison between the two, the Renault influence expressed by Mark Smith can be immediately seen, especially in the shape of the sidepods with the new V inclination of the intake entrance and in the aerodynamic appendages applied to the barge boards behind the front wheels. The double flaps on the front wing were of the McLaren school.

SEPANG

The sidepod intake entrance had a sort of protrusion (1) in order to accelerate the air on entry and improve cooling. Small lateral apertures were also used in the early races for the same purpose. The horizontal fin (2) was much pronounced in the lower part of the flat bottom, as was the triangular fin (3) connected to the barge boards of Renault derivation. The slot (4) in the lower part of the sidepods was also notable.

Red Bull RB1

Red Bull RB2

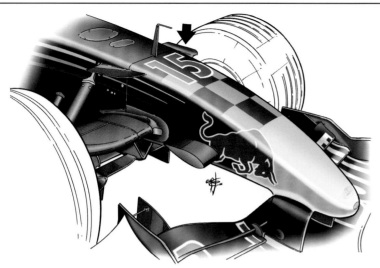

MELBOURNE
Another element of Renault inspiration was the introduction of these small fins in Australia, initially produced in a rather rudimentary manner for the purpose of better directing the air flow towards the body of the car, a feature that was taken up again as the season continued.

IMOLA
There was a curious sophistication in the area in front of the rear wheels with these small teeth, the purpose of which was to generate a series of mini-vortices that interfered with those that were more substantial and harmful created in that zone.

MONTREAL: FRONT WING
Red Bull reduced the front wing to a single flap while retaining the rounded section with a bigger chord in the central area. This sector of the plane was highly sophisticated, with its peripheral zone rather "pot-bellied" compared to the central area. Note above the definitive versions of the fins on the sides of the nose that first appeared in Australia.

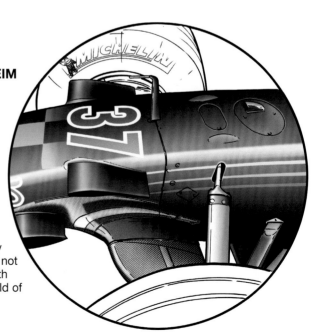

MAGNY COURS
The fins at the sides of the nose were integrated with the small end plates that Coulthard wanted to be transparent for better visibility, while on Klien's car they were painted blue.

HOCKENHEIM
At the subsequent Grand Prix of Germany, FIA imposed an almost obligatory location for these fins on Coulthard's indication. They were moved slightly forward so as not to interfere with the driver's field of vision.

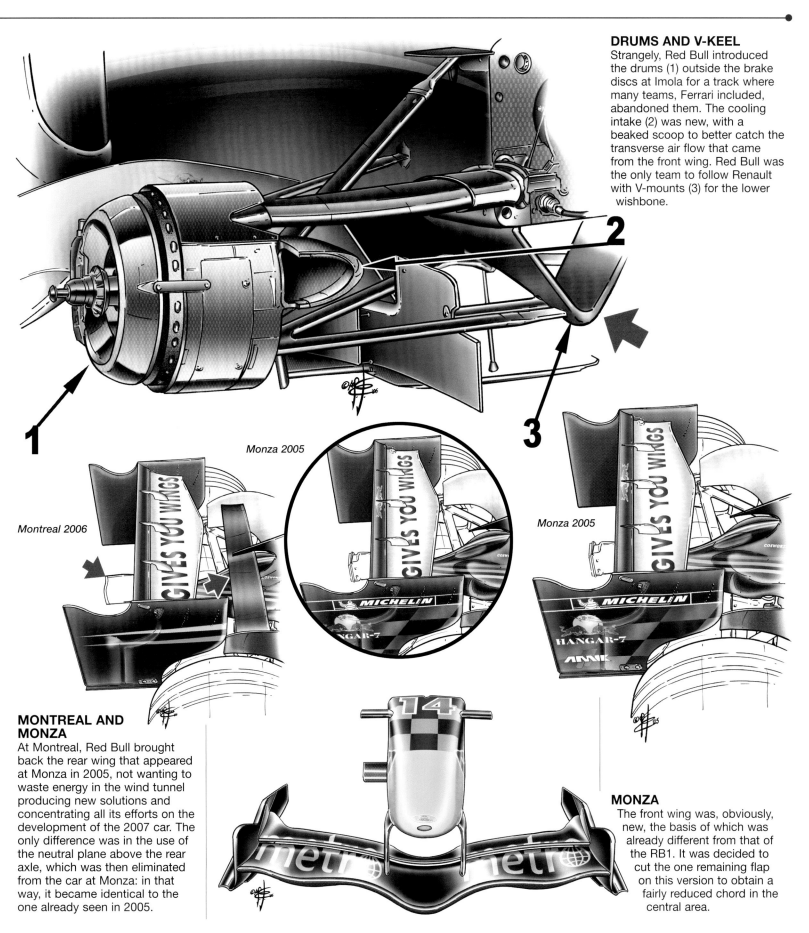

DRUMS AND V-KEEL

Strangely, Red Bull introduced the drums (1) outside the brake discs at Imola for a track where many teams, Ferrari included, abandoned them. The cooling intake (2) was new, with a beaked scoop to better catch the transverse air flow that came from the front wing. Red Bull was the only team to follow Renault with V-mounts (3) for the lower wishbone.

2

1

3

Monza 2005

Montreal 2006

Monza 2005

MONTREAL AND MONZA

At Montreal, Red Bull brought back the rear wing that appeared at Monza in 2005, not wanting to waste energy in the wind tunnel producing new solutions and concentrating all its efforts on the development of the 2007 car. The only difference was in the use of the neutral plane above the rear axle, which was then eliminated from the car at Monza: in that way, it became identical to the one already seen in 2005.

MONZA

The front wing was, obviously, new, the basis of which was already different from that of the RB1. It was decided to cut the one remaining flap on this version to obtain a fairly reduced chord in the central area.

WILLIAMS

CONSTRUCTORS' CLASSIFICATION			
	2005	2006	
Position	5°	8°	-3 ▼
Points	66	11	-55 ▼

Williams FW27
Sao Paolo

Williams FW28
Presentation

Williams FW28
Monaco

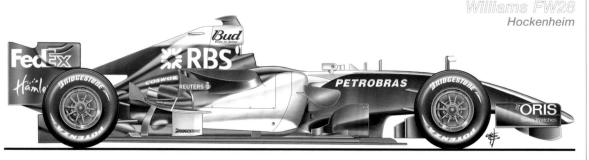

Williams FW28
Hockenheim

Williams FW28
Shanghai

For Williams, the 2006 season was a "real disaster" according to Patrick Head, without him searching for excuses and entailed, even if not directly, the disappearance of the name Cosworth from modern Formula One. A chronic lack of reliability, often due to minor details but still determinate, caused a loss of about 35-40 points, which meant the team dropped three places in the end of season constructors' classification. The FW28 was also a heavier car than its predecessor, reducing the opportunity of manipulating weight distribution in order to better adapt the car to the characteristics of the various circuits. After a very positive start at Bahrain, linked to the fact that the Cosworth was the only engine able to rev at 20,000 rpm at the time and the result the team had achieved in the November tests, the unreliability problems started to appear from the Grand Prix of Malaysia. One of the strong points of the engine was that the old Ford 10 cylinder did not use variable height trumpets, the banning of which by the new regulations seriously penalised other constructors. The same went for fuel pressure, which was limited to 100 bar compared to the values used by the top teams of over 230 bar. A separate book could be written on the evolution of the Williams cars during the course of the season; but while that was not a positive factor it did confirm the team's absolute determination to re-emerge and the spasmodic research on a firm technical basis on which to develop the car, which was modified for every race. The principal changes appeared at Monaco, in Germany and China, but the car still remained relatively uncompetitive. However, there was some satisfaction: the seamless gearbox that so impressed the heads of Toyota, which the Didcot team offered in exchange for engine supply in 2007.

CHASSIS

The FW28 had a layout without a keel, but with the lower wishbone mounts in the inferior part of the chassis, which was particularly raised from the ground, as indicated by the arrow. The front view shows the concave shape of the sidepods, which were, however, very high and rounded in the upper area. That was to ensure greater air flow to feed the rear of the car.

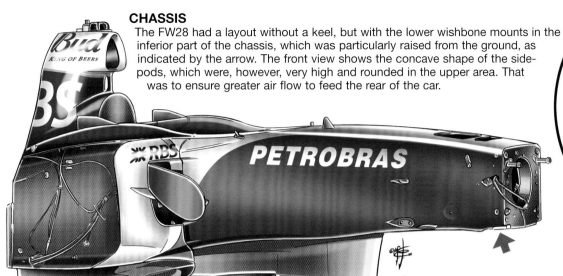

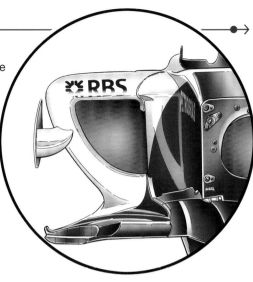

Loic Bigois, responsible for Williams's aerodynamics, carried out a strange experiment at Monza, bringing the front plane four centimetres closer to the body of the car and in that way renouncing the maximum exploitation of the overhang permitted by the regulations. The last important evolutionary package was introduced at the next race in China, with elements also developed for 2007. The chief new feature concerned the adoption of a Renault style full width raised flap together with two small stabiliser fins also of the Renault school for the air flow in the upper part of the chassis. The bargeboards inside the wheels united with a large vertical fin containing ballast were also new, as were the new V-shaped mini-planes behind the engine air intake, the new fins with three vents in the area ahead of the rear wheels and the new extractor plane.

As far as the car was concerned, the brake air intakes also completely faired the discs at the front end. This technique was applied to the rear end of the FW27 from the previous year's Grand Prix of Turkey and was retained for the FW28. This feature had never been used for the front, unlike Ferrari and BMW-Sauber, both of whom adopted it from the start of the season.

NO KEEL

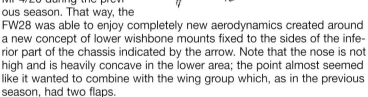

After the "walrus" experience of 2004, when the car had a generous twin keel, and the return to the single keel with the FW27 in 2005, it was decided to jump into the deep end once more by deciding to have the no keel solution, analogous to the one tested by McLaren on the MP4/20 during the previous season. That way, the FW28 was able to enjoy completely new aerodynamics created around a new concept of lower wishbone mounts fixed to the sides of the inferior part of the chassis indicated by the arrow. Note that the nose is not high and is heavily concave in the lower area; the point almost seemed like it wanted to combine with the wing group which, as in the previous season, had two flaps.

COSWORTH

Williams had the honour of bringing back the glorious Cosworth to Formula One. The new 8 cylinder shone, especially during the early races when it was the only engine able to reach 20,000 rpm; but later it was at a disadvantage compared to the power units of other teams as it had been developed less.

SIDEPODS

There were few links with the previous FWs if one excludes a certain similarity of the bargeboards behind the wheels (1) with two teeth in the lower area. The sidepods were new and represented a mix between those of Sauber and BAR. Compared to the former, they retained the almost triangular shape in the aperture, while from the latter they inherited the double aerodynamic appendages in the upper (3) and lower (2) areas. An embryo of (2) was seen on last year's FW27.

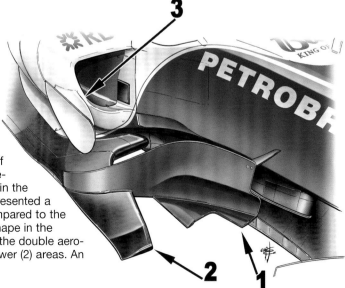

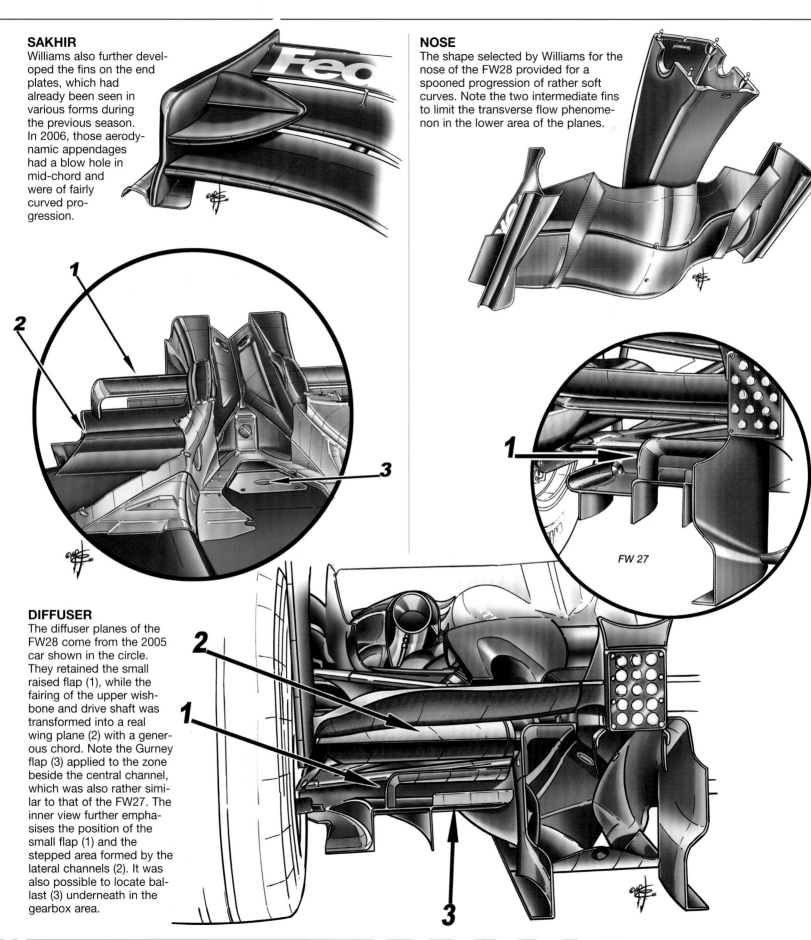

SAKHIR

Williams also further developed the fins on the end plates, which had already been seen in various forms during the previous season. In 2006, those aerodynamic appendages had a blow hole in mid-chord and were of fairly curved progression.

NOSE

The shape selected by Williams for the nose of the FW28 provided for a spooned progression of rather soft curves. Note the two intermediate fins to limit the transverse flow phenomenon in the lower area of the planes.

FW 27

DIFFUSER

The diffuser planes of the FW28 come from the 2005 car shown in the circle. They retained the small raised flap (1), while the fairing of the upper wishbone and drive shaft was transformed into a real wing plane (2) with a generous chord. Note the Gurney flap (3) applied to the zone beside the central channel, which was also rather similar to that of the FW27. The inner view further emphasises the position of the small flap (1) and the stepped area formed by the lateral channels (2). It was also possible to locate ballast (3) underneath in the gearbox area.

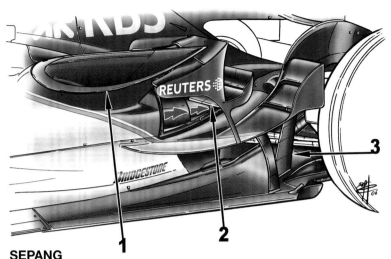

SEPANG

The chimneys were opened as much as possible (1) and the maximum lateral apertures were used to beat the Malaysian heat (2).The vertical fin added (3) to the area inside the wheels was also new, and better channelled the air to the rear of the car.

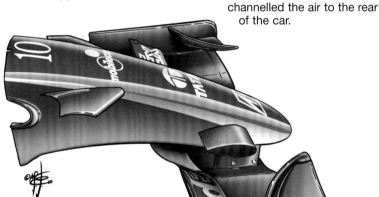

SILVERSTONE

The debuting front wing had a new flap, the principal purpose of which was to direct the airflow in such a way as to improve the efficiency of the rear end, a feature already seen on other cars.

IMOLA

The new fairing of the rear suspension, in particular, had a wing plane at the anchorage point of the push rod in order to direct the airflow towards the lower part of the rear wing.

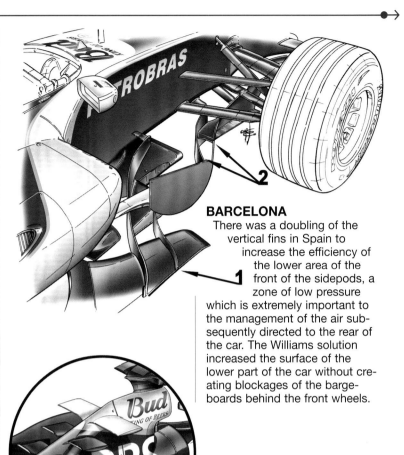

BARCELONA

There was a doubling of the vertical fins in Spain to increase the efficiency of the lower area of the front of the sidepods, a zone of low pressure which is extremely important to the management of the air subsequently directed to the rear of the car. The Williams solution increased the surface of the lower part of the car without creating blockages of the bargeboards behind the front wheels.

MONACO

Williams and Toyota were the only teams that took up the three plane feature behind the engine air intake once more, as shown in the circle, a technique used the previous season at Budapest. In the case of Williams, the first two planes were conceived so as to create negative lift, while the third was to normalise the airflow again towards the rear wing.

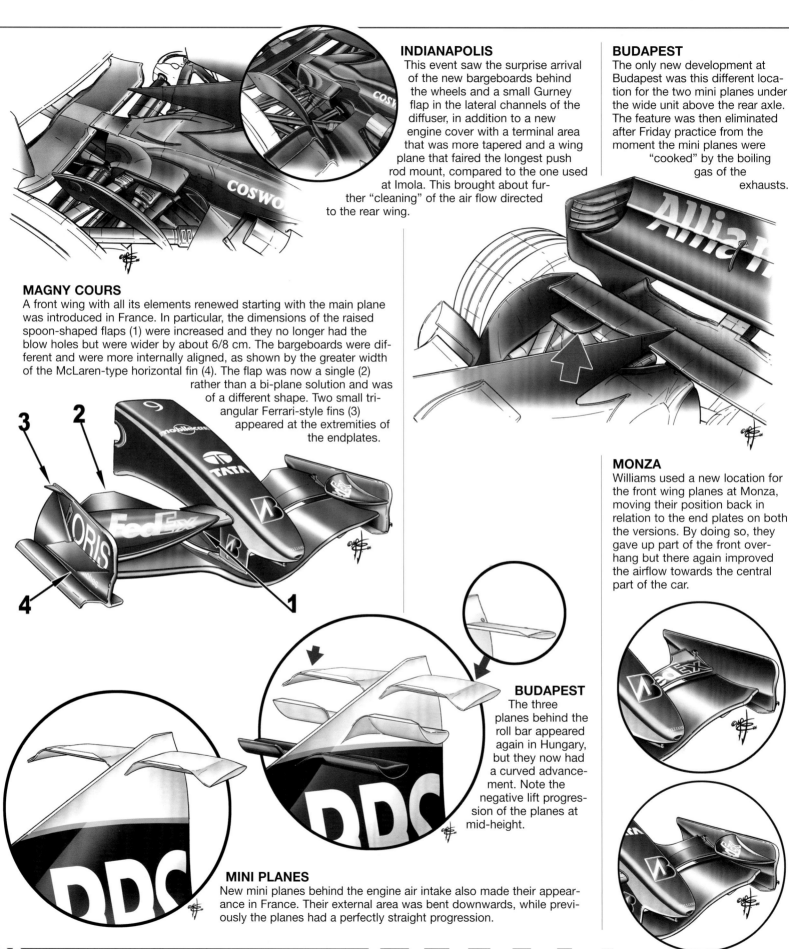

INDIANAPOLIS

This event saw the surprise arrival of the new bargeboards behind the wheels and a small Gurney flap in the lateral channels of the diffuser, in addition to a new engine cover with a terminal area that was more tapered and a wing plane that faired the longest push rod mount, compared to the one used at Imola. This brought about further "cleaning" of the air flow directed to the rear wing.

BUDAPEST

The only new development at Budapest was this different location for the two mini planes under the wide unit above the rear axle. The feature was then eliminated after Friday practice from the moment the mini planes were "cooked" by the boiling gas of the exhausts.

MAGNY COURS

A front wing with all its elements renewed starting with the main plane was introduced in France. In particular, the dimensions of the raised spoon-shaped flaps (1) were increased and they no longer had the blow holes but were wider by about 6/8 cm. The bargeboards were different and were more internally aligned, as shown by the greater width of the McLaren-type horizontal fin (4). The flap was now a single (2) rather than a bi-plane solution and was of a different shape. Two small triangular Ferrari-style fins (3) appeared at the extremities of the endplates.

MONZA

Williams used a new location for the front wing planes at Monza, moving their position back in relation to the end plates on both the versions. By doing so, they gave up part of the front overhang but there again improved the airflow towards the central part of the car.

BUDAPEST

The three planes behind the roll bar appeared again in Hungary, but they now had a curved advancement. Note the negative lift progression of the planes at mid-height.

MINI PLANES

New mini planes behind the engine air intake also made their appearance in France. Their external area was bent downwards, while previously the planes had a perfectly straight progression.

GEARBOX

The quick shift gearbox casting of the FW 28 was extremely clean, with the torsion bars set into its interior. Note the sophisticated brake air intake shown in the circle. The AP calipers were inclined in an "S", as on all other cars with the exception of the Super Aguri.

SHANGHAI: FRONT WING AND SMALL WINGS BEHIND THE ROLL BAR

The umpteenth aerodynamic revolution by Williams appeared at Shanghai and included a nose much inspired by that of Renault at the Grand Prix of Germany, but with the plane raised and more curled. It was a feature that guaranteed more load for the front end and also improved the quality of the airflow towards the central and rear areas of the car. The two Toyota style triangular fins at the sides of the nose were replaced by another two that were positioned above the front part of the chassis and were also inspired by those of Renault. The mini planes behind the engine air intake were also new and were no longer mounted horizontally, but in a V format.

SHANGHAI

All the rest of the front aerodynamics were profoundly modified, starting with the fairing of the brake intakes, which completely covered (1) the front discs for the first time. Once again, they were combined with the sophisticated cooling intakes (2) with a conveyer directed at the calipers. The doubling of the low, long vertical endplates (3) was new and ran along the sides of the shadow plate. The voluminous vertical fin (4) was also new and was brought in to move the ballast into a slightly more advanced zone in relation to the previous position. Obviously, the Renault type "ears" (5) were retained in the upper area of the chassis and were part of the new aerodynamic package.

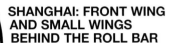

REAR BRAKE INTAKES

The rear end of the Williams retained the sophisticated brake intakes with the double fairing of the drum duct type (1) and inside of them (2), introduced in 2005 at the Grand Prix of Turkey. Also note the double series of vertical fins (3) and the small shield (4) in the area inside the rear wheels to "clean" the airflow towards the extractor plane as much as possible.

TORO ROSSO

CONSTRUCTORS' CLASSIFICATION			
	2004	2005	
Position	10°	9°	+1 ▲
Points	7	1	-6 ▼

Minardi PS05
Imola

Red Bull RB1
Sao Paolo

Toro Rosso STR01

the Toro Rosso STR01 and the Red Bull RB1 was limited to the Brembo brake callipers combined with Hitco discs in place of those of A+P fitted to the Red Bull during 2005. Unfortunately, Gabriele Tredozzi, the Minardi designer, was not confirmed by the new team owner and technical responsibility passed to Alex Hitzinger. His responsibility was to follow the developments of the season and prepare the ground for a new 2007 car project by Adrian Newey, who was engaged to design both the new cars under the aegis of Red Bull.

ENGINE AIR RESTRICTOR
Toro Rosso was the only team to take the opportunity of installing a 10 cylinder 3000 cc engine in its cars for 2006, with the limitation of adding a 77 mm restriction flange and keeping maximum revolutions at 16,700 rpm.

The Toro Rosso that competed in the 2006 Formula One World Championship was, in fact, the old Red Bull and was a car that had certainly not distinguished itself with new or interesting features. Indeed, some layouts like the rear end even harked back to those the team inherited from Jaguar. A real shame because the new team, which had an adequate budget, could have further developed the 2005 Minardi PS05, which made its debut at the Grand Prix of San Marino and was considered a concentration of interesting and technically valid solutions with good development potential. The choice, of course, was dictated by purely financial reasons, and among other things had its influ-

ence on the evolution of the car during the season. Toro Rosso was the only team to use a 10-cylinder engine – the Ford – with the air restrictor imposed by the regulations. A decision that did not penalise a lot the team during the first part of the season, in part because the Ford V10 was the only unit that did not use variable height trumpets in 2005, which were prohibited by the 2006 regulations. This limitation created quite a few problems for the new generation of V8s, especially in the early stages of the season. Then progress made with the new engines by the leading constructors with units reaching a maximum of 20,000 rpm against the 16,700 imposed on the Ford V10, created an

unbridgeable difference in favour of the eight cylinders, even with their reduced cubic capacity. The lower performance of the engine enabled Toro Rosso to reduce the opening of the entry inlet of the sidepods, divided in the lower area by about 7-8 cm. During the second half of the season a front wing was used with end plates derived from those utilised by Minardi in the closing stages of the 2005 season. The only technical difference between

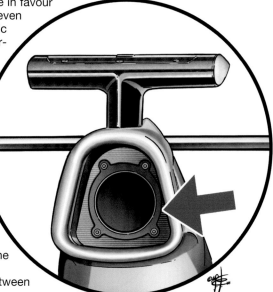

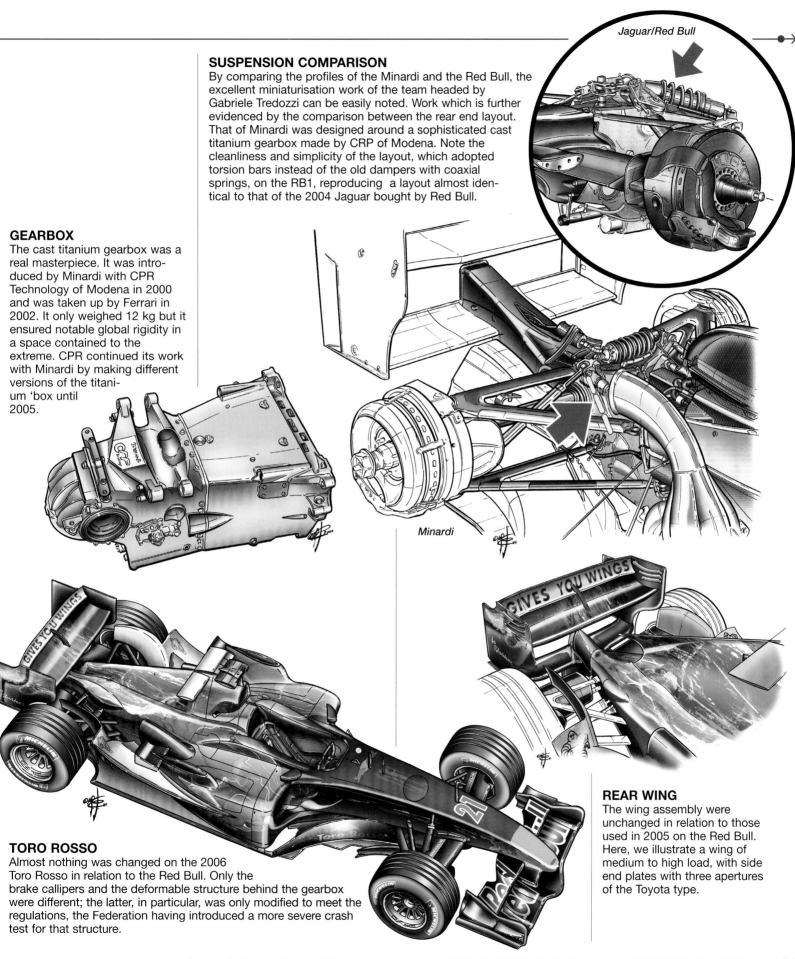

SUSPENSION COMPARISON

By comparing the profiles of the Minardi and the Red Bull, the excellent miniaturisation work of the team headed by Gabriele Tredozzi can be easily noted. Work which is further evidenced by the comparison between the rear end layout. That of Minardi was designed around a sophisticated cast titanium gearbox made by CRP of Modena. Note the cleanliness and simplicity of the layout, which adopted torsion bars instead of the old dampers with coaxial springs, on the RB1, reproducing a layout almost identical to that of the 2004 Jaguar bought by Red Bull.

GEARBOX

The cast titanium gearbox was a real masterpiece. It was introduced by Minardi with CPR Technology of Modena in 2000 and was taken up by Ferrari in 2002. It only weighed 12 kg but it ensured notable global rigidity in a space contained to the extreme. CPR continued its work with Minardi by making different versions of the titanium 'box until 2005.

Minardi

REAR WING

The wing assembly were unchanged in relation to those used in 2005 on the Red Bull. Here, we illustrate a wing of medium to high load, with side end plates with three apertures of the Toyota type.

TORO ROSSO

Almost nothing was changed on the 2006 Toro Rosso in relation to the Red Bull. Only the brake callipers and the deformable structure behind the gearbox were different; the latter, in particular, was only modified to meet the regulations, the Federation having introduced a more severe crash test for that structure.

FRONT SUSPENSION

The car also retained the substantial fairing of the front suspension's upper wishbones. Exploiting the regulations to the full, which permitted a ratio of 3.5 between the thickness of the arms and the width of the plane, Toro Rosso incorporated in a single and notable chord plane both the upper wishbone and the steering linkage, as in the case of the 2005 Red Bull.

MONZA: REAR WING

The Monza version of the two teams' rear wing were almost identical and harked back to the one brought in on the RB1 during the 2005 season at the same circuit, then used again for the Grand Prix of Canada.

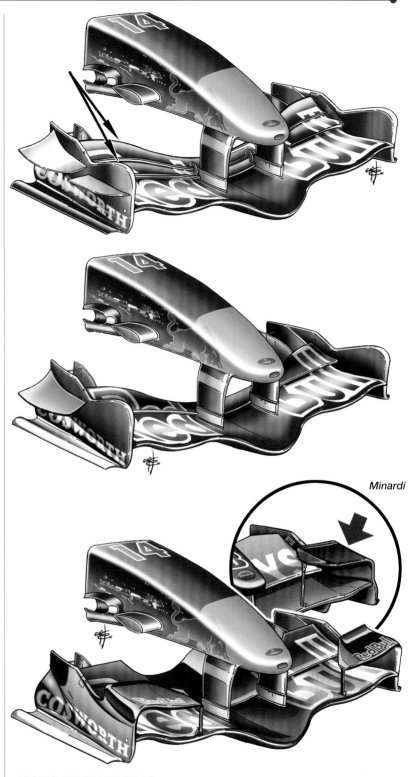

Minardi

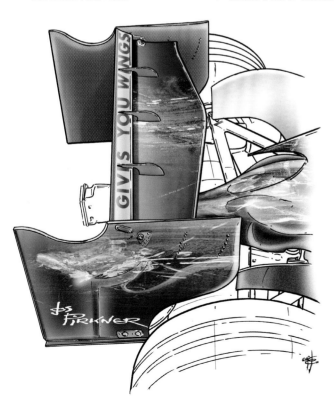

SMALL FRONT WINGS

Development of the small front wings also progressed in step with those of the team's Red Bull cousin. Both introduced a doubling of their flaps at the start of the season, obviously required by Adrian Newey who had specified them for the McLaren. The feature was also identical at Monza, this time a single flap with a much reduced chord. Finally, the solution brought in for the last Grands Prix of the season, initially carried out by fitting Minardi end plates and then moving on to the definitive feature illustrated here and derived from the Red Bull end plates.

SUPER AGURI

CONSTRUCTORS' CLASSIFICATION		
	2005	2006
Position	0°	11°
Points	0	0

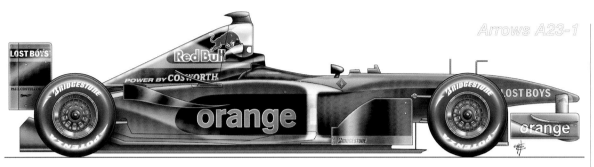

Arrows A23-1

Super Aguri
Presentation

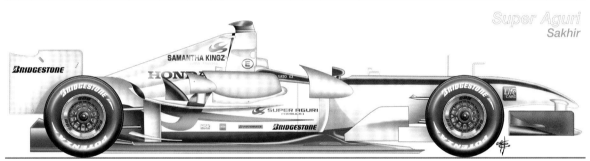

Super Aguri
Sakhir

Super Aguri
Hockenheim

Super Aguri
Sao Paolo

Not many would have put money on a brand new F1 team being able to race a more than adequate four year old car. That result was achieved by Super Aguri and Mark Preston, who took four old Arrows A23 chassis in hand and transformed them bit by bit into suitable cars with which to compete in the 2006 F1 season. The first pre-championship tests were carried out with a car that was in almost its original configuration, while another chassis was used for the crash test in order to satisfy the new regulations brought in by the Federation, which were more severe than those of 2002. The car that began the season retained the old Arrows chassis, front and rear suspension and carbon fibre gearbox. It also had the same wheelbase, despite the adoption of an eight cylinder engine by using spacers. It was, of course, a heavy car with many limitations such as its obsolete power steering, which meant using 2005 tyres in the first four races. It was only for the fifth Grand Prix with the introduction of the new power steering system that the car could be fitted with the latest specification Bridgestones. The new team used McLaren's old wind tunnel at Teddington, and the support of Honda's research and development department obviously helped it a great deal. Super Aguri was able to create a new gearbox, which constituted the basis for the final version of the car called the SA06, which was given its debut at the Grand Prix of Germany. All the electronics were provided by Honda and a large part of the aerodynamic modifications and front end arrived at the last minute. The definitive version of the car appeared at Hockenheim for the first time. The faired sidepods were new, with completely differ- ent, raised intake mouths with a concave part a la Renault, but more important still the car had a

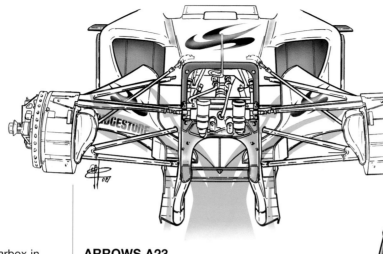

new rear end. The gearbox in cast aluminium ensured the redesign of the suspension in line with new and adequate parameters. To be able to have a determined suspension geometry, Mark Preston made a choice against the general trend, moving the brake caliper upwards at the front of the disc, it having previously been in a horizontal position. A change that permitted him to make up for the inevitable raising of the centre of gravity, bringing with it advantages in terms of the use of the suspension itself and, therefore, the rear tyres wear. The SA06 was about 10% more aerodynamically efficient than the car fielded at the beginning of the year and was notably lighter, a factor that enabled the team to use ballast to set up the car for the demands of the different circuits. The young team naturally paid the price in lack of reliability, due in part to the few private tests carried out during the season; only two, compared with the over 50,000 km of the top teams.

ARROWS A23

The new Super Aguri was the old 2002 Arrows, the car that had interpreted in a more than extreme manner the twin keel concept, as can be seen in the illustration: it shows a chassis particularly high from the ground with two large vertical members to which were fixed double lower wishbones that permitted the exploitation of the maximum amount of air possible in the lower area of the car. The end plates were extremely sophisticated at the sides and pushed as far as the reference plane in the central 50 cm area.

NOSE

Clearly derived from the Arrows was the nose, which retained the shape of the deformable central structure and, vaguely, also that of the long vertical supports. The Super Aguri illustration shows the new front wing introduced at the Grand Prix of Australia, with raised flaps of the Renault school.

SHANGHAI

The final phase in the development of the Super Aguri reached its conclusion at the Grand Prix of China with the arrival of these new end plates on a front wing of the beginning of the season. They were, obviously, retained until the last race in Brazil. They had a horizontal fin at mid-height (1) and another small, triangular unit of the Ferrari school above (2) in the area in front of the wheels.

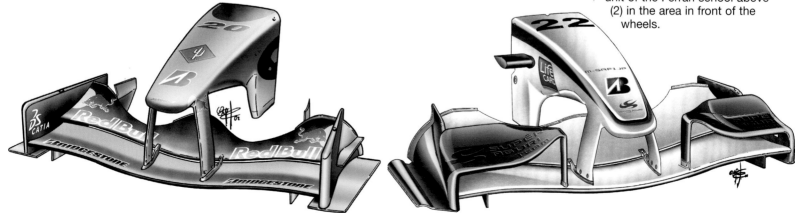

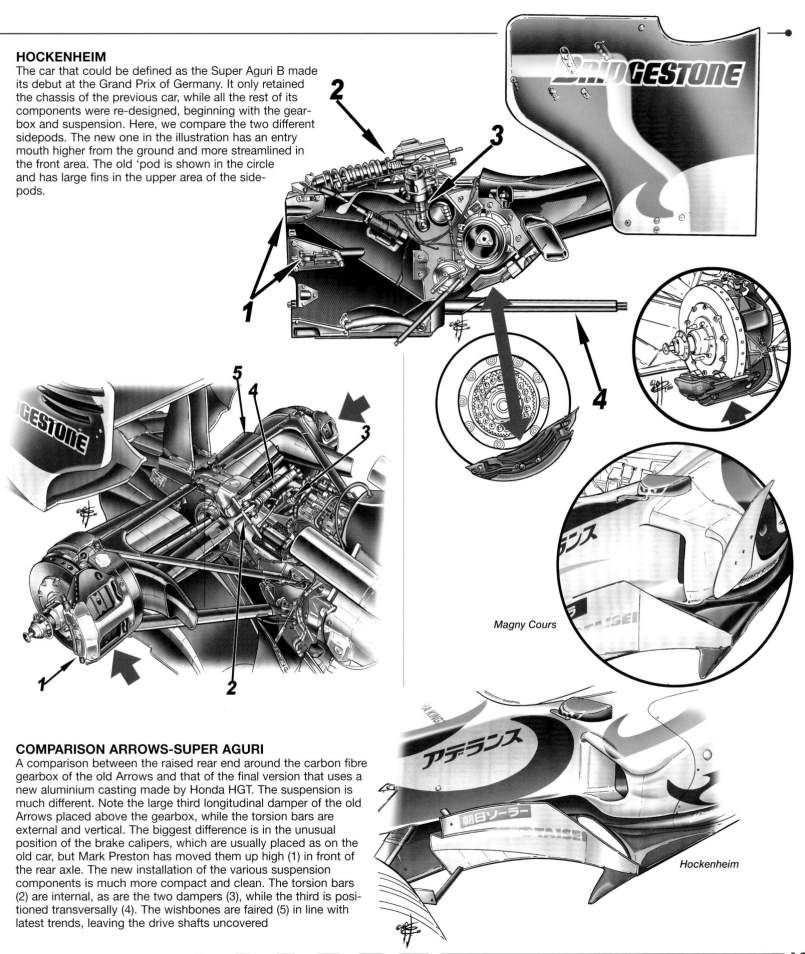

HOCKENHEIM

The car that could be defined as the Super Aguri B made its debut at the Grand Prix of Germany. It only retained the chassis of the previous car, while all the rest of its components were re-designed, beginning with the gearbox and suspension. Here, we compare the two different sidepods. The new one in the illustration has an entry mouth higher from the ground and more streamlined in the front area. The old 'pod is shown in the circle and has large fins in the upper area of the sidepods.

Magny Cours

Hockenheim

COMPARISON ARROWS-SUPER AGURI

A comparison between the raised rear end around the carbon fibre gearbox of the old Arrows and that of the final version that uses a new aluminium casting made by Honda HGT. The suspension is much different. Note the large third longitudinal damper of the old Arrows placed above the gearbox, while the torsion bars are external and vertical. The biggest difference is in the unusual position of the brake calipers, which are usually placed as on the old car, but Mark Preston has moved them up high (1) in front of the rear axle. The new installation of the various suspension components is much more compact and clean. The torsion bars (2) are internal, as are the two dampers (3), while the third is positioned transversally (4). The wishbones are faired (5) in line with latest trends, leaving the drive shafts uncovered

SPYKER

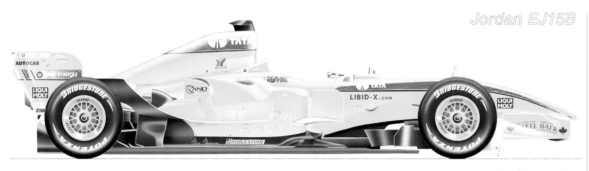

Jordan EJ15B

Midland 01

Midland 01
Indianapolis

Spyker
Shanghai

2006 provided to be a difficult season for Midland, the team failing to score a single point compared with the 12 from the previous championship. This meant a drop of one place in the Constructors' Championship standings. The team's efforts were largely frustrated by budget problems that eventually com-

promised the development of the car. At first sight, the M16, the first car designed from scratch under the responsibility of James Key (who had already signed off the 2005 B version) appeared to be the logical development of the Jordan EJ15 B, although it was actually an all-new design. The wheelbase remained unchanged

thanks to a spacer placed between the engine and gearbox which compensated for the reduced length of the Toyota V8 engine compared with the previous V10. When it came to installing the new V8, having maintained the same supplier made life easier for the new designer who had come through

the ranks under Mike Gascoyne during his time at Jordan. The Key-Gascoyne pairing was then revived during the summer when the latter rejoined the team after his divorce from Toyota, this all happening at the same time as Midland was being taken over by Spyker. The cars then lined up for the Chinese Grand Prix in the colours of the new owners. Compared with the EJ15B, the changes prevalently concerned the aerodynamic package and new front and rear suspension, in particular the brand new front lower wishbone mount introduced by Key. The Midland-Spyker was in fact the only car in 2006 to feature a form of dual mini-keel either side of the lower part of the chassis, the other teams (with the exception of Ferrari) instead opting for one of two interpretations of the "zero keel" configuration: the V-shaped keel seen on the Renault in 2005 (a path followed by Red Bull alone) and that of the 2005 McLaren taken up by all the others. There was an interesting use of rotating dampers (abandoned instead by Toyota which has used them on the 2005 car) on the rear suspension together with a transverse element equipped with a coaxial spring. The development of the car saw minor modifications introduced at most races, but the main steps coincided with four Grands Prix: Imola, with the introduction of a new front wing, Monaco, with changes to the suspension, France, with the introduction of new front suspension and Turkey, with a different front wing and shields behind the wheels. The McLaren-style dual flap introduced at Imola, combined with the Renault-style raised flap, already used in the 2005 season, considerably improved the car's handling.

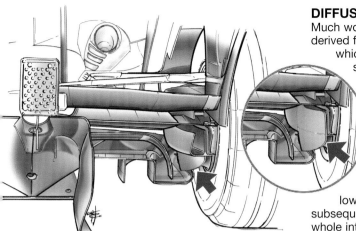

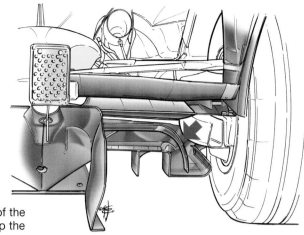

DIFFUSER

Much work also went into the diffuser derived from the Jordan design of which it retained the characteristic small arching profile over the lateral channels, highlighted by the arrow. There was also greater integration with the brake air intake, which had gradually become a true aerodynamic device. The drawing shows the first version of a vertical fin added to the lower part of the intake, a fin that subsequently became an integral part of the whole intake with the aim of cleaning up the air flow (in the circle).

TURNING VANES

The Midland M16 retained relatively low twin turning vanes, the forward section of which led back from inside the front suspension (like those of the 2005 Jordan). During the course of the championship these elements were subjected to continuous micro-development.

FRONT WING

Departing from the Renault-style raised flap introduced in 2005 on the Jordan, the M16's front wing was revised on a number of occasions. McLaren-style dual flaps with a significantly reduced chord were adopted at Imola while in Japan the main plane had a more pronounced central dip that was better suited to the Suzuka track (a circuit requiring greater aerodynamic loading).

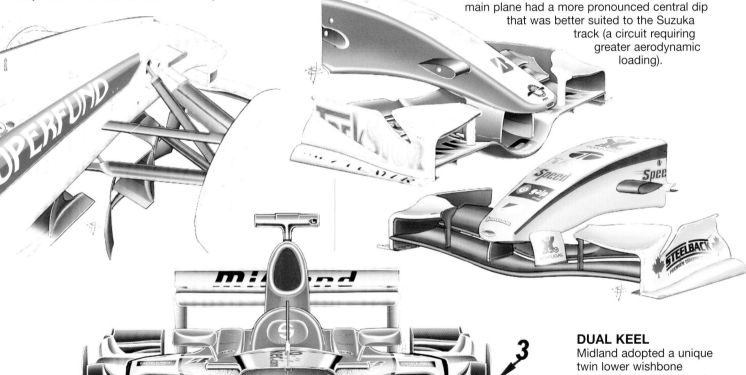

DUAL KEEL

Midland adopted a unique twin lower wishbone mount that can be seen in this front view. There were in fact two very short mini-keels (1) on the lower section of the chassis. Note that Midland did not use shrouds (2) on the external part of the brake discs. The side plates (3) on the shoulder wings located above the front of the sidepods were also subjected to development.

THE 2007
SEASON

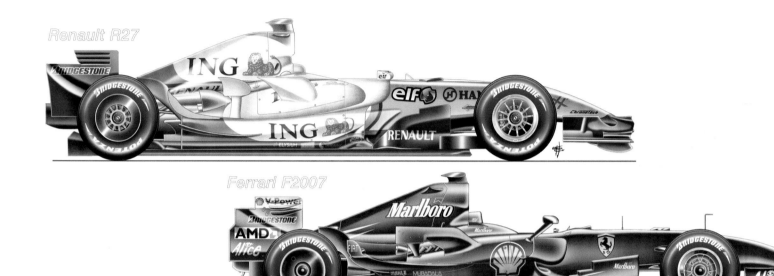

Renault R27

Ferrari F2007

McLaren MP4-22

Honda RA107

BMW-Sauber F1-02

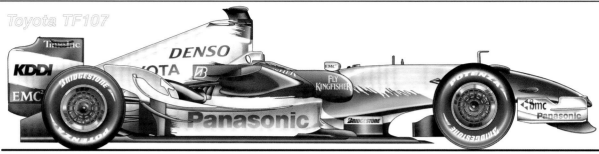

Toyota TF107

Red Bull RB3

Williams FW29

Toro Rosso STR2

Super Aguri SA07

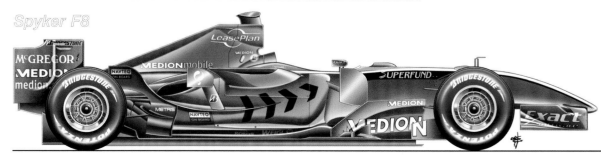

Spyker F8

The 2007 season began with a certain stability of regulations, but the factor that most distinguishes it from recent years is the return to a tyre monopoly after the retirement of Michelin of France at the end of 2006. There had been similar situations in 1999 and 2000, when Japan's Bridgestone was the sole tyre supplier and, going further back in time, from 1962 to 1964 with Britain's Dunlop and 1992 to1996 with American Goodyear.

Each weekend every driver has available to him 14 sets of dry weather tyres, four for the wet and three for extremely heavy rain. Friday testing is longer, with two 90 minute sessions, but above all else each driver must fit and use during the race tyres of both tread compounds – the same for everyone – brought by Bridgestone. Another new element is the opportunity of using a different engine for Friday testing, with a ban on changing the power unit coming into effect on the Saturday morning. The use of a third car is not allowed, but a third driver may take out one of the two race cars during Friday testing. The last regulation change concerns the safety car on track: competitors are not permitted to call into the pits until all cars are lined up behind the Federation's vehicle and are not allowed to refuel during that time. As well as the modifications to the regulations which, as always, are having severe repercussions on the progress of the season, on the technical front the key new elements concern safety, with the modification of the front and lateral crash tests and the dimensions of the rear deformable structure. The only new dictate in the technical regulations affecting car performance relates to the rear wing, and that is the obligation to locate two stiffeners 250 mm from the end plates to completely anchor the flap and main plane to avoid flexing after the controversy of the 2006 season.

Further development of the engines was put on hold at the end of the 2006 championship and the situation should stay that way until 2010; up to then, only limited adjustments to the external parts of the engine are permitted, for instance the induction system manifold, the exhausts and the shape of the trumpets, which was fixed from 2006. The last 10 cylinder with a bottleneck, used in 2005 by Toro Rosso, disappeared in 2006.

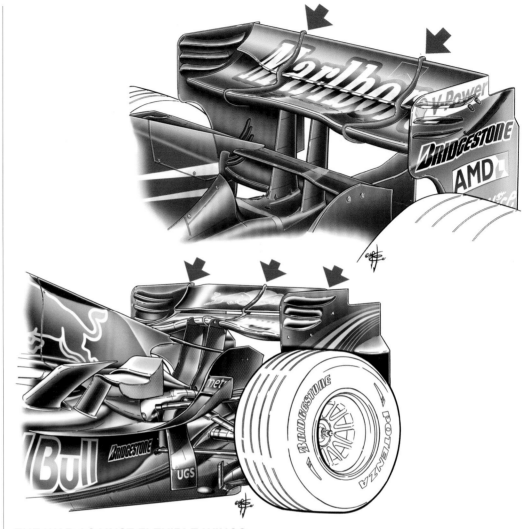

THE WAR AGAINST FLEXIBLE WINGS

To limit the flexible wing phenomenon, the Federation dictated that reinforcements should be applied 250 mm from the end plates, as in the case of Ferrari, or one in the centre and one at each extreme as with Red Bull, with the purpose of firmly fixing the flap and the principal plane. A decision that the F1 technical group reached at a meeting during the days of the Grand Prix of San Marino.

V-KEEL

The Renault R27 is the only 2007 season car not to adopt the "zero keel". The team remained faithful to the barge boards of the permeable V-structure introduced in 2005 and retained during 2006.

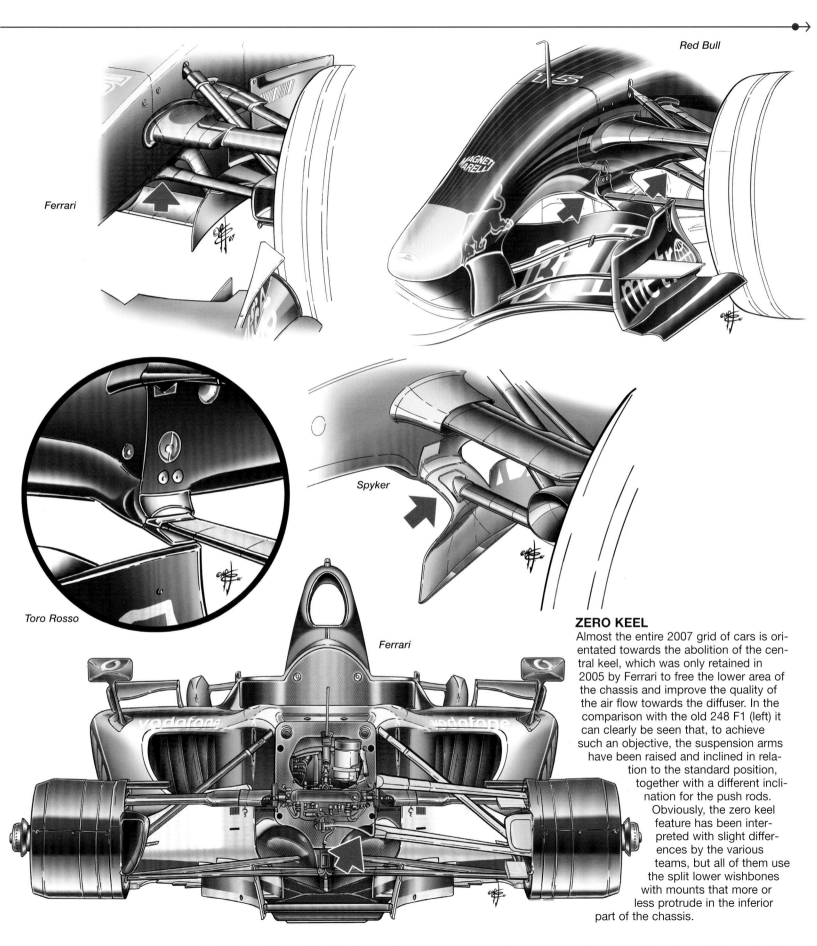

Ferrari

Red Bull

Toro Rosso

Spyker

Ferrari

ZERO KEEL

Almost the entire 2007 grid of cars is orientated towards the abolition of the central keel, which was only retained in 2005 by Ferrari to free the lower area of the chassis and improve the quality of the air flow towards the diffuser. In the comparison with the old 248 F1 (left) it can clearly be seen that, to achieve such an objective, the suspension arms have been raised and inclined in relation to the standard position, together with a different inclination for the push rods. Obviously, the zero keel feature has been interpreted with slight differences by the various teams, but all of them use the split lower wishbones with mounts that more or less protrude in the inferior part of the chassis.

REAR VISION MIRRORS/ AERODYNAMIC DEVICES

FERRARI 248 F1

Rear vision mirrors have become true aerodynamic devices, which work with the chimneys and flaps positioned in the sidepods, as can be seen in this view, where the mirror becomes the first turning vane in alignment with the chimneys.

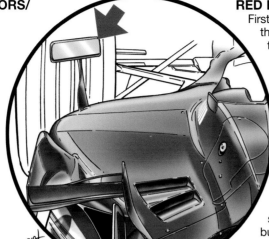

RED BULL

First of all, Coulthard contested the positioning of the Ferrari type rear vision mirrors (indicated with an arrow) developed by Adrian Newey. He wanted them close to the cockpit for the opening race of the world championship. The mirrors were subsequently mounted with higher and sophisticated supports, but still close to the cockpit.

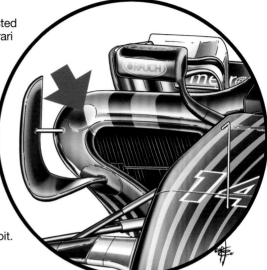

McLAREN

Mirrors close to the body of the car or a long way from it? The doubt continued at McLaren during various private test sessions, in which the two combined versions were tried out. After that, the team chose the standard position.

RENAULT

The further sophistication by Ferrari in 2006 have taught other teams a lesson, so much so that the rear vision mirrors on the Renault are integrated with the fins, as on the BAR Honda, in the upper area of the sidepods. Before the championship got under way, there was controversy concerning the effective visual capability of these mirrors as far as the drivers were concerned, to the point that the Federation carried out surprise tests.

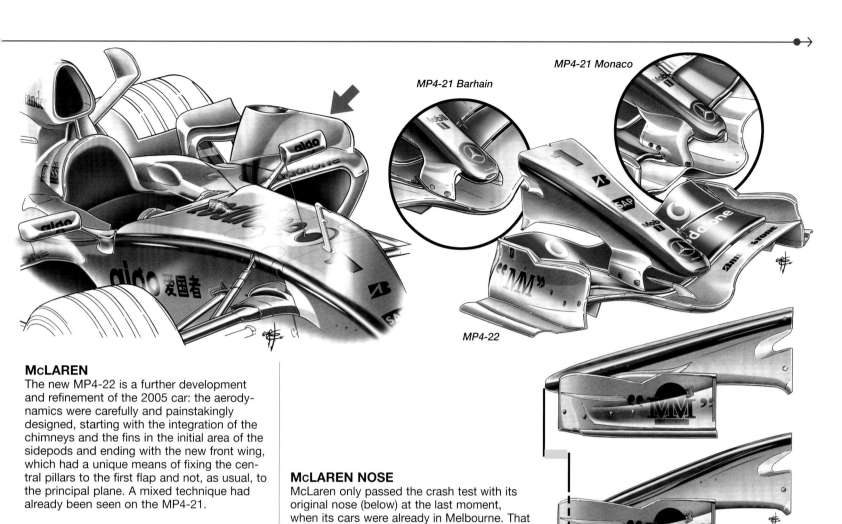

MP4-21 Monaco

MP4-21 Barhain

MP4-22

McLAREN

The new MP4-22 is a further development and refinement of the 2005 car: the aerodynamics were carefully and painstakingly designed, starting with the integration of the chimneys and the fins in the initial area of the sidepods and ending with the new front wing, which had a unique means of fixing the central pillars to the first flap and not, as usual, to the principal plane. A mixed technique had already been seen on the MP4-21.

McLAREN NOSE

McLaren only passed the crash test with its original nose (below) at the last moment, when its cars were already in Melbourne. That is why there was another much higher nose in the pits: it was straighter and longer, and had immediately passed its test.

SUPER AGURI: THE CLONED CAR

There was controversy concerning the use of a cloned car by Super Aguri and Toro Rosso. The former fielded a car directly derived from the previous year's Honda but with small aesthetic differences. A new front wing was also produced, which was a mix between that of McLaren and Renault, but it was dropped in favour of the Honda style wing (circle).

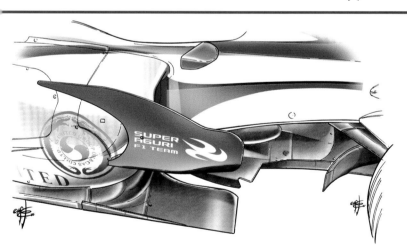

TORO ROSSO

The Red Bull and the Toro Rosso cars are practically identical, even in details such as this large fin applied to the brake air intake, with evident aerodynamic benefits.

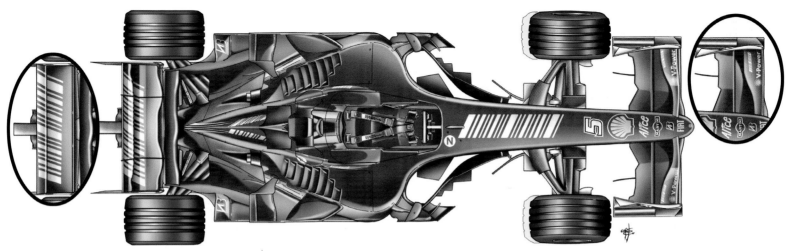

FERRARI

The F2007 is, perhaps, the most revolutionary car in relation to the 2005 version. The main difference is the lengthening of the wheelbase by about 8 cm, which was achieved by moving the front axle forward. In that way, the cockpit has been moved further away from harmful turbulence generated by the wheels, to the advantage of the exploitation of the aerodynamics. After having been presented with wings derived from the 248 F1, the real new developments appeared during testing before the start of the world championship. In the ovals are the wings shown at the presentation; it can be seen how the new rear wing has two longitudinal stiffeners imposed by the Federation.

NOSE

A new front wing (right) was tried out in the pre-world championship tests with a raised flap, which was a much different design that was higher in the centre and lower at the sides.

MANIFOLD

The intake manifold of the F2007 is split at the beginning of the entry mouth of the air box in order to direct air to the supplementary radiators of the hydraulic system.

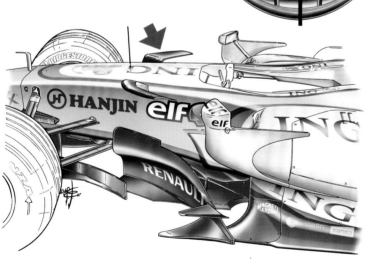

RENAULT

These boomerang-type pins are unique and have been brought in by Renault to stabilise the airflow in the central area of the car; small "ears" were used during the previous season, but the new devices are more effective.

RENAULT NOSE

The central body of the Renault's nose is decidedly large in relation to those of the competition. The disposition of the planes derives from those introduced at the previous year's Grand Prix of Germany.

BMW-SAUBER

At the BMW-Sauber presentation, the F1-07 was shown without the McLaren-style "horns" that were first seen on the old car the previous year during the Grand Prix of France. Those appendages were fitted from the first contact with the track in the early afternoon. Looking at the car in profile, note its strict derivation from the 2006 model, even though the aerodynamics seem more extreme. The F1-07 has also adopted conspicuous fins. There are others of the Honda type in front of the sidepod entrance, in part already seen in the second half of the 2006 world championship, even if the shape was more contained. The lower area of the sidepods is more concave.

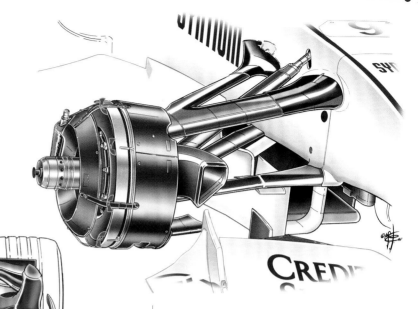

BMW-SAUBER BRAKES

BMW-Sauber have devised a new solution for the brake cooling intakes. It is a blend of techniques that had been seen in part before, such as the internal drums that were also used on the previous year's car, the external ones on the Ferrari and little used by the various teams in the 2006 season. The new element concerns the internal drum, which almost completely covers the disc brakes, while the external one has been moved by several centimetres in order to leave an empty space through which hot air is extracted.

TOYOTA

A comparison between the Toyota nose seen at the presentation and the one used during the first race of the season. The former was different in all its elements from that of the TF106: the nose was more tapered towards the lower area in relation to the TF106, the main plane was spooned but with a less brusque shape; the flaps were also different, more linked to and integrated with the end plates, the external part of which had been modified. The fins at the side of the nose were also fairly different and there were only two of them with a more arched shape of the Renault school. The definitive version made its debut in Melbourne and had a Renault-style raised flap with a new link with the central part of the nose.

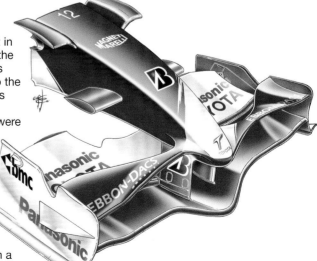

Toyota TF107

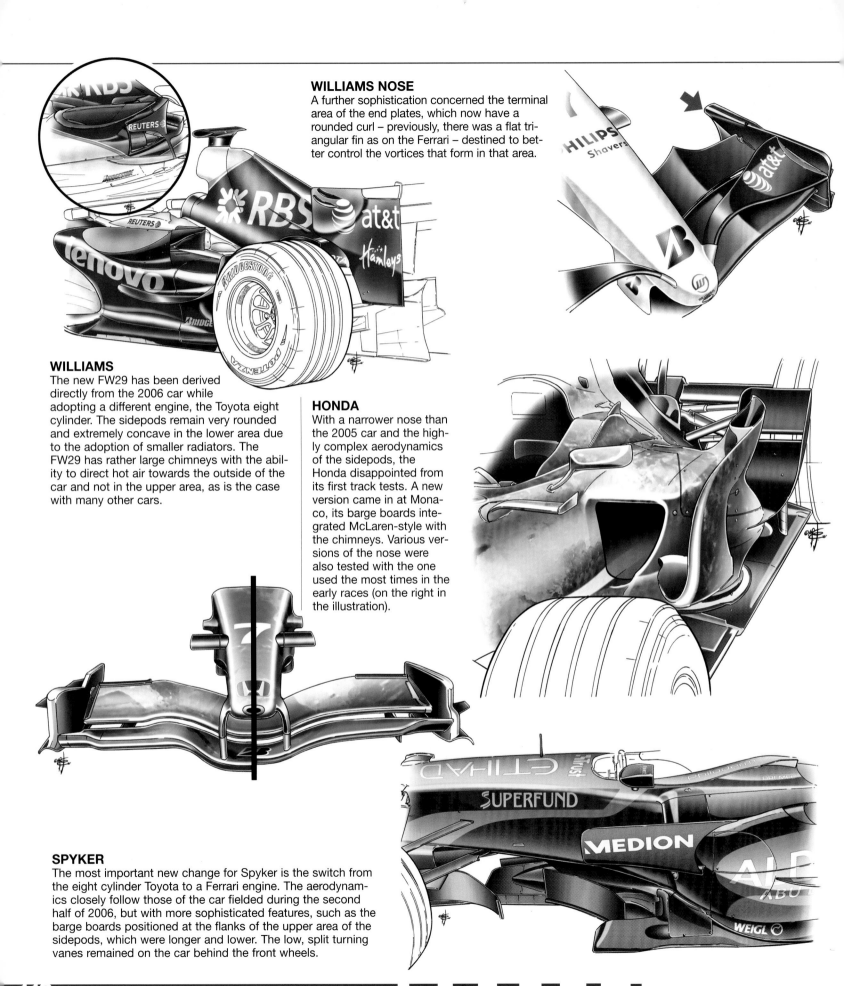

WILLIAMS NOSE

A further sophistication concerned the terminal area of the end plates, which now have a rounded curl – previously, there was a flat triangular fin as on the Ferrari – destined to better control the vortices that form in that area.

WILLIAMS

The new FW29 has been derived directly from the 2006 car while adopting a different engine, the Toyota eight cylinder. The sidepods remain very rounded and extremely concave in the lower area due to the adoption of smaller radiators. The FW29 has rather large chimneys with the ability to direct hot air towards the outside of the car and not in the upper area, as is the case with many other cars.

HONDA

With a narrower nose than the 2005 car and the highly complex aerodynamics of the sidepods, the Honda disappointed from its first track tests. A new version came in at Monaco, its barge boards integrated McLaren-style with the chimneys. Various versions of the nose were also tested with the one used the most times in the early races (on the right in the illustration).

SPYKER

The most important new change for Spyker is the switch from the eight cylinder Toyota to a Ferrari engine. The aerodynamics closely follow those of the car fielded during the second half of 2006, but with more sophisticated features, such as the barge boards positioned at the flanks of the upper area of the sidepods, which were longer and lower. The low, split turning vanes remained on the car behind the front wheels.

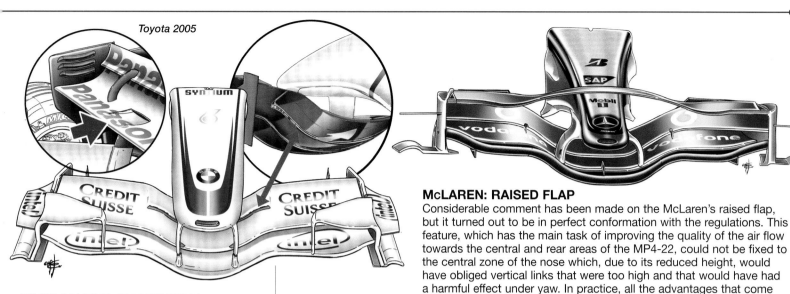

Toyota 2005

BMW-SAUBER: FRONT WING

The vent by Willy Rampf that was on the BMW-Sauber from the first track test was new and relative to the central section of the second flap of the front wing. Its purpose is to improve the efficiency of the plane and permit a lesser angle of incidence.

McLAREN: RAISED FLAP

Considerable comment has been made on the McLaren's raised flap, but it turned out to be in perfect conformation with the regulations. This feature, which has the main task of improving the quality of the air flow towards the central and rear areas of the MP4-22, could not be fixed to the central zone of the nose which, due to its reduced height, would have obliged vertical links that were too high and that would have had a harmful effect under yaw. In practice, all the advantages that come from this feature would have been completely annulled.

STEPPED BOTTOM FIXING

McLaren immediately requested clarification from the Federation concerning the anchorage of the stepped bottom at the opening race in Australia. The illustration shows the system used by Maranello, which had been on the Ferrari for the last four seasons and which is shown in the profile of the Rosse in the 2004 Technical Analysis. Strangely, it was not until the 2007 world championship that suspicions were raised. A fact that emerged and had the effect of modifying the scrutineering procedure of the front part of the stepped bottom. The scrutineers checked the flexibility of the bottoms without any elastic system. Flexing was not allowed to exceed 5 mm when subjected to a 50 kilo load. The curious thing is that the F2007s were not at the top of the list of the teams that had to carry out the most substantial modifications. At the top was Red Bull, followed in this order by Honda, Renault and BMW: they all preceded fifth placed Ferrari.

THE TORO ROSSO AND RED BULL QUESTION

This is one of the few interchangeable details between the cars of Red Bull and Toro Rosso cars. It is a fixing of the shadow plate of the stepped bottom, complete with technical designs presented to the scrutineers by the heads of Spyker.

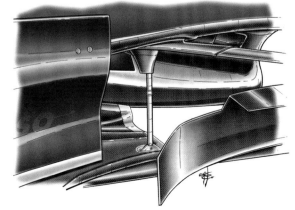

Giorgio Nada Editore S.r.l.

Editorial manager
Luciano Greggio

Editorial coordination
Leonardo Acerbi

Product development
Studio Enigma

Graphic design and cover
Aimone Bolliger

Contributors
Mauro Forghieri and Mauro Coppini (engines)
Michele Merlino (engine tables)
Kazuiko Kasai e Mark Hughes (tyres)

Computer graphic
Belinda Lucidi
Cristina Ravetta
Marco Verna
Gisella Nicosia
Alessia Bardino
Matteo Nobili

Printed in Italy by
Grafiche Flaminia S.r.l.
Sant'Eraclio (PG)
august 2007

Giorgio Nada Editore
Via Claudio Treves,15/17
I - 20090 VIMODRONE MI
Tel. +39 02 27301126
Fax +39 02 27301454
E-mail: info@giorgionadaeditore.it
http://www.giorgionadaeditore.it

Formula 1 2006/2007 - technical analysis
ISBN: 978-88-7911-398-4